CROSSING OVER

Also by John Edward

Books

ONE LAST TIME:
A Psychic Medium Speaks to Those We've Loved and Lost

WHAT IF GOD WERE THE SUN? (a novel)

Audio Programs

CROSSING OVER: The Stories Behind the Stories (audio book)

DEVELOPING YOUR OWN PSYCHIC POWERS

UNDERSTANDING YOUR ANGELS AND MEETING YOUR GUIDES

UNLEASHING YOUR PSYCHIC POTENTIAL

WHAT IF GOD WERE THE SUN?
(audio book)

CROSSING OVER

THE STORIES BEHIND THE STORIES

JOHN EDWARD

JODERE
GROUP

Jodere Group, Inc.
San Diego, California

Published by: Jodere Group, Inc., P.O. Box 910147, San Diego, CA 92191-0147
(800) 569-1002 • www.jodere.com

Design: Summer McStravick

"Beyond The Blue," reprinted by permission of Debra Swift/Carl Perkins dba Brick Hithouse Music, December 17, 1991.

"Precious One," reprinted by permission of Annie Haslam/Annie Haslam, Michael Dunford, March 8, 1999.

Cataloging-in-Publication Data available from the Library of Congress.

ISBN 1-58872-002-0

04 03 02 01   4 3 2 1
1st printing, August 2001

Printed in the United States of America

In memory of Shelley Peck.

This book is dedicated to Bonnie Hammer, who brought *Crossing Over* to television. Taking a huge chance on a guy she barely knew who claimed to talk to the dead, she has done more than anyone to change how millions of people view death. I will be forever grateful for her personal belief and professional support. She is the wind beneath the wings of many, both on this side and the other.

CONTENTS

ACKNOWLEDGMENTS

I owe a great debt of gratitude to a great many people whose talents, energy, and support have made *Crossing Over*—both the book and the show—possible.

Simple words don't do justice to the intense energy and unwavering support that Debbie Luican has demonstrated since the very first phone conversation I had with her three years ago. Her guidance and assistance in helping me tackle and overcome some of my toughest obstacles have been vital to me. And my success would not mean what it does if she were not there to make me realize how important it is to take control, honor the process, and above all, to laugh.

I want to express my deep thanks to Rick Firstman, not only for his collaboration on this book, but also for the energy and skill he poured into *One Last Time*. Reliving your own life and recounting the endless experiences of others is a difficult, often painful process, unless you are taking a friend on that journey with you. Rick's ability to fashion my thoughts and experiences into an absorbing narrative have made it possible for me to share my story. For that, and for the sensitivity and intelligence he has brought to a difficult and controversial subject, I am grateful.

The thanks I could give to Mark Misiano could fill a page, but for the purposes of this book, what I must acknowledge most is the support he has shown me in my work the last three years. He would be in my corner no matter what I chose to do in life, but he kept me on track when that's what I needed most. If Mark has been like one brother to me, Ernie Santopatre has been the other. I'm not sure how I would make it through all the ups and downs of my work without his friendship.

It's hard to imagine what kind of television show *Crossing Over* would have been without Paul Shavelson. As an executive producer with tremendous creativity and intelligence, he has helped me achieve my vision of honoring the process and helping people understand the messages of the other side. As my colleague, he has made the journey worthwhile and great fun. As my friend, he has been a gift. I couldn't have anticipated teaming with someone I would have such a great connection with.

I extend a huge thank you to the other key players in the production of *Crossing Over:* the Glow in the Dark team of Shirley Abraham, Dana Calderwood, and Charles Nordlander. In my book, they are the Dream Team of television. Only this group of talented and dedicated professionals could have taken such a complicated subject and made it possible for so many to understand and embrace. I also thank coordinating producer Liz Arias for her devotion, hard work, and great spirit. "La Liz" has made my experience in television much easier than it might have been without her.

Crossing Over never would have happened without the belief that the great ladies of Media-Savvy had in me. Ramey Warren Black, Adora English, and Jean Wiegman are the godmothers to history. I thank them for their loyalty, faith, and unending support.

I can't imagine a day without Carol Spadaro, my amazing assistant, who has organized my life and become a good friend. She is a driving force and an eternal source of encouragement. She makes me feel as though all those people who call the office are interested in the work I do, when I know it's her they're calling for.

I have appeared on many television talk shows over the last few years, but I want to acknowledge the hosts of two of them. I thank Leeza Gibbons for handling my work with respect, and for her kindness. I will never forget her compassion and understanding both on her show, and most important, on the phone one day not long ago. She is a special person. I also have great admiration for Catherine Crier, who has dealt with mediumship with both tenacity and straightforwardness. During my second appearance on her show, she validated information that came through for her off the air the first time I was on. She didn't have to do that, and it was a brave thing to do.

My deepest thanks to the following people for sharing their experiences for this book: Donna Marie, Carol Maywood, John Shauder, Debbie Swift Perkins, Terri Kaplowitz, Pat Price, Jamie Talan, A.J. Korn,

Acknowledgments

Nicole "Segue" Aflague, Allison Blecker, Doug Fogel, Garesh Bhargava, and the family of Louis Acompora. Special thanks to my good friend Rick Korn for his invaluable help in bringing to life the chapter on Carl Perkins, and for other support he has given me on this project and others over the past three years. And to Gary Schwartz and Linda Russek for their courage in scientifically exploring after-death communication.

Pardon me while I offer a private thank you to Karen: I believe everything happens for a reason. I believe that God sent you in to help me understand the pressures and new experiences I would encounter by being in the public eye. I thank you for being my friend, and for seeing me as "just John" and not "John the guy that talks to the other side." I hope we are able to maintain our connection and our friendship for years to come.

I would also like to thank the following people: Stephen Chao, Angela Mancuso, Valerie Schaer, Nancy Bocchino, Steve Rosenberg, Susan Kantor, Madeline McBride, Russell Friedman, Roger Guillen, Tahira Bhatti-McClure, Libby Gill, Larry King, Kristen Green, Lydia Clar, Todd Pettengill, Naomi DiClemente, Steve Harper, Annie Haslam, Chad Murdock, Judy Guggenheim, Shelley Peck, Suzane Northrop, Linda Williamson, Ellen Toomey, Denise Silvestro, Antoinette Kuritz, Marc Gurvitz, Lisa Jackson, Linda Ellerbee, and Dorothy Bonardi.

Finally, *Crossing Over*, the television program, has been the result of a lot of dedicated work by many people: Jim Moroney, Diane Wheeler-Nicholson, Helen Tierney, Lisa Tucker, Kevin Moriarty, Lori Levine, Michele Wasserman, Lauren Bright, David Cook, Joanne Longo, Christine Cipriani, Kimberly Dunn, Beth Archipoli, Leslie Becker, Deke Hazirjian, Mary Schmid, Linda Benya, David Cripton, Christian Jacobs, Aaron Moore, Jesse Shafer, William Jones, Juan Carlos Otero, Debra Ellenoff, Chris Fosdick, Kerri Neville, Claudio Sasso, Sharon Tassielli, Eileen Walsh, Wendy Stuart, Risa Lupardo, Maddy Schlesinger, Beverly Alkow, Richie Wirth, Al Centrella, Jorge Silva, Steve Watson, Frank Brown, Jeff Leib, Juan Rodriguez, Mary Dubois-Goldstein, Jeffrey McRoberts, Kevin West, Susanne William, Walter H. Kaiser III, John Meiklejohn, Jim Scurty, Manny Gutierrez, John Kosmaczewski, Tim Quigley, Dante Pagano, Alain Onesto, Lisa Rosenberg, Greg Barna, Tjeerd Belien, Ernest Albritton, Craig Mahan, Mitch Blazer, Ken Ortiz, Pete Loughran, Richie Mazzacca,

Joice Lee Stewart, Trinsha Matthew, Cliff Schwartz, Debi Mae West, Nina Bhargava, Christina Carr, David Powitz, Jennifer Simons, Deke Hazirjian, Duncan Cameron, Karl Dawson, Jill Hendelman, Greg Pope, Paul Rachman, Jerome Wallin, Mary Schmid, Liz Kyler, Mike Barrett, Joe Just, Aaron Moore, Jesse Shafer, Kerri Neville, Aaron Sorg, Lou Russo, Tjeerd Blelien, Debra Ellenoff, Chris Fosdick, Zuri Russell, Claudio Sasso, Sharon Tassielli, Eileen Walsh, David Cripton, Gregory Costa, Brian Miklas, Phil Sorrenson, Walter Berry Jr., Pamela Dale Blum, Barry Rosen, Rick Siegal, John Harrison, Jake Ostroff, Yahel Herzog, Larry Farkas, Chris West, John Asaro, Daniel Berry, Stan Gregory, Giovanni Lima, Migdalia Gutierrez, David Alan Comstock, Gracie de Arellano, Julian Middleton, David Caban, Robert Acevedo, Charles Lee, Richard Apman, Juan Vargas, Charlotte Hitchcock, Rennie DiCuia, Herman Gutierrez, and Herbert Orduz.

PREFACE

This is a book about Crossing Over. Not just the television show. Not just the metaphysical process that inspired the television show. To be sure, you'll read a lot about both the show and the process. But this book is also a chronicle of personal transition. It seems like a lifetime ago—and it seems like last week—that I was a young, suburban newlywed with a job in a hospital computer department and some unusual part-time activities. Okay, so maybe ballroom dancing isn't so strange. I guess it's the other thing that gets all the attention. Even as recently as 1999, I was doing readings in my house, and you had to be pretty plugged into the psychic world to know who I was. Two years later, I'm on TV five nights a week, and reading about myself in newspaper and magazine stories with headlines like, *"My Next Guest is . . . Dead."* I'm a media medium who not too long ago had stage fright on the radio. Talk about crossing over. This is the story of that wild ride.

If you have read any books by or about psychic mediums (including my own), you will notice that this is not like the others. No disrespect intended—some of them are excellent books by fine mediums, and I have them to thank for paving the way. But I intend this book to break some new ground, not only in demystifying the process of spirit communication—my whole reason for doing my work so publicly—but in offering a glimpse of this world I live in. I want you to know how things look from inside my head. Because, I've got to say, you have no idea what it's like being a psychic medium these days. I hope you will after reading this book. That's why you'll find me discussing some difficult and controversial questions—money, motivation, celebrity, and the private and public battles I have to confront in my work. These are issues I can't avoid if I'm going to stand up and do what I do in front of television cameras.

This book was written in collaboration with Richard Firstman, an author and journalist with whom I wrote my first nonfiction book, *One Last Time*. As you will read in the coming pages, Rick and I first connected in 1996 through circumstances that only now seem to make complete sense. For this book, as for the first one, we spent many hours together discussing and exploring my work and my life. Unlike with *One Last Time*, we also spent a lot of time talking about what it's like to be the first television medium. We retraced all the steps that got me here, and Rick filled out the picture by spending many days on the set of *Crossing Over*, observing the action and interviewing and getting to know many members of the production staff and crew, as well as the key players in the show's development and creation.

One of Rick's most important contributions to both books has been to bring his journalistic skills to bear on the stories I wanted to tell. I realize that some of these stories are so extraordinary—even to me—that a skeptic could be forgiven for being, well, skeptical. That's why we've both felt it was important for Rick—an accomplished reporter and a skeptic himself by nature—to completely and independently verify everything in this book. In all the work we've done together, Rick has had free reign to interview anyone he wanted or thought necessary, and, weaving together the recollections and perceptions of the participants with my own, to write the episodes as he saw fit. It has not been uncommon for him to discover much more about a story than I ever knew from the limited scope of a reading. In all cases, we present here an accurate portrayal of my experiences, without embellishment or exaggeration.

One final word: I know you picked up this book either intentionally or by what you might consider chance. But I don't subscribe to coincidence, so I believe you are reading this book because you are seeking a higher understanding of life after death, most likely because you have had a difficult loss in your life and want to know about the possiblity of spirit commmunication. But it's vital to understand that connecting with the other side cannot take the place of the natural grieving process. You still must confront and accept the physical loss of that person. As beneficial as it might be to connect with a loved one on the other side, either through a medium or on your own, it is imperative that you honor yourself and that loved one by grieving for them properly. That might mean reading this book only after you have sought out a counselor, a member of the clergy, or a friend. Only after you have accepted the loss can true healing begin.

I hope that what you find here is helpful to you on your path of learning and for your own soul's progression. And as I am a continuing student of this field, now you are, too. May the student in you become the teacher for another.

J.E.

PROLOGUE

Unitel Studios, New York City
June 14, 2000

I'm standing in shadows, waiting to walk out in front of a hundred people and explain that I'm about to connect some of them with their departed relatives. *To your side means husbands, wives, brothers, sisters, above you parents, grandparents . . . appreciate the messages . . . just answer yes or no. . . .* I've given this litany a thousand times before, in living rooms and offices and Holiday Inns in states I can't even locate on a map. But this is different. This is like nothing I've ever done before. It's not something I've ever really aspired to. But here I am.

Across the dimly lit set, I see Doug Fogel watching me. He's the stage manager, a Martin Shortish man with a twinkle in his eyes who's done *Cats* and *The Lion King*, Radio City and the Metropolitan Opera. Now he's working on a TV show about a guy who talks to dead people. He's in control of what's happening, unlike the person he's looking at, the person whose name is in the title of the show. I'm told that this studio was the original home of Big Bird, Bert, Ernie, and Oscar the Grouch. They shot *Sesame Street* right where I'm standing. And right before me, Chris Rock did his HBO show here. So I guess I fit right in. I like to think that this show is going to be educational. I won't break the news to the network just yet. I'm sure they think it's entertainment.

Doug hears the cue from the control room over his headset and begins counting me down with one hand. *Five, four, three, two. . . .* He points to the irregularly shaped white screen that plays the opening montage of the show. He looks at the audience, extends his arms, and begins clapping with a purpose, turning himself into a human APPLAUSE sign.

Then he points to me. It's showtime. Time for me to walk out from side-stage, make a quick left as I reach the middle of the screen, and bound onto the illuminated disk that will be my new home.

Something tells me we're not in the Holiday Inn anymore, Toto.

I scan the audience—the gallery, as it's being called—and try to smile the way I think a TV host is supposed to smile. Regis? Jerry? Oprah? I'm not comfortable. I am extremely *un*comfortable. I'm not wearing clothes, I'm wearing wardrobe. I have makeup on. There's all this *stuff* around me. Up there, a constellation of lights. Over here, a contraption that looks vaguely like a camera. Back over there, a rolling screen that feeds me little bits of monologue to wrap around the taped segments.

And there's, like, an entire industry of people laboring over a cosmic version of something I've been doing for years by myself. Up until now, I've been pretty much okay with just God's help. Now I'm relying on Doug. Everywhere I look there are people in headsets talking to the producers and the director who's in a room somewhere staring at fifty-two TV screens with my face on more of them than really seems necessary. It's called the control room, and that makes me nervous. I'm a control freak—ask anybody. And I don't like surrendering so much control that they need an entire room to hold it.

Will I be able to do what I do under these conditions? Will I get swallowed up like that *mad-as-hell-and-not-gonna-take-it-anymore* guy in that movie that came out when I was in, like, second grade? Was this really such a good idea?

How the *hell* did I get here?

— CHAPTER 1 —

GREAT EXPECTATIONS

A PSYCHIC
IN LADIES' LINGERIE

I was not a happy medium in 1998.

An example: Denver in November. I'm sitting in a radio studio, near the end of a two-week, city-a-day tour to promote my first book, *One Last Time*. The night before, at a signing at a bookstore, I spoke for about twenty minutes, then asked if anybody had any questions. A woman raised her hand. "Can you start over?" she asked. "You talk way too fast."

It's been that kind of tour right from the start. Back in New York, the publicity people booked me at a Bradlee's department store—in the ladies' underwear section. *Attention shoppers, come see the psychic in ladies' lingerie on the lower level.* I'm standing among the bras and panties, talking about dead people. *Uh, the lady by the I-Can't-Believe-It's-a-Girdle girdles—did your father pass?* My spirit guides—*The Boys,* as I call them—have one fine sense of humor. They're just hilarious.

No, things are not going well. Bookstores where I'm appearing bring out plenty of copies from the back room, but the others—one or two stashed in the New Age section, or no books at all. In a town on Long Island where I *live,* I went to a bookstore and they tried to sell me James Van Praagh's latest. The sales clerk said it was way better than the one by that John Edwards guy. And this one by Sylvia Browne's good, too. I ask if she's read the one by the Edwards guy. She says no. I introduce myself. Doesn't help. It's still Edwards to her.

There have been worse days lately. Last month, Montel Williams and Larry King canceled on the same day—my birthday. Definitely a message from The Boys. But what were they trying to tell me? The Larry people said we'd reschedule, but the Montel producer said I'm been-there-done-that. Yet another psychic, another guy who talks to the dead—so what else is new? They need a new angle. I don't think I have one.

So now I'm doing this radio show in Denver. "Last week we had a psychic on, and he was a big phony, a total fraud," says one of the hosts. "We don't believe any of this crap." That's my introduction. There are times when I can handle the cynics, take all the slings and arrows in stride. And then there are other times. By this point on the book tour, I am, shall we say, a little cranky. I'm so drained, so frustrated with the entire publishing industry, that I'm pretty much a man without a personality.

I love doing radio. I like the exposure it gives my work without making my face—by that I mean *me*—the focal point. As long as I have a headset on—for some reason, handsets don't cut it—I'm good to go. And nobody can accuse me of reading facial expressions or body language. So for me, radio is the medium's medium. But the last thing I want to do on this particular day in Denver is another call-in show, with hosts who are giving me the morning-zoo treatment, even though it's four in the afternoon.

I'm pretty good with the first few callers, although a couple of them seem to take the hosts' cue and don't make this easy for me. A man to the side comes through for one caller. He's saying he had a brain tumor. I pass on some other details, and I ask the caller if he understands that.

"Well," he says, "is there something, you know, something you can tell me that's a little more detailed?"

He's neither validating the brain tumor nor denying it. He's just ignoring it. I repeat the messages I've given him, and ask him again if he understands them. It seems he doesn't want to say yes. The host asks him who he's trying to connect with. He says a friend with a brain tumor. I snap.

"Did I not just *say* that? What's wrong with you people in Denver? Is it the altitude?" I actually say that on the radio. At which point Kristen Green, the book publicist accompanying me on my tour, comes flying in from the control room with her face wrapped in an extremely tight smile. "Do you think you might have been a little *short* with that last caller?"

I'm fuming, ready to leave, but the Rocky Mountain DJs think this is fantastic. *Hey, this is a New York psychic! He's like a psychic with an attitude!*

SOMEWHERE ON THE ROAD, it hit me like a punch in the face. Things are not turning out as I thought they would. No, as I *knew* they would. Go ahead, say it: *Some psychic you are.*

I was about to turn thirty, and I could look back across the years and see where I came from and how I got here. And I had thought I could see around the bend, because my spirit guides had given me glimpses. They had told me years earlier that I would be a teacher in this field. What they didn't tell me was when or how. I would have to find that out on my own. Not that they didn't shine a light. They always had.

Years ago, the summer I was fourteen, my Aunt Joan took me on my first real excursion, a cruise to the Caribbean. Docking in St. Thomas, we spent hours shopping, eating, and walking along the shore. Mostly walking. And walking. And walking. After seven or eight hours, we thought it might be a good idea to turn around and head back. About twenty minutes into our return hike, my feet tired and burning, I looked across the horizon and saw our ship in the far distance—about half an inch wide in my perception. "Oh, my God," I said, "look at how far we still have to go."

My aunt laughed, reminded of something her mother, my paternal grandmother, Mary, used to always say: "Don't look at how far you have to go. Look at how far you've already come."

My grandmother's favorite saying was prophetic—she didn't know she was passing down from her daughter to her grandson nothing less than words to live by. Trying to look too far ahead, worrying how and when and even if you're going to get where you're supposed to go, can stop you in your tracks. It's a lesson I would have done well to remember fifteen years later, when all I could do was squint at the half-inch ship across the horizon and stop to rub my burning feet. I wasn't in much of a mood to look back and appreciate how far I'd already come.

There was irony in this, because I had spent a lot of effort recalling my earliest years for the opening chapters of *One Last Time*—how, as a young child, I had experiences that only years later would I realize were not part of the average childhood. How I knew things I shouldn't have known, family events that happened before I was born that no one had told me about. How I knew who was going to call on the phone or walk through the door. And how I could spell complicated words I'd never heard by actually seeing them in front of me. My dad, a cop, thought this was very cool—his boy was a genius. From an early age, I also had several experiences where I found myself momentarily outside my body, transported to another place in my house, or outside on the street, and then brought back. And I had the sense that I'd had a prior life, of having done things "before I came down here," as I explained it to my family. In elementary school, I saw auras around my teachers, and sometimes told them so. Not a great idea. My mother was always telling me I was "special," but only later did she tell me she wasn't just being a mom. *So let me get this straight. You're telling me having out-of-body experiences in nursery school is* not *normal?*

It wasn't until I was a teenager, after an encounter with a psychic named Lydia Clar, that I began to explore what was going on inside my head, and by college I was spending my free time as a psychic medium. But I never considered "psychic medium" as a viable career choice. It never even entered my mind. Imagine putting *that* on your tax return. I got a degree in public administration and went to work at a large hospital, first as a phlebotomist, drawing patients' blood, and later in the computer department. I continued doing private and group readings at night and on weekends, and developed a small following around Long Island. But I envisioned a fulfilling, upward career in hospital administration, and a normal life. I married my dance instructor, and we bought a house on a quiet cul-de-sac. I turned professional and began to teach ballroom myself, and on weekends, Sandra and I traveled the country competing— sometimes against each other—on the pro-am dance circuit.

I had always loved to dance—there were always big parties with bands and DJs in my large Italian family—and Sandra turned me into a real pro (and gave me a steady partner). I found that doing the rumba and the cha-cha—anything Latin—was a great physical and creative release, and it kept me grounded as I tried to balance the different compartments of my life. To most of the people I knew at that time, I wasn't John the medium, or even John the dancer. I was "Sandra's husband." Most of my dance crowd didn't even know about my psychic work. I never talked about it.

By 1995, my spirit guides were pushing me to put more time and energy into that part of my life. In fact, they wanted me to change course—in their direction. They were leading me to the understanding that I was on a path to a life's work connecting the physical world to the spirit world. I didn't leap into it. I loved my job at the hospital, and had serious reservations about building my life around my psychic work. For one thing, I was very insecure about how people would perceive me. *What do you do? Oh, I talk to dead people.* But the stakes were even higher than that. What my guides were telling me was that I would be more than a practitioner. I would be some sort of noted figure in the field, and I would help a lot of people. Go ahead, roll your eyes—who is this guy, some possessed cult leader? But as pompous as that might sound, it wasn't anything that I aspired to. I had no interest in being well known—in fact, it's still not important to me. Celebrity is fleeting. It's the work that endures, if you're doing it right.

I had a major life decision to make. Stay with a job and a career I loved—and the financial security that came with it—or cross over into a peculiar blend of spiritualism and entrepreneurship. I had always followed my guides, and they had never steered me wrong.

That year, I made the biggest leap of faith of my life. I left the hospital and actually did put down "psychic medium" as my occupation on my tax return. I gave private readings in my home office, group readings in the living room, and started giving lectures to larger groups in hotel meeting rooms. Even those who had heard I was young were taken aback when they saw me, this twentysomething guy in jeans and a T-shirt who was now going to unite them with their departed loved ones. You didn't need to be a psychic to know what they were thinking: He's *a kid.* But because of my abilities, people old enough to be my parents or even grandparents treated me with a sort of deference I found a little unnerving. I was your average suburbanite, except for the parade of nighttime visitors to my front door. Some had out-of-state license plates. So you *know* what the neighbors thought. Two of them had moved past the awkward preliminaries and were onto a running discussion of whether it was cocaine or marijuana. They brought my next-door neighbor Hope into it, and she set them straight. *No, no, he's not a drug dealer, for Chrissakes. He talks to dead people.*

Not long after I left the hospital, my guides let me know that I needed to begin working on a book. My human reaction was puzzlement. Who wants to read a book by a twenty-six-year-old kid who says he has special access to "the other side"? But this became a persistent refrain, so I took it pretty much as a given, no more complicated than following a "bear right" road sign without having to slow down, as if just following someone's instructions. I started thinking about it, making notes of the points I wanted to make in the book and the stories I wanted to tell. I started keeping a file of letters that validated past clients' readings.

I didn't have an agent. I wondered if I should get some help writing it. But my guides told me specifically no—I would do it by myself. I didn't find this surprising, or a daunting prospect. I felt I was a good writer, and was emboldened by the confidence boost my guides were giving me. Then one night in February of 1996, something very unusual happened. They slammed on the brakes and did a screeching U-turn. *You need help with the book.* This confused me. It was very odd for my guides to tell me one thing, stay with that for more than a year, and then suddenly do a 180. I was reminded of the 1982 movie *Poltergeist*—you remember, *"They're ba-ack"*—in which a medium named Tangina, who is an "earthly guide," seems to jerk around the parents of a missing little girl. At first Tangina instructs them to tell their daughter Carol Ann to stay away from the light. But later she tells them Carol Ann should go *to* the light. The lesson was that different decisions and tactics apply at different times. I wasn't sure why my guides were suddenly leading me in a different direction, but I wasn't going to argue with them. They're called guides for a reason.

THE NEXT NIGHT, a slender woman with long, dark hair came to my house for a private reading. She was very friendly and had a smile that lit up her face. Her name was Jamie, and when we sat down for the reading, I felt the kind of positive, open energy around her that makes my job so much easier, and a lot more fun. If this story starts to sound familiar, it's because I told it in *One Last Time*. But not completely. Jamie was called "Randi" there. And, for reasons that will become apparent, the context of the story was removed. I simply presented it as an intriguing and memorable reading, which it was. But I left out the ending, which was, for me, the most important thing about it.

Almost from the start, Jamie's reading was like an unfolding book—interestingly enough, as it turned out. I was getting information with clarity and detail. Jamie brought a notebook and began scribbling as names started coming quickly. Not the usual sounds or initials, but complete, unmistakable names: Helen. Jacques—not Jack, but *Jacques*. These were Jamie's grandparents. And they were with a younger male. "He's telling me Jon," I said. "But you know him as Jonny." That was their grandson, Jamie acknowledged—her younger brother. I told Jamie he was coming through more like an older brother. No, she said, he was nine years younger. She was like a second mother to him.

"He's telling me that now he's your older brother. He's telling me that you have a piece of his clothing. A jacket, or maybe a sweatshirt. I'm seeing both."

"I have two things of his," Jamie said with a calmness she seemed to be working to maintain, as if trying to not let her emotions overtake her objectivity. "His jacket and his sweatshirt."

Then suddenly, I felt a sharp pain at the back of my head, and in the next instant a startling realization. "Oh my God," I blurted. "This guy was hit with a baseball bat! He woke me up this morning!"

Jamie looked at me with a mixture of astonishment and confusion. I quickly explained that early that morning, I had been jarred awake by a voice that said, *"John, wake up!"* I knew it was the spirit of someone who had been hit in the head with a bat—I just didn't know who it was or why he was showing up in my bedroom before daybreak. I'd assumed a spirit so bold would be connected to me or my family, so I had spent most of the day calling friends and relatives, asking if they knew anyone who had been killed by a blow to the head with a baseball bat. Nobody did.

"Wow—it was your brother," I told Jamie. "I guess he couldn't wait."

Jamie explained that her little brother, eighteen at the time, had been killed by a stranger in a video arcade in New York City on New Year's Day, 1984. "These kids came in looking for someone else," she said. "They had a bat. They wanted to hurt someone. My brother tried to leave, and this kid just hit him in the back of the head."

Jonny told me that his spirit had left right away, but his body lingered.

"He was on life-support," Jamie said. "We took him off the next day."

A strange look came over her face. "This is so weird," she said. "I wasn't going to tell you this because you'd think I was some nut. But I had a dream about your mother this morning. You know how you just know something in a dream? It was your mother. She was shrouded in smoke."

"My mother died of lung cancer," I said. "She was a heavy smoker." I was blown away by that. I did not know this woman, and how would she know my mother had died? There was something very unusual about this whole thing. First, a spirit barges into my bedroom and wakes me up.

Then I hear that my mother has dropped in on his sister at just about the same time. Yes, weird. Even to me.

The reading continued for more than an hour, and after Jamie's family pulled back, she and I began to talk. We were both intrigued by what had taken place.

"You know," Jamie said now, "I'm a science writer, so I'm skeptical by nature. But I've always believed in this. I know that my brother has come to me. My husband doesn't believe in any of this. He wasn't too happy I was coming. He thinks this is all a bunch of baloney. "

"What does he do?" I asked, not something I normally ask a client.

"He's a writer, too."

At that instant, it was like my guides were saying, *Ta-dahhhh*. Without even a second's hesitation—without asking what kinds of things he wrote, or knowing if he was any good, or even stopping to consider that Jamie had just said that he thinks I'm full of shit—I said, "That's why you're here. Your husband is going to help me write my book."

Jamie let out a big laugh. "I don't think so," she said. "You've got the wrong guy."

I LOVE LARRY

ONE FORTY-PAGE PROPOSAL LATER, I started making the rounds of New York publishers with my new writing partner—guess who? Jamie had gone home that night and read from her notebook, and a few days later, her husband was sitting in my living room observing a group reading that—as I had warned it might—included a few stray messages for him. Rick was indeed a confirmed nonbeliever when we met, a when-you're-dead-you're-dead kind of guy with a lifelong fear of the great abyss that Woody Allen would be proud to own. But now Rick was undergoing a readjustment in the metaphysics department. Talk about reconsidering your world view. When he told his friend Josh that his latest project was a book with a psychic medium, a guy who makes contact with "the other side," Josh thought it was just about the funniest thing he'd ever heard. He snickered at the ridiculousness of it. Josh was a magazine and book writer who specialized in the Internet. It's obvious where this guy's getting his information, he told Rick: Off the Net. He had only one thing to say anytime Rick told him about a reading: "Research."

I told Rick how I believed our collaboration had been arranged—how my guides had been telling me I would write the book myself, and then suddenly reversed field. Going back over the events, we realized that on that very Sunday night that they had given me the new plan, I got a call on my office answering machine from someone scheduled to have a reading the next night. She couldn't make the appointment. I called the next person on my waiting list to see if she could grab a late opening the following night. And that, of course, was Jamie.

The timing struck me as even more interesting when Jamie told me she had been trying to get a reading for months. That's a long, involved story in itself, but all you need to know is the part about the chance encounter a month before at Abel Conklin's, a well-known steakhouse on Long Island. Jamie and I had unknowingly sat back-to-back at adjoining booths, each of us at a table with our spouse and another couple—who happened to know each other. Jamie told me that among the hot dinner topics at her table was how hard it was to get an appointment with a medium these days. And then, on their way out, the two other couples saw each other, unleashing a chain of Oh-my-Gods that ended with Sandra insisting on taking Jamie's number down and promising she'd get a call. I just stared at Sandra—she never, ever did that kind of thing.

Now it all made sense. My guides had not really reversed themselves. They had merely orchestrated the timing. They wanted to prepare me to write a book, but if they had told me everything at the outset, I would have been sidetracked by the plan. I would have spent too much energy looking for the person I was supposed to work with, rather than doing what I needed to be doing: diving into the swim of being a full-time medium, gathering experience, and—without the crutch of a collaborator—envisioning the book. Thinking it out, writing an outline, keeping notes. If they had to deceive me to get me ready, I couldn't quarrel with their shrewdness. Because now I was ready.

Visiting some of the big publishing houses that expressed interest in our proposal, I knew there would be polite requests for me to read the editors who would be deciding whether to buy the book. It didn't strike me as unreasonable, and I read anyone who asked. We had some nibbles, but nobody was beating down any doors for the honor of publishing the memoirs and collected wisdom of a twenty-seven-year-old psychic from Long Island. Not coincidentally, the best reading I gave was around a conference table with a group of editorial, sales, and marketing people at the company that eventually bought the book, an imprint of Penguin Putnam called Berkley Books. They made the only offer. It was about equal to the starting salary of a public school teacher—all of which went toward the expense of getting the book written.

While working on the book on and off over the next year or so, I continued trying to follow the path my guides had laid out for me, to be something more than a neighborhood psychic. I had actually taken the first step years earlier, while still working at the hospital. One morning in 1994, a colleague of mine named Pat had come up to my desk and informed me that I *had* to call WPLJ, a popular radio station in New York. Right away. Pat was a very assertive and precise person who looked just like Teri Hatcher, the actress. She did not give suggestions. She gave statements of fact. I had to call the radio station, and I was *going* to call the radio station. Okay, what? Today's trivia question is who played Dr. Bellows on *I Dream of Jeannie?* No, Pat said—Scott and Todd had a psychic on, and she gave Naomi bad news. Naomi DiClemente was the morning jocks' sidekick, the darling of the show, loved by all, and the butt of many jokes. Apparently this "psychic" had told Naomi she should cancel her wedding. Pat wanted me to call up the station and uncast this evil psychic spell.

"I'm not gonna do that," I said. "I can't call up a strange woman on the radio and say, 'You don't know me, but I'm a psychic, too . . .'"

"Would you like someone to do that to Sandra?" Pat said. Sandra and I had just gotten engaged. I freaked. I called. I left four messages, including the last one with someone in the office who hung up on me, saying Naomi had heard enough from psychics for one day. But Naomi called me back, sounding nervous but apparently in desperate need of a Good Psychic of the East to counteract the Bad Psychic of the North. So there I sat at my desk in the hospital computer department, asking Naomi the Plucky Morning Sidekick how this psychic had performed this reading. Did she use astrology? No. Numerology or cards? No, Naomi said, none of the above. Did she say anything that was validated in any way to let you know that she was accurate at what she does? Well, no. Then *why* would you pay *any* attention to her? Naomi thanked me for calling, said she felt better, and went on to become happily married.

A few months later, my friend Ernie and I went to a Tower Records store in a shopping center on Long Island. He had just bought a new car and insisted on parking in the next zip code to avoid that dreaded first scratch. The long walk to the store took us past a Filene's Basement where we saw that WPLJ was doing a remote. We recognized Naomi, who was smiling, signing autographs, and posing for pictures. Ernie wanted me to go over and say hello, but there were too many people around, and I opted for lunch at Ben's Kosher Deli. But sitting in the restaurant, I felt this urgency to do what Ernie said and go over and introduce myself to Naomi. The Boys pushing me? I didn't know. "I'll go over there and say hello," I told Ernie, "but only if they make it so there's nobody around." (Just so you know—since we'll be hanging out for a couple hundred pages—whenever I refer to "they," and there's no one else around, it means I'm talking about my guides.) It was a safe promise, since there were dozens of people around the WPLJ table when we went into Ben's. But then we left the deli and went to check the situation at the table, and there wasn't a soul around. Ernie and I looked at each other, then headed over. I walked up to this beautiful blonde woman sitting in a chair and said, "Naomi?"

She turned and looked at me. "John Edward!" She jumped up and gave me a big, gleeful hug. I don't know who was more shocked—me or Ernie. His face said, "I thought you said you don't know this woman." One of the people from the station moved in, looking on warily, not having seen that all I did was walk up and say hello. Naomi said later she recognized my voice, although to this day, I can't imagine how. All I said was "Naomi." We chatted for a few minutes, and Naomi asked, "When are you coming on the show?" Uhhh, well, umm . . . just the suggestion that I go on the radio—on a big New York station—was enough to unhinge me. Hadn't she had enough of wacko psychics anyway? I'll call you, Naomi said. Great, I said.

Naomi kept asking. I kept saying no. Besides doing her morning-show job, she had her own show that was taped and aired early on Sunday mornings. I told her I wasn't ready. I did go on a Long Island radio station, with Steve Harper on WBLI, to promote an event where I was appearing. But Long Island I could handle. I wasn't ready for the big city. Then, a few months later, I got a call from a producer at the biggest radio station in Miami, Power 96, asking me to come on. A cousin of mine who booked commercials for the station had mentioned me to the producer. I was feeling pressure. My guides were letting me know that they were starting to lose patience with me. They were like, "Why are you wasting our time? You know you're going to do this." Like I was a child running around the doctor's office trying to avoid a shot, when everyone in the office knew I wasn't getting out of there without it. And, truth to tell, I was running away from media as if it *was* a shot.

I called Naomi and asked her what she thought about Miami. She gave me a long list of reasons why I should do it, probably figuring that it was her best shot at getting me on WPLJ. Once I got my first time out of the way, I'd relax—and if I did Miami, I couldn't say no to her anymore. "And if you suck," she said, laughing, "it doesn't matter. It's Florida. Nobody up here will know." I went on in Miami, and it went fine. I found that I could do readings just as well on the phone as face-to-face. I called Naomi to tell her. "Now you have to do my show," she said. And I did. After that, Naomi spoke to her colleague Todd Pettengill, who called me at an event I was speaking at and invited me on his show. I said yes, and immediately thought, *Oh God. This is New York—and New Jersey, Long Island, and Connecticut.*

I went on in August of 1995. Between my appearances on WBLI and WPLJ in New York, I was becoming better known. Steve Harper, Todd Pettengill, and Scott Shannon began e-mailing friends in the business. Radio is a small business, and word-of-mouth travels fast.

Over the next year or two, I assembled a small network of stations around the country whose hosts treated me seriously—though not *too* seriously—and put me on the air regularly. I wasn't paid for this. It was just something I felt was worthwhile, and something I enjoyed. I liked the hosts, some of whom became far-flung phone friends, and I looked forward to the occasional trips I began making to their studios. It also led to an offbeat request. The owner of a restaurant in New York called Serendipity 3, which had been Andy Warhol's hangout, wanted to gather Andy's friends and have me bring him back for a visit. So I did. It was actually at that event that I received the call from Todd From WPLJ to come on his morning show.

I was content with radio as my medium. I had no burning desire to be on television, even if I'd the audacity to try. I liked the simplicity of radio, but more than that, the physical anonymity. People didn't need to know what I looked like because it wasn't about me; it was about the work. When my guides told me I would be well known, I saw it as the message getting the attention, not me. I've always felt that way. I remember that when I was doing readings at my grandmother's house, she would look at what I was wearing—shorts or ripped jeans and a T-shirt, no shoes—and ask, "Is that what you wear to see your clients? Don't you think you should—"

"What—wear a shirt and tie?" I'd say.

"Don't you think you should look . . . presentable?"

"Oh, Granny," I'd say, "they don't care what I look like. They just want to know what I'm gonna say."

My jeans aren't ripped anymore, but I still feel basically the same way. I try to be appealing, but as long as the information is good, people wouldn't care if I was Mister Rogers.

After establishing good relationships with a few radio shows around the country, I began going on the road. I would schedule a lecture at a hotel, then fly out and do a radio show in the same city. The lectures, which I had been doing regularly in the New York area, were part seminar and part group reading. I'd get anywhere from 50 to 200 people. But I was far from a household name. By 1997, James Van Praagh had burst onto the scene with his big bestseller, *Talking to Heaven*. I was thrilled about the success of the book because it was great for the field. It introduced so many people to the idea of a conscious, interactive afterlife. It brought the idea more into the mainstream, made it okay to talk about. More eyes were looking at this than ever before. When his book reached the top of the *New York Times* bestseller list, I called James from Dallas to congratulate him. "Wow, number one," I said. "A book about talking to dead people. This is huge. You're making all our lives easier."

James's book was a landmark, just as Joel Martin and Patricia Romanowski's *We Don't Die*, about George Anderson, was in the late 1980s. But two things were different when James's book came out. One is that our society had become much more interested in examining "the soul" and what it means. Gary Zukav's *The Seat of the Soul,* published in 1990 and a perennial bestseller, was a leader in advancing the idea that the human race is undergoing a great planetwide transformation—that we're coming to understand that "authentic power" comes not from what we can see and hear and touch, but from the internal perceptions of the soul. Zukav wrote in a very accessible way that humans are immortal souls who can stimulate their spiritual growth and become better people once they begin to bring their personalities in line with their souls.

The other thing that had changed was not so esoteric: We had become much more defined by the media and celebrity culture. There were more TV news magazine shows tripping over each other for the same stories. There were endless entertainment and celebrity magazines and TV shows. There was cable. The Internet.

Everyone knew who James was. Few knew who I was. But I had to figure, based on what I had been hearing from my guides for a while now, that this would change once my book was published. I believed that George had blazed the trail, and that James had paved the road. Now I would widen it. I wasn't being presumptuous or smug—at least I didn't feel that way. Probably just unsophisticated. Berkley had paid little for the book and was planning to publish it in trade paperback, which, if I had known anything about publishing, would have given me an indication of how much they would put into marketing it. But I just believed in the book. It was human, I thought, and it was honest: Here you go, this is who I am. And these are the people I've known, and here are their experiences.

There was the story of a little boy named Mikey DiSabato, who had drowned in a pool in 1994 and whose spirit had become a regular visitor to me. There was Andrew Miracola, a teenager killed while riding his bicycle who was one of the strongest and most amazing spirits I had experienced. And Tracy Farrell, a car accident victim who got me to surreptitiously order a lab test that wound up saving a girl's life when I was working as a phlebotomist at the hospital. Rick, my once dubious collaborator, spent many hours interviewing their families. I badly wanted to believe that these stories would touch a lot of people.

And I wanted to believe I had accomplished my most important goal: demystifying my work and giving people an understanding of the process. I've always hoped that when people encounter me, whether in a private reading or in a lecture, whether it's their first time or their tenth, they leave with a new perspective about spirit communication. The emotional stories of Mikey and Andrew and Tracy were gripping and revealing, but my favorite chapter in the whole book was about the process: Chapter 8—"Appreciating the Messages."

By the spring of 1998, the book was finished and set to be published in the fall. I couldn't wait. It would reach so many more people than I ever could through lectures. I also liked the fact that with a book, there was still a measure of anonymity in a funny way. I insisted that the picture of me on the back cover be one I had taken a couple of years earlier and used on my business card. The lighting and angle gave a kind of mystical tone to it, and somehow it looked like me but it didn't look like me. So I could be known for my work, not my face. Pay attention to what I do, but leave me out of it.

With that, I hoped, would come something I craved. Credibility. For as long as I had been working professionally as a psychic medium, my goal was to be respected by my peers, and for my work to be understood and accepted by the public. There was no denying I had chosen a field tainted by the stereotypes of phonies and flakes, and ridiculed by cynics. If you were prominent enough to be written about in newspapers or magazines, it usually meant they were going to make fun of you. What other profession deals with such a profound subject and is taken less seriously? In my mind, a book was a way for me to take some control of how I—and the whole idea of spirit communication—was perceived. And it meant that I had attained a certain stature. A book was something you could hold in your hands and keep on your bookshelf. It wasn't going to be lining someone's birdcage. To have the prestige and credibility of a major publishing company behind me meant that smart, careful people believed in me. At least my editor and the people I worked closely with believed in me. I'm not sure what the people at the top believed, other than that, whether I was talking to the dead or not, I was convincing enough to sell books.

And make no mistake—selling books is what I wanted to do. I saw no reason to be embarrassed about seizing this opportunity to be paid as much money as I honestly could for my hard work. I am no different from anyone else. I only had to make sure of one thing: Money could be a by-product of what I do. But it could not be the *reason*. If I let the balance tip, if money became my driving force, I would have problems. It was a lesson I had to learn over and over and over. If I had a mortgage payment due and saw five readings on my calendar that would get me over the top, all five would cancel.

To get the book out there, I knew I would have to essentially stop earning my living and focus all my energies on promoting it. The publicists said I would have to get on TV. I didn't wait for them to do it. I started calling people who knew people. I made cold calls to talk-show producers. I sent out promotional tapes. It seemed that after James Van Praagh went on *Larry King Live* twice within a couple of months, he started his phenomenal rise to the top of the *New York Times* bestseller list.

I figured Larry was a good place for me to start, especially since a close friend of mine had a brother who was a top-ranking executive at CNN. Larry seemed to like mediums. I went on one night in June, four months before the book was due out. I did well enough with Larry to leave with an invitation to come back when the book was out. A few days later, the publisher decided to publish *One Last Time* in hardcover. The power of Larry! My first lesson learned.

The book arrived in November of 1998. The publisher sent me to the big cities, and others where I had relationships with radio stations. Dallas, Denver, Cincinnati, San Francisco, Seattle. I would go on the air, do some readings and horse around with the morning-drive hosts, then appear at bookstores. I had made friends with a woman named Ramey Warren Black, a veteran TV talk show producer who had recently left the *Leeza* show to start a media consulting business. She made some calls and helped get me on the one-name-TV-host circuit. Roseanne. Maury. Donny and Marie. Catherine Crier, a former judge, had me on her show and was amazingly honest and objective about a topic that was risky for her to embrace. After they preempted me on my birthday, the Larry King producers offered me a night when Larry would be away, the day before Halloween. His fill-in would be Greta Van Susteren, CNN's legal analyst. I said sure. She would do an interesting interview. And she did. She asked me about my burden of proof.

"WHERE'S THE PATHFINDER?" Sandra asked over the phone. It was a few days before Thanksgiving, and I had arrived in Los Angeles for another stop on the book tour. She wanted to know where I'd left the car. In the driveway, I told her. No, really, she said, where is it? *In the driveway, I said. Right where I left it.* It's not there, she said. *Sandra, you saw me get in the cab to go to the airport. The Pathfinder's in the driveway.* Well, it's not there, she insisted. I was getting annoyed. I had a lot to deal with— *Entertainment Tonight* was doing a story, and there were problems—and I didn't need my wife calling from home to say she'd misplaced the car. *Sandra! It's in the driveway!*

A pause. "Well, psychic boy. One of your *Boys* should have told you that your damn *car* was going to be stolen right from your *driveway*. Because it's not there."

Not a good way to start a day on a book tour. Something tells me I'd better stay a little more tuned in than usual today.

I was scheduled to appear at a Barnes & Noble in Santa Monica that night, and a crew from *Entertainment Tonight* was going to be there to shoot footage, and interview me for a segment they were doing. The show's producers told our publicist that it would be the cover story. My guides said this was a bad idea. Don't let *ET* be there. Not tonight. I had no idea why. But I figured I missed something about the Pathfinder being stolen; I'd better pay attention now.

If you wonder what it's like to live inside my head, this is what it's like sometimes: I have to call the publicist for a major New York publisher, which is spending a lot of money to send me around the country to get as much attention as it is possible to get in two weeks, and tell her that under no circumstances should she allow *Entertainment Tonight*, which is doing a *cover story* on me, to come to a public event and shoot footage of me in front of several hundred people who think I'm terrific—and I have no idea why. Poor Kristen, the publicist. The conversation goes like this:

"They can't come. Not tonight. You've got to change it."

"What? *Why?*"

"I don't know."

"You don't *know?*"

"My guides are telling me they can't be there. I don't know why.

They're just saying they can't be there."

"Well, I'm not canceling because of *that*."

"Well, then, I'm not going."

"You're not *going?*"

"I'm not going if they're coming. My Pathfinder was stolen out of my driveway, and I didn't get a heads-up. They didn't tell me about that, but they *are* telling me this. They can't come tonight."

"Your Pathfinder was stolen so I'm supposed to . . . John, you're being ridiculous."

"Kristen, do I have to show you my business card?"

"I'm not canceling them."

I called Ramey. She didn't question it for a second. She called the producer from *ET*, who was, like just about every talk TV producer in town, a friend of hers. Listen, Ramey told her. Forget Barnes & Noble. That's pedestrian. How about this—John's doing *Leeza* tomorrow, my old show. Shoot him doing that. Much better stuff. And then you've got the whole cross-promotion thing. They're Paramount. You're Paramount. Sold.

Thank you, Ramey. "So what do you think's going to happen tonight?" she asked me.

"I don't know. They're not telling me. All I can think is either nobody's gonna show up, or I'm gonna suck."

I arrived at the Barnes & Noble with two of my close friends, Mark Misiano and Rick Korn, who were with me on the tour. We looked around. It was a good-sized crowd. And when I began my talk, they were extremely receptive. Everything seemed fine. Maybe I was just out of sync today, some kind of psychic jet lag.

About halfway through my talk, a tall woman in a long coat entered the store and walked along the back wall. She came in unobtrusively, but she had a dark energy that everyone in the room seemed to sense. People turned to look at her as she made her way left to right and found a place to stand in the corner. The positive energy I took from the crowd abruptly shut down. *Okay, this might be a problem,* I thought as I kept talking. I knew this woman was the reason *Entertainment Tonight* had to be deflected over to *Leeza*. I didn't know why, didn't know what she was going to do, but it was definitely going to be something I wouldn't want to see on television. Her negative energy was so strong that she was blocking out spirits that I had felt on that side of the room before she entered.

Then the woman screamed out, *Where's the proof?*

Everyone turned to look.

You can't prove this scientifically! This is nonsense!

The audience started murmuring. A man yelled at her, "Go write your own book. Shut up or leave."

You're all stupid fools!

Before it got too ugly, I stepped in. "Wait, wait," I said. "Let's respect everyone in the room. This woman obviously has her own belief system, or disbelief system. So why not listen? I always tell people to keep their skepticism. This lady will play the role of the skeptic. I'm not here to convince anyone of anything, but let's entertain her questions. But first"— I looked at her—"I have just one question for *you*. Do you believe in God?"

No!

"Well, then I don't think I can help you, because this is something that is driven by a belief in God. It's the energy from that force that I think allows us to create *this* energy."

The people applauded. This woman was my first heckler. And this nasty little scene would have been the centerpiece of the *ET* report. No doubt about it.

I got back to the audience. I closed my eyes, breathed deeply, rubbed my hands. "I'm coming over here," I said, walking to my right toward a middle-aged woman. I noticed that a man had been sitting with her but had gotten up and left. The woman acknowledged a few things. Meanwhile, Darth Vader was rolling her eyes. I tried to stay focused. It's your daughter who's coming through, I told the woman. She's saying she was murdered. The woman validated virtually everything I told her over the next few minutes. "I only wish my husband was still here to hear this," she said finally.

"I did," came a soft voice from an unseen corner of the store.

The audience heaved a collective sigh. Darth Vader stormed out. It was as if it was good versus evil, and good won.

On the way to the airport, Mark said, "They really watch your ass. That is an amazing, amazing thing. They totally protected you tonight. Don't you ever not listen to them."

DO PUBLISHERS HAVE SPIRIT GUIDES?

AFTER THIS WHIRLWIND TOUR, after all the national television exposure, I was sure the book would take off. This just in from The Boys: *Surprise— not happening.*

One of the standard caveats I give people before I do readings is to leave their expectations at the door. Whatever happens, happens, and for a reason. Value whatever you get, even if it's not what you wanted or anticipated. I should have remembered that. I mean, my favorite chapter was all about that—"Appreciating the Messages." But I was clueless. *One Last Time* was going nowhere, at least by the standard of my own inflated expectations, and I saw nothing to appreciate in *that* message. Was I naïve? Arrogant? Maybe both. But mostly I was too caught up in the Big Sell to realize that my guides wouldn't stand for it. Yes, they protect me. But sometimes that means protecting me from myself.

I have a rock on my desk, a paperweight, that says "Trust." It has a very specific meaning for me. I don't easily trust people. I have learned to always trust my guides. I just need to remember that sometimes their schedule is not necessarily the same as mine.

As far as I can tell, publishing conglomerates don't have spirit guides. The sales and marketing people thought they might have made a mistake by using my title. *One Last Time* was too generic, they thought, not memorable or to the point enough. You had to read the book to know that *One Last Time* alluded to a wish I had shared with my mother many years ago—that people should have one last time to connect with their loved ones, not just before they passed, but *after* they passed. I didn't think the title was the problem. I liked the title. It meant a lot to me. But it wasn't a title that was on a lot of people's lips.

The Berkley people may well have considered the book a success. They'd paid me only a small advance, so they didn't have to sell a huge number of books to make money. Then they could push the paperback, which is what they'd had in mind in the first place. And if that went nowhere? Well, that's big-time publishing. Churn out three hundred titles a year, give each one about six weeks to make a splash, then move on to the next one. I had always suspected they didn't have great expectations for me, anyway. Through its various imprints, Berkley's huge parent company, Penguin Putnam, published all the established psychic stars—

Sylvia Browne, James Van Praagh, George Anderson. I was the rookie, trying to break into the big leagues. My editor was wonderfully supportive and enthusiastic. But she couldn't get books in the stores any more than I could.

I tried not to dwell too much on the disappointment, still holding out a glimmer of hope that word-of-mouth would somehow build slowly but surely enough to get the book off the ground. Meanwhile, thanks to Rick Korn, I had some other things going on that distracted me from my frustrations and kept me going. I'd met Rick only a year earlier, but we had clicked immediately, and he had wasted no time trying to help me broaden my horizons. Rick was a great talker who told great stories. He had all kinds of experience in television and music marketing, and he was always bubbling with ideas, never at a loss for contacts. It was the phone call to his brother at CNN that first got me on *Larry King Live.*

I had made a video version of *One Last Time* that was ready before the book was. Rick thought I should use the Larry King opportunity to sell it. "Everyone who goes on there promotes something, a movie, a TV show, a book," he said. "Why not you?" He asked the show's producer if Larry would hold up the video for a couple of seconds at the end of the show and give an 800 number. The producer said they don't usually do that, but I guess they made an exception because of Rick's connection.

Rick set up a phone bank through a telemarketing company where he had once worked. The night of the show, Larry held up the tape, and the producers were nice enough to flash the number on the screen. I don't know how many people wanted the video, but enough calls came in to crash the phone bank. Most people got busy signals. So then they started calling CNN's offices in Atlanta and Washington, and blew out *their* phone lines, which the network did not appreciate. A few thousand people did get through and placed their orders. But the company we hired to duplicate and ship the tapes . . . well, there's no other way to put this. They ripped us off. They took the money, twice or three times from some customers, and didn't send out the tapes. Some people threatened legal action—they're probably still out there thinking it was some sort of TV scam. We had to scramble to get a new company to get these tapes out, and we had to pay for priority shipping.

The whole debacle cost me a lot of money—about the starting salary of *two* public school teachers. Meanwhile, I was having problems with the freelance producer who had made the video. We had met in 1997, after I gave a talk at Starchild Books, a New Age store in Florida owned by Sandi Anastasi, the only person in this field who can claim to be a teacher of mine. This producer came up to me and said we should do a video together. I wasn't interested. He kept calling, saying how much money we would make. I told him to go away. Then he came back with a different pitch: Think of how many people will hear your message. I bought it. While putting the video together, he was all about what a beautiful thing this was, how important this was, how we would touch so many people. Looking back, though, he seems to have been more about the money.

I might have taken the hint, that I can't be out there hustling the spirit world. But no. Let me keep trying this. At least One Last Time. The Larry King snafu was a night to forget, but the guys in the direct marketing business took notice. I mean, it can't be that easy to blow out the phone lines of a company that only sells stuff over the phone. They asked if I'd be interested in making an infomercial. I began talking to them, and eventually agreed to offer a package that would include a revised video and a copy of the book, as well as another video on developing your own spirit-communication abilities, called *Building Bridges to the Spiritual Realm*. And, courtesy of Rick, a CD he produced with Annie Haslam, the lead singer of the British group Renaissance. It featured a song Annie had written after reading the book, called *Precious One*. It was about Mikey DiSabato, the little boy whose spirit had become so close to me over the years that he had gotten his own chapter.

Books don't sell on TV, the direct marketing people told me, so it would be the tapes they would focus on. *One Last Time* would be a "premium"—a giveaway. Hey, whatever it took to get the book in people's hands. Any qualms I had about hawking myself through that much-maligned art form, the infomercial, eased considerably after I met Chad Murdock, the guy the marketing company wanted to hire to produce and direct the show. The first time I met Chad, I wanted to see if he was right for the job. I asked him about his background and his ideas. But then I realized he wasn't there to be interviewed by me. He was there to interview *me*. When he had first been approached by the marketing people, he was wary. They told him I was legitimate, but he wanted to make sure I wasn't one of those 1-800-Dial-A-Psychic charlatans. So when we met, he came with a lot of questions about *my* background and work. And it slowly dawned on us that we were interviewing each other.

Chad and I were on the same page from the get-go. I saw the infomercial as an opportunity to introduce my work to a lot of people and broaden the awareness of spirit communication. I hoped they would buy the tapes and get more out of it, and I wouldn't mind if it made a lot of money, but I saw the infomercial as an end in itself. Chad was excited, too. He saw an opening to do something special, not the usual infomercial. In fact, he didn't even want to make an infomercial. He wanted to do a quality half-hour show. At the end, we could simply say something like, "If you're interested in this, call this number."

Unfortunately, the marketing company had no such thoughts. The head of the company was new to the creative aspect of the infomercial industry—in fact, he had never even been on the set of a television production of any kind—so he brought someone in to oversee things, much to Chad's dismay. And quickly, mine. Forget being on the same page— this guy wasn't even in the same *book*. He came in like Yosemite Sam, guns ablaze. *Now here's what we're gonna do. You—psychic guy—over there.* When he thought someone was slacking off—like going home for Christmas when there was vital work to be done—Yosemite demanded that they "*BUCK UP!*" So we didn't figure to see a lot of peace, love, and understanding around our sweet little project. I wanted to put a lot of educational information in the infomercial. Fat chance. I wanted it to show me doing readings so people could see how the process works. Forget it—you can't just *give* it away. I wanted Judy Guggenheim, co-author of *Hello from Heaven!* and probably the world's leading documentarian of after-death communication, to be the host. Sure, sure, she can be in it, but we're going with a pro, a redhead, real nice-looking. So don't expect to see this Judy in the final cut.

In other words, Yosemite Sam, and his boss, Elmer Fudd, were hell-bent on making an *infomercial.* A yell-and-sell, as they call it up there on the high channels, with the standard-issue infohost dripping with contrived sincerity, selling me like I'm the latest remedy for Male Pattern Baldness. A lot of people saying how great I am, how I changed their lives, blah, blah, blah, and if you call in the next sixty seconds, you'll get this great eight-in-one knife sharpener, absolutely free. "You can't sell spirituality," I told Elmer, in all earnestness. "It's something that people have to acquire on their own." Oh, they can acquire it on their own all right—for $29.95. The phone call's on us.

Fortunately, the infomercial never saw the light of day (or night), aside from a few small test markets, where it went over like a pitch for a treadmill that only goes backwards. It didn't convey who I was or what I do. It was disjointed and unconvincing. It was what you might expect: a sitcom-length commercial for soul survival. My guides gave it two thumbs way, way down.

"I can't believe it," Rick said. "This should have been a grand slam." The marketing company wanted to recut it—make it "edgier." I told them to forget it. I wondered if my guides just didn't want these people to make any money from me. And maybe The Boys thought I could do better.

AFTER THAT, IT WAS CLEAR: Let's go back to what I know. Just me and a room full of people. No cameras, no phone lines, no used-car salesmen with camera crews. Rick organized an event at a hotel in Dallas for which we booked ballroom space for five hundred people. But after I went on a radio show the day before the event, the response was so strong that we decided to expand the room to a thousand seats, a major commitment of money. It would be the largest crowd I had ever appeared in front of. That was fitting. With me on the trip was Lydia Clar, the psychic who had gotten me started when I was fifteen. My guides had picked her to put me on my path. Now I guess they wanted her to have a look at where the path was leading me.

The phone lines were fine this time. Everything was looking good. And then there was a slight problem. The company we contracted to handle the event had hired a telemarketing outfit to process reservations over the phone. And they lost the credit card information of everyone who called, or so they said. Rick was on the phone all day, and finally demanded that the head of the company we were dealing with fly to Dallas from Philadelphia. But all he did was apologize a lot. The other guys—they're all under federal investigation. Why didn't I know this was going on? What's the use of being a psychic if you can't see danger ahead? I'm no different from anyone else. I'm here to learn lessons, too.

That night, Rick and a coordinator we brought with us sat at a table at the door, furiously writing down the credit card numbers of all 600 people who came. They had no idea who had paid and who hadn't. The rest of the people didn't even show up because they hadn't gotten confirmations. It was a financial nightmare, but it was really worse than that. Rick took it really hard. He was a successful marketing consultant. He knew stuff happens sometimes. But he wasn't used to the kind of spectacular fiascos that were occurring all around me. Rick was a master of marketing who was just doing what came naturally. Lesson for me: Putting business over the work—not a good idea. Lesson for Rick: See Lesson One.

On the flight home, we were a defeated bunch. Rick opened *USA Today* and showed me an article about the success of several psychic mediums. I was very happy for them and for the field. They were both getting the recognition they deserved. But I couldn't help but wonder what I was doing wrong. You want me to write a book, I told my guides, I write a book. You tell me it will reach a lot of people, do a lot of good. I work hard to get it out there. So why is it a flop—and why is everything I touch a financial disaster?

My ego was taking a beating, for sure, but not as brutal as the pummeling my bank account was getting. Traveling to promote the book, I was not earning my living giving readings and seminars. And, of course, I didn't have a job to fall back on. Meanwhile, Sandra and I had invested borrowed money so she could become a partner in a dance studio. By December, we were really struggling. A lot of people outside my immediately family and closest friends assumed I'd hit it big. I had a book out, I was on TV—I must be a millionaire. It couldn't have been further from the truth.

I couldn't imagine how this could possibly fit into the universal plan I thought I was following. But it did. I was just too close to see it. Perspective is everything.

LIFE'S A BITCH—AND THEN YOU DON'T DIE

I HAVE A SIMPLE PHILOSOPHY about the whole idea of destiny and choice. If you meet with obstacles, you try to overcome them. You fix what you need to fix to reach what you believe is your goal. If you still can't fix it, if you're hitting a wall, it probably means you're not doing what you're supposed to be doing. Change careers. Change direction. You're meant to be doing something else.

For me, the wall was this: I was playing by the rules—at least I thought I was—and yet I was becoming weighed down by some of the nastiest energy I'd ever known. The downside of the Information Age is that the bad stuff is impossible to control. It spreads like a retrovirus. All of a sudden, people I'd never met were attacking me with a vengeance on psychic message boards and Amazon.com. Most of the comments on Amazon were very positive, but of course I focused on the negative ones. That the book was cookie-cutter, new-age stuff, or worse; that I was a fraud preying on gullible, grieving people, using stories that were obviously fabricated. Taking the hits in stride had been a struggle for as many years as I'd been a medium, but now I was a bigger target—even if my book was a flop. I didn't read the criticism on my computer, but people faxed me printouts. Hey, thanks for thinking of me. I tried to shrug them off. But it was infuriating that these Internet critics—the kind of people who give free speech a bad name—were telling the world that the stories in the book were made up when I knew they were completely true, verified by a respected journalist, and written without any exaggeration.

After the book tour, I came home and got back to doing private readings. I had moved my office out of my home and into a commercial building after I'd had one too many drive-bys, one too many "Just in cases," as in "Just in case you had a cancellation, I thought I'd knock on your door." The new office was in a two-story building on a busy Long Island thoroughfare called Jericho Turnpike, upstairs from the salon where I had my hair cut. It was a corner office with lots of windows to let in the light.

I was in a different place emotionally as well. Coming off the frustrations of the past six months, I was much more sensitive than usual to the ups and downs of my workaday world. Private readings have always been important to me; they are my roots, and they keep me on the ground. Like a comedian who goes on television and appears in movies but needs to come back to standup in small clubs to keep his balance, I need to be doing one-on-one readings in my little office with nobody else there. I need that intimate, personal connection. But the last thing anybody needs is my filling the room with negative energy. Step *away* from the medium.

I would read someone in my office, and the person would let me know she was disappointed that her son didn't come through, or that I didn't get her husband's name. Or I would have what I thought was a great session with someone, both on a professional and personal level, and two days later I would go to my mailbox and find a scathing letter from that same person, who had apparently decided after leaving my office that it was outrageous that I charge money for what I do. These kinds of attacks were not new to me. Nor was my own dismal reaction. A particularly wounding comment or incident, or a personal attack on my integrity, was entirely capable of putting me out of commission for a couple of days. But I'd gotten better at letting the shots whiz past my ear, usually with the help of a nice letter from a happy client telling me how much peace and comfort her reading had brought. But now I was finding it harder to climb out of the hole.

I'd never been this chewed up. The closest I'd come was in the spring of 1997, at a time when I was stressed out about the physical and emotional demands of my work and feeling a little sorry for myself. "People don't understand how hard this is," I had told Sandra. "They don't realize how much energy it takes. And they're only too quick to criticize. 'Why didn't my mom say this instead of that? Why didn't Grandpa come through instead of that Uncle Tony that I hated?' How could these people not appreciate the gift they're getting? Their people are trying to come through for them, and I'm working like hell to get them through. But they're not satisfied. They want more. What's wrong with them?" Nothing worse than a pissed-off medium.

I was scheduled to appear in Albany at an event organized by Todd Pettengill, the WPLJ radio personality whose show had a lot to do with getting my full-time professional career off the ground. On the way upstate, Sandra saw how down I was. She has never wavered in the conviction that connecting people and spirits is what I'm supposed to be doing. She's like an earthly guide. But nothing she said could snap me out of it.

We reached Albany and headed to the auditorium at the College of

St. Rose. When I appeared on-stage, I was greeted by an incredible sight: People were giving me a standing ovation. I was stunned. Nothing like that had ever happened before. I didn't know why it was happening now. The energy in the room zapped me back to life. I had a great night, and at the end, I hugged Todd. "You have no idea how much I needed that tonight," I told him. I looked at Sandra, and we smiled. The way I saw it, they weren't standing and applauding for *me*. They were applauding for the work I did. They appreciated it. That's all I needed to know. It was a pivotal moment for me, because had I not come out of it I might well have gone back to work in the hospital, or done something else.

Now, two years later, I began to think that not only was I hitting a wall, but there might be handwriting on it. I withdrew from Sandra and from my friends. Rick Korn called me, and I could barely talk to him. I had nothing to say.

I will never forget this night: I'm sitting back in my chair, sneakers off, as usual when I do private readings. I'm alone in my office after finishing the last reading of the night. It's about ten o'clock. I look down at my white socks. They're dirty from walking around without shoes. I wonder if my clients saw them. They're probably thinking, *The guy's charging $200 for a reading; the least he could do is have clean socks.* It makes me think of my grandmother, and I chuckle out loud. Granny would definitely be getting on my case. And then I sit back in the chair some more, and finally I say to myself, "I'm done."

I add it all up: I'm having the longest period of discontentment I've had as a medium. I haven't had a worse six months since my mother's dying days. I'm tired all the time, I'm expending a lot of energy, and not getting a whole lot in return. The past six months have been a paradox. With all the exposure I've had, I'm getting more attention—more letters and phone calls than ever. But I'm not making enough money to be anything but a one-person operation. I don't want to raise my fees. I have a rule I wouldn't break: I only charge what I would pay. I was so sure the book would be my big turning point. Maybe it was. I went to school for nearly five years, got within a few credits of a master's. I can do something else. It's time to move on to the next thing.

The phone rings. It's Mark. He and I have been friends since the age of twelve, back when I was telling teachers about their auras. Even twenty years later, we're like very tight brothers. We chose different careers. I'm a medium; he's an accountant. Great combination: death and taxes. There are only two times when Mark and I go even a day without talking. One is during tax season. The other is when I'm going through a funk. This time, I'm in a funk during tax season. My meager income for the preceding year doesn't help. We haven't talked in days. He'd gotten a call from Rick Korn. I sounded so bad on the phone. Rick was worried.

"What's going on?" Mark asked.

"I'm not doing this anymore," I told Mark.

"Okay, what's wrong?" Mark wasn't new to this. He'd seen me completely sapped, zombie-faced and shut down after lectures. I'd go into a two-hour zone-out, fall asleep, then bounce back the next morning. He'd also seen me do my share of dwelling on perceived slights. He once tried to pump me up after an event with a forty-five-minute monologue. I just sat there. "I just wasted the last forty-five minutes, didn't I," he said finally.

Now I gave him the I-don't-feel-appreciated speech, which he'd heard before.

He gave me the but-you-bring-a-lot-of-comfort-to-people speech, which I'd heard before.

"This is different," I said. "I think I want to do something else."

"Really," Mark said.

"I don't want to deal with people."

"What would you do instead?"

I had been thinking about when I was the happiest with what I was doing. It was back in the hospital. And not when I was the computer guy with lots of responsibility and a promising future. It was when I was drawing blood. The actual job was irrelevant. What I loved was connecting with the patients. I would see them before and after surgery, and I felt like I could affect their lives in a positive way, calming their nerves with some encouraging words, a gentle tease, or just a smile at the right time. *Hey, tomorrow's the big day. I'll see you when you get out. You'll be so drugged up you won't even have the pleasure of feeling me draw your blood.* When I was nineteen, just a couple of years before I began working in the hospital, I had spent day after day at my mother's bedside as she lay dying of a cancer that had been diagnosed just a few months before. Now I felt as if every patient I saw was my mother. Every person who came in to visit was me. To make it a little easier for them was tremendously rewarding. Now *that* was appreciated. I missed it—I still do.

"Then you should go back to the hospital," Mark said. "Go back to health care."

But I didn't want to go back to the hospital. I wanted to return to the feeling of contentment I'd had, but not to the actual job. The hospital was filled with, you know, people. I'd recently added a second Bichon to our family. Now Jolie had a little sister, Roxie. Sandra and I referred to them as "the girls." I loved those dogs.

"I'm going to vet school," I told Mark.

— CHAPTER 2 —

My Three Signs

PRINCESS

When I was starting college, I thought I'd eventually like to go on to medical school. It was a step up from my earlier ambition, which was to own a deli. I could imagine becoming a surgeon. What I couldn't imagine was how I would pay for school. My parents couldn't afford it. Even if they could, I wasn't sure I had the patience to wait until I was almost 30 to finish my schooling and start my career. So I lowered my sights a little. I thought about training to be a physician's assistant. I even looked into becoming a cardio pump perfusionist. That's how seriously I wanted to work in health care.

Eventually, I settled on health administration. But even before I graduated, I was starting on a different career path, even if I didn't fully understand it at the time. It was the experience surrounding my mother's passing when I was nineteen that is the reason that I find myself, a decade later, conversing with the dead for a living. I don't have to stretch too much to see what I do as health care of a sort.

My mother was a major force in my life, and she always seemed to be closely connected with everything psychic that happened to me. She introduced me to it as a child, in a gradual, unthreatening way. Later, when I got a glimpse of my abilities, she gently encouraged me to develop them. When I had questions about the meaning of it all, she helped me answer them, even if she sometimes didn't even know that's what she was doing. But her biggest lessons of all came at the end of her life and in the dozen years since she has been on the other side.

Her given name was Perinda, but everyone called her Prin, short for Princess, a nickname given to her when she was only a few days old. A nurse thought she looked like a little princess in her bassinet, and the name stuck. So the ninth of eleven children was the princess of the family, even if she felt like anything but. She told me years later that she had always thought of herself as the ugly duckling of the family, a self-image others did nothing to dispel.

My mother's family moved from Brooklyn out to Glen Cove, Long Island, when she was a teenager. A decade later, she met and then married Jack McGee, who later became a city cop and a career military reservist. They moved back over the city line, to Queens, where I was born. I was christened John Edward McGee. To answer the question: Yes, John Edward is my real name, just not my full name at birth. But it is now. I no longer answer to McGee. And for the record, it's Edward. Not Edwards. Some of my friends think I should just get it over with and change my name to Edwards, just add the damn "s."

I was born two days and three subway stops away from the 1969 Miracle Mets' crowning moment of glory at Shea Stadium. You would think this might make me a sports fan on some organic, karmic level. But I've never had much interest in baseball, or any other sport. (This is why things like this happen: During a reading, I was shown a Baby Ruth candy bar. It turned out that the spirit had given this person a bat signed by Joe DiMaggio. Not quite getting those sports references, guys.)

So back to my mother. She worked for seventeen years as a secretary and office manager at a factory that made typewriter ribbons and carbon paper. Then she moved up to a job in Manhattan. And to her, it really was moving up. She was no longer working at some little factory on Long Island that made a product that was starting to look like a relic. She was the office manager for a multimillion-dollar venture capital firm, responsible for keeping things running on six floors of offices. She felt as if she had arrived. But I don't think she ever quite shook the ugly-duckling feeling, so she spent her money on clothes, and on getting her hair frosted and her nails manicured. It was important for her to look good. To try to live up to her nickname.

By that point, she and my father were separated, and Mom and I were living with my grandmother on Long Island, in the house my mother had lived in as a teenager. The reasons for the disintegration of my parents' marriage were complicated . . . and they weren't complicated. Isn't that the way it usually is? She was a strong-willed Italian. He was a strong-willed Irishman. It was a culture clash that was evident in the way they regarded their own families. That my mother refused to cut the cords with her mother and siblings was an issue. As was my mother's devotion to me, her only child. To her, I always came first, even if it came at the expense of her personal life. On some basic level, my mother and father had an intense love bond, but it was broken by their inability to understand each other. My mom would tell me that they loved each other too much. They just couldn't live together.

My grandmother instilled in me a great sense of family, always having big parties with lots of music in what came to be known as "the dancing room." But as tight as my bonds have always been to the maternal side of the family, I have not been able to match that closeness with my father or much of his family. This isn't easy, given my philosophy of life. A few years ago, recognizing that I was always telling people to appreciate and validate their loved ones who had passed, I realized I should expand the message to the obvious: We shouldn't focus so much on communicating with those on the other side that we neglect to appreciate and validate the people in our lives on This Side. But, of course, sometimes, despite the best of intentions, that's not possible. The simple answer in my case is that my father and I have never been able to be close, for whatever reasons of personality, distance, and experience.

My closeness with my mother's side, especially my grandmother and aunts, developed naturally after my parents split up. With my mother off at work in the city, my grandmother was the one who looked after me when I got home from school. I'd come through the door and find her in the same spot every day, crocheting and watching the soaps from a chair between the living room and dining room. And I do mean soaps. She would have two TVs on: One, a big, old RCA console with family photos sitting on top, would be slightly turned toward the dining room and tuned to *Another World* on Channel 4. The other, the hottest new Zenith, was turned toward the living room and tuned to *Guiding Light* on Channel 2. My grandmother sat in the middle and actually watched and followed both shows simultaneously, her head moving back and forth as if she were watching a tennis match from center court.

I would have preferred cartoons, but that wasn't an option since Granny didn't have a third TV. We make our choices in life. I went to the *Guiding Light* side because it seemed to have better stories. I learned to tune out *Another World*. Granny wouldn't surrender the TV until 4:30, at which point I would flip over to reruns of *Batman*. But I usually stayed with that only if Batgirl came zooming across the opening montage on her motorcycle. That meant that the episode would feature Commissioner Gordon's librarian daughter, who would turn into the red-hot Batgirl, who was played by Yvonne Craig, who I had a serious TV crush on—no matter which character she was playing. And if you got both Bat-girl and Catwoman . . . well, life was good. But it turned out that like most crushes, the love didn't last. It was *Guiding Light* that I got stuck on. And eventually, my grandmother gave up on *Another World*. We would sit there on the couch, Granny and I, watching the impossibly complicated goings-on in Springfield.

My mom, the family breadwinner, would take the train home and walk through the door precisely at 6:30 each evening, looking more like the dads than the moms I saw on TV. She'd be tired after a long day at the office, and not in too good a mood. You didn't talk to her. You waited for her to talk to you first. Everyone was better off that way. But that was just her—you had to accept that it wasn't always sunshine and rose petals around my mother. But she was as fiercely devoted a mother as anyone could have, all the more so because it had become clear that I would have a minimal relationship with my father.

Here's a little thing that tells you a lot: I was a pudgy kid, the one who always got picked last in choose-up games. My mother would take me shopping at Mays' & JC Penney's department stores, and I noticed that before she sent me into the dressing room to try on pants or jackets, she would surreptitiously rip a tag from each one. I found out later that these were the tags that said "Husky." She didn't want me to see them.

For a long time, I thought my mother was also a nut. It was the psychic thing. She was always going to psychics and psychic fairs, having psychic house parties. My father wanted no part of it, and wanted no part of it for me, either. You just make sure Johnny's not home when you bring these people over here, he'd tell her. That was just fine with me.

She wasn't into mediums. I only remember hearing the word *séance* once as a child. My mother's brother, Joey, had invited a medium by the name of Reverend Craig to my grandmother's house for one. I was thrown out of the room for being a child. This five-foot small-framed white-haired medium put her finger in my face and told me to leave, that I would have enough time for this later in my life. An interesting state-ment given my career choice. But, beyond that, I never heard the word until I was a teenager. My mother wanted to know about the here-and-now, and if you don't mind, a little bit about next week. And, if possible, anything important in the next twenty years or so. As I got older, I would tease her about being a psychic junkie, but besides finding her obsession inane, I found it irritating as hell. Mom, I'd say, these are con artists. They're taking your money, and for what? To tell you about your life? You're *living* your life. Predict your future? Okay, Mom. Sure. Whatever you say. That I had always been able to know things I couldn't know did not enter into it. Seeing auras around people and having dreams that seemed to take me outside my own body was just stuff that was a normal part of life, as far as I knew. It had nothing to do with all these "psychics" my mother hung around with.

When I was fifteen, my mother's latest psychic came to our house and read various members of the family in my bedroom. Her name was Lydia Clar. From the living room, I'd hear my aunts and cousins go into my room and shut the door, and then the door would open a little while later and the next one would go in. One after another, all night long. When my cousin Roseann came out, she came over to me and said, "John, she's good. You should get a reading." No thanks, Ro. But she badgered me until I said okay, okay. Looking back at it now, there was no way my guides would have let Lydia leave our house that night without reading me. She was their messenger.

I wasn't in the room two minutes when Lydia told me that I was the reason she was here. "You have highly evolved spiritual guides, and they are ready to work with you," she said. "I was sent here to introduce you to this world, to open you to your future." You can imagine how that went over. Psychic schtick, right? Oh, brother. She must tell that to all the psychic-reading virgins. What are you, the Mrs. Robinson of the psychic set? (Okay, so *The Graduate* came out two years before I was born. I've still heard of it.) But when Lydia sat in my bedroom and told me I was destined to become famous as a psychic, I thought she was laying it on just a bit too heavy. I didn't even think *she* could do this, and I'm supposed to believe her when she says *I* can?

I figured I'd play along. Lydia told me some things about my family that were true, but I dismissed them as either lucky guesses or just a trick. She could have known all of it from talking to my mother. That was my mind-set, always picking apart the things these psychics were telling my mother at all those psychic fairs she'd go to on the weekends. But then Lydia talked about some things in my life that she couldn't have known.

And about events that would happen in the future. Within a few weeks, everything she said would happen *did* happen—nothing momentous, teenage stuff mostly.

I had to admit I was curious. What's this all really about? I started reading about spiritualism and psychic phenomena. *This is weird*, I thought. The books describe all those things I thought were normal, things I've been doing ever since I could remember. When I asked my mother about the possibility of my "being psychic," she told me, "Well, you know I've always told you that you were special."

"You had to say that; you're my mother."

She laughed. "I didn't mean it as your mother. I was talking about your . . . abilities."

It must have taken some self-control for her not to say anything more than that all these years, especially when I was telling her, at age seven, that we had to get home quick because Cousin Phyllis was coming over. That's Cousin Phyllis from Florida, making an unannounced visit. My mother never made a big thing out of this stuff. She just wanted me to be a kid. My abilities would develop, she figured, or they wouldn't.

You know how, when you're young, you open your mind to something, and then all of a sudden you're really into it? Well, it was that, squared. When I get involved in something, I get *involved.* It was as if I was being introduced to a new person—and it was me. I was driven by a need to know who I really was. I started spending a lot of time at the library. I began studying tarot and other metaphysical philosophies with a woman named Sandi Anastasi, who ran a little "psychic institute" on the South Shore of Long Island. She agreed with Lydia. She invited me to a class, and halfway through said it was a waste of time for me to be there—my abilities were already too advanced for this class. She convinced me to try working at psychic fairs. "What is it that you do?" the woman who ran the fair asked me when I showed up the first time. "I don't really know," I said. "I don't know what I do." She had me do a reading, and I was terrible. But she was another one who thought I had "ability." I was hearing that word a lot. I was trying to get a grasp of what that meant.

I started doing psychic fairs on weekends. I wanted to be around psychics, to speak to them, learn how they worked. The most impressive one I met was a woman named Shelley Peck. She was an amazing psychic, but was also known for her astrology and mediumship, which I didn't know anything about yet. She had a background in psychology, and also taught metaphysics and was a certified hypnotherapist who did past-life regressions. That was a lot to digest, but Shelley became one of my closest friends. She was closer in age to my mother, but it didn't matter. We would talk about our work for hours at a time.

At the psychic fairs, I was a novelty. I could hear people talking about me, looking at me. It had nothing to do with my "ability." Sitting at a table among a roomful of middle-aged, tarot-reading, suburban mystics, I looked like I'd gotten lost on my way to the SATs. I was a kid telling people decades older than I was what I thought was happening in their lives.

Pretty quickly I got my first call for a "house party," a group reading at someone's home. I went on the appointed day and rang the doorbell. Through the storm door, I could see a woman on the phone in the kitchen. She looked out, saw me, and yelled, "I just paid you!"

I just looked at her. "Um, I'm not who you think I am," I called to her through the door. She thought I was the paper boy.

She looked again, and suddenly seemed very worried. "You're not John, are you?" she asked. I nodded yes. "*What?* Why didn't you tell me you were just a kid? Oh, God. I have a house full of people coming." She opened the door. "Okay, come in quick. You'll have to read me first. And hurry. Because if you can't do it, you have to get out of here before anyone comes. I might have to call everybody and cancel. Why didn't you tell me how old you are?"

I wound up spending six hours in this woman's house. She asked me to come back. I declined.

NOT LONG AFTER I STARTED doing psychic readings, something very weird started happening. One day I was doing a card reading for my Aunt Anna, mostly for fun because she didn't take it very seriously. As I was doing the reading, a woman appeared behind her. She was sixtyish, wearing a black dress. She had only one leg, but there was a serene smile on her face. When I described her, my aunt said it sounded like her late mother-in-law. Then a man appeared, slender, with salt-and-pepper hair. I didn't know who he was, and neither did my aunt. To me, it was if these people were actually there, standing right in front of me. The images were fast and fleeting. I registered the smallest details—a flower brooch the woman was wearing, a pocket watch the man was holding. He was nattily dressed, albeit a bit out of fashion. When I asked him who he was, he took a barber's comb out of the pocket of his beige-and-blue pinstriped suit.

Oh, my God. *I see dead people.* Sorry—I've been waiting to say that.

And then, at the psychic fairs, I started feeling a different kind of energy. It struck me that I was doing something other than what I thought I was doing. Not that I had any idea *what* I was doing. Shelley and others had news for me: I was connecting with the spirit world.

Oh, really. This was not that interesting to me. I was a kid. I didn't want to talk to dead people. I wanted to predict people's futures, like Lydia. That was fun. And I was good at it. I was even getting a reputation for it, and people were coming to the fairs specifically to get a psychic reading from me. The kid. But over time, the people I met in the little subculture of the New York psychic circuit encouraged me to develop my skills as a medium, to take them in whatever direction was intended.

And then, a turning point. Shelley Peck wanted to try putting me through a "past-life regression." Here's what was supposed to happen: Through a series of meditations, I would be taken on a trip to a different plane of consciousness, where I could retrieve facts and essences of one or more of my soul's previous lives and convey them unconsciously to her. Sort of a cross between hypnosis, meditation, and time travel. Literal soul searching.

But the regression went in an unplanned direction. Let's just say that on the way to my past lives, we stopped off for a meet-and-greet with my spirit guides—The Boys, as they were destined to become known. In retrospect, I think they chose Shelley to make the introduction that day because we had such a great connection. She thought of me as her protégé, this young kid always hypothesizing about the potential of "our work." I saw her more as an earthly guide of sorts.

LOOKING BACK, I HAD ALWAYS FELT the presence of my guides. I remember telling my mother when I was a young boy that I felt as though I was living the opening of the Scooby Doo cartoon. It showed Scooby Doo outside in the dark of night, and then all these eyes opening and looking down on him. When I felt this presence, I didn't know it was my "guides," of course. I didn't know who they were or why they were there. I didn't feel any particular guidance. I just felt that *someone* was looking in on what I was doing. Five or six of them, in fact. Now we had finally been introduced.

My mother was thrilled that I had come into the fold. I was now one of them. She became a psychic stage mother, bragging to her friends and relatives about her son, the psychic. More than a few relatives thought she was ridiculous—no less ridiculous than her son. She assured them that I would be famous someday.

Late in 1987, my Uncle Carmine died of a heart attack. It happened just two months after I'd had a vision, during a meditation, of him clutching his left arm and collapsing. I told my cousin Ro, Carmine's daughter, and she said her father was scheduled for a physical that very week. She called me the next day and said her father had been given a clean bill of health. His death shook me: Somehow I felt responsible. I had this "ability." I should have done something. Blame it on the doctor? I had to do better than that.

At his wake, I learned from relatives that the man I had seen when I was trying to read cards for my Aunt Anna was Carmine's father. He was a barber. It was totally confusing to me then, but now I realize that not only was the vision of Carmine's heart attack a heads-up, but so was the appearance of his father. He was waiting to greet his son on the other side. That was a major turning point for me. Spirit messages began coming through so much more strongly. It was as if Carmine had gone into a house, leaving me outside in the dark, and then flicked a switch to an outside light. But it was more like a sixty-watt lamp than a halogen floodlight. I had a long way to go before I could call myself a psychic medium, even if I wanted to.

UNTIL I WAS NINETEEN, I regarded my psychic work and mediumship as a kind of hobby. I was just okay at it. I had a hard time keeping up with the images and sounds. They came and went so fast. And my interpretations of the symbols were often off the mark. I wasn't that motivated to work on it and develop my abilities. But then everything changed.

In April of 1989, my mother was diagnosed with terminal lung cancer. It is the mother of all understatements to say it knocked me off balance. I kept my sorrow, my panic, tightly under wraps. I wanted to stay strong for her.

One day a few months after my mother was diagnosed, when it was evident that she would not survive the year, we began to talk about her transition to the other side. The sense I had gotten from my early experience doing readings as a medium was that the other side was all about peace. None of the things that troubled you on earth mattered anymore, and it made you feel—maybe not superior, but promoted to a way more advanced level, maybe even the difference between kindergarten and graduate school. Evolved, to use a cliché. It was a like a variation of one of those self-help mantras from the '70s: "I'm Okay; You're Worried about the Will." But of course, nobody on this side could know for sure if this was true, or if everyone had such a blissful existence once they were liberated from their earthly shackles. We couldn't know what the trip was like until we took it ourselves, and we couldn't know what life was like in that form until our time came to live it. We could only surmise and hope, and devise from that a belief system we could live with. After all, maybe we only heard from the happy ones—a scary implication for everyone else.

I made my mother promise she would come through to tell me she was safe.

"Johnny," she said reassuringly, "when I get to the other side I'll talk to you all the time."

I told her it wasn't that simple. I knew too much, and I would be hurting. How could I distinguish between an actual spirit message, and a thought conceived from my own emotional need? I was a medium; I needed to be objective to do my work. This would be like a surgeon operating on himself. My mother could come to me in an "astral visit" while I slept. Those were unconscious, and I would be able to distinguish between a visit, which is incredibly vivid, and an ordinary dream. That would be fine. But it would be like watching something on tape. I wanted conscious, live, real-time messages confirming that she was okay. There was only one requirement: They had to come through other people. She would have to use other mediums, so I could be sure I wasn't tricking myself. We decided on three signs that she would use to validate that it was her.

First, an easy one. Princess. She could show Diana, she could show a crown. She could even show a pink telephone. Or she could just say her name.

The next sign would be something that was special between us. Ever since I was a little boy, I'd had a thing for Winnie the Pooh. I mean, a real obsession. I started out in kindergarten with a singular Pooh who came with me to school. I kept him in my knapsack. Nobody knew he was in there but me. Right. At lunch, I would take him out so he could breathe. Soon I tired of just the one Pooh, and demanded more and more Poohs. And Pooh wasn't even that popular then. I'm sure my memories are exaggerated, but it seemed like my mother almost never came home without a Pooh bear for me, and sometimes a Tigger, too. No matter how many I had, I had to have more. I had Pooh sheets, Pooh music, Pooh posters. My mother started calling me Winnie. I dragged her to see *Winnie the Pooh and Tigger Too* seventeen times. Then I wanted to leave. But she made me sit through some Sinbad movie seventeen times. I'm sure there was a lesson in there somewhere. She couldn't have liked Patrick Wayne that much.

I wasn't a fan of the classic Pooh, whom I felt lacked personality. It wasn't until the outfits like Sears and Disney got the Pooh rights that Pooh's charm was done much justice by the merchandising industry. That's just my opinion. They have whole teams of people in lab coats working on the "cuteification" of storybook characters. Even when I was a little too old for this, I saw a Pooh that was so adorable, I had to have it. My mother laughed. "You big idiot," she said. "How many of these things do you have?" I know, but he's so cute. She bought it for me.

The second sign had to be Pooh bear.

And then, the last sign. I wanted my mother to make an allusion to something that had become a ritual for me: *Guiding Light,* three o'clock, Channel 2. I had been watching it religiously for more than ten years, and now, in these grim days watching my mother slip away day by day, the soap became an essential diversion for me. My mom wanted to die at home, so I arranged for hospice care. I would spend hours with her, taking only one break when the hospice caretaker was there. Each afternoon at three, I would excuse myself and go to the living room to watch *Guiding Light* with Granny. "I'm going to Springfield," I'd say. Not to be flip—

I'm sure my mother would appreciate the humor in this—but things weren't much better there.

The trouble in Springfield—even more trouble than usual—had started a few years before, when I was in high school. My mother called me at the deli where I was working and said gravely, "John, I have a little bad news for you. I just want you to be prepared for this when you come home."

My heart sank to my intestines. "Is it Grandma? Is she okay?"

"No, she's fine. But I watched *Guiding Light* today."

"Yeah?"

"Reva jumped off a bridge."

"*She jumped off a bridge!?*" Everyone in the deli turned around. "Who? Who jumped off a bridge?" they all started asking. "What happened? Is she okay?"

Reva Shayne was my favorite character on the show. She was an amorous live wire played lusciously by an actress named Kim Zimmer. Three years later, Kim wasn't renewing her contract, so the writers pushed Reva off a bridge (*again*) in the Florida Keys, leaving her husband devastated. So now as my mother was in her last days, my only distraction was to mourn over a TV character I had loved since I was in junior high school. I tried to imagine what Reva's children were going through, how they were dealing with the same thing I would be facing in a few months . . . or weeks, or days.

Reva's body was never found, but years later she was back in Springfield. When I saw her for the first time, I thought: *Wouldn't it be great if in just this one way, life imitated—well, if not art, maybe daytime TV?* We have the potential of spirit communication, but that is never enough. No matter how much I believe in reaching across dimensions, it can't ever be the same as when they were here.

"*Guiding Light*," I told Mom at her bedside. "That's the third sign." But I realized that might be a hard one for her to get across, unless I happened to be with a medium who was a fan. So I gave her an easier way. "Take me to Springfield," I said. "I don't care if it's Springfield, Illinois, or Springfield Boulevard. You can show a spring and a field. I don't care how you do it, but just get me to Springfield. Get me to *Guiding Light* in some way."

"Johnny, I'll do my best," she said.

That night, I made a vow that I would not reveal the three signs to anyone. I wanted to be sure, beyond any doubt, that when they came, they came directly from her.

ONE DAY A COUPLE OF WEEKS LATER, with her room crowded with relatives, my mother looked at me and started telling me how sad she was that she wouldn't live to see my twenty-first birthday. The others began to get teary and started clearing out to leave us alone. My mother and I didn't cry. We wanted to be strong for each other. This was the moment some people never get to have, a One Last Time on this side. She gave me a gold ring and a matching diamond bracelet for the birthday she wouldn't be around to celebrate with me. She wanted to leave me with this moment of love, and I wanted to give her the same thing to take with her on her impending journey. We were both absorbing the power of this bond that we knew would not end just because she was leaving me physically.

My mother departed at four in the morning surrounded by her family. A few seconds after she took her last breath, I walked out of her bedroom and into mine and began to talk to her, trying to help her make the transition to the other side. I told her she would be okay, that soon she would be greeted by her father and by Uncle Carmine. And then I asked her to give me a quick sign that she had arrived, that it was as blissful and blessedly unworldly as I thought. I wasn't asking for one of the signs we had talked about that needed to come through another medium. Something tangible that I would see. I asked her to show me a white bird. It had to be personal, not just a random white bird flying in the sky. It had to be obvious that it was meant for *me*. I had to know that there really was an other side, and that she had arrived there safely. A sickening wave of uncertainty was washing over me; suddenly I had the same fear of the unknown that everyone else feels. I told my mom to go toward the light. And let me know she's safe.

On the afternoon of the last day of the wake, my cousin Anthony came over to comfort me. "So many flowers," he said. "Yours stand out the most. Those white birds are beautiful." I went over and saw that there were two plastic, feathered white birds nested in a colorful arrangement. I'd overlooked them for three days.

"Why did you say they were *my* flowers?" I asked my cousin.

"I don't know," he said. "Roseanne and Joey picked them out for you."

I asked my cousins if they'd requested the birds. They said they hadn't. I called the florist and asked the owner why there had been birds in my flowers. "Oh, I'm sorry, those are for confirmations," he said. "We were really busy yesterday. One of my girls must have put them in there by mistake. I'm very sorry." No apology necessary, I said. They were beautiful.

On that last day of the wake, I found my favorite Pooh bear, the one I had gotten when I was too old, and brought it to the funeral home. After everybody left and I was alone with my mother for the last time, I tucked the bear in next to her in the casket. The next day, she was buried with it.

My mother's death was, of course, a profoundly sad time in my life, one that stays with me all these years later. But it changed my life in a positive way, too. My sense of loss, my need to somehow stay connected to my mother although we were separated by this mysterious dimension between the physical world and the spiritual one, was so powerful that it was nothing short of a revelation: Oh my God. So *that's* how these people feel. Mothers, fathers, sons, daughters, husbands, wives—they all went to mediums to lessen their pain, to keep the kind of bonds that I needed so desperately now. If I can do this for them, I realized, then I have to.

BUSTED

"I GOT AN APPLICATION TO VET SCHOOL," I told Mark almost exactly ten years later.

"Shit, you're serious," he said.

"I went on the Internet and did some research."

"Explain this to me. You're doing this because…"

"So I don't have to deal with people. I'll be able to heal, like, dogs and cats. It seems like animals give you unconditional love. Not that I'm Dr. Doolittle here, but I do feel like I understand animals."

Mark just sat there, looking at me with a face that said, *What's wrong with this guy?* "You know these unconditional beings of fur?" he said finally.

"Yeah?"

48

"They're attached to *people*. It will be *people* who will be bringing them in. It will be *people* who will be paying the bill. It will be *people* who will be complaining to you when their dog dies."

I hadn't thought of it that way. Accountants—they can be so damn smart.

"Shit," I said. "You're right."

"Look," Mark said. "Stop feeling sorry for yourself. You've been through this before; you'll go through it again. God gave you this great ability. How can you think of not using it? What other work could you do that would bring so much peace to people? Look at *me*. I'm an accountant. How much peace and comfort do you think I bring people? I call people and say, 'You owed fifty dollars, but I got it down to ten.'"

I laughed and told Mark, all right, you made your point. But I still felt lousy. I didn't rip up the application to vet school, not yet.

I didn't tell Sandra what I was contemplating. I didn't want to give her the opportunity to say what I knew she would: that this was what I was supposed to be doing, helping people, et cetera, et cetera. I could take it from Mark. He's like Cher in *Moonstruck*. He's in charge of smacks in the face. *Hey—snap out of it!* But if I heard it from Sandra, it would bring me to a place I didn't want to go. Ultimately, she would support whatever I decided. But I hated disappointing her.

We Libras, we're terrible with choices. That's the big joke among the people close to me—don't give him options. But like my mother, when I finally decide something, I'm done. I won't talk about it anymore, and I won't change my mind. But it can take a while to get there, which is not easy for the people around me. First, I will argue both sides, as if I really want both sides. I will argue so passionately why we need to do something on one day and argue just as passionately the next day why that would be the worst possible thing to do. Then I'll work out a line of probabilities for both options. If we do this, this might happen, then this might happen, then this . . . but if we do *this*, then this might happen and this might happen, then . . . being a psychic only complicates things. If it needs to be a consensus decision and I'm pulled in one direction by my guides, which happens all the time, I get very frustrated when people don't listen to me. Another occupational hazard that sometimes makes me feel like I'm alone on the planet.

Anyway, as you've probably surmised, I decided not to become a pet doctor. Which meant I had to confront what the past nine months had been all about. It wasn't as simple as That's Life. That's not how my life works. Things happen for a reason. As I slowly climbed out of my little abyss, I began to realize that it wasn't unappreciative people who were making me so unhappy. I was basically using them—the very people I had set out to help—as scapegoats for what was really bugging me: I was angry at *myself*. I had let my guides down. I'd failed to achieve what I was supposed to. I had screwed up.

By this time in my life, my guides and I had been through a lot together. It's a unique relationship, to say the least. Everyone has guides to assist them and give them insight, but for most people, the connection is subtle, even imperceptible. I may be more in tune with my guides, but they're no different from anyone else's. They aren't there to make my decisions for me, but to help me find my way to the right ones—even if it sometimes means making things happen so the decision is a little easier. They shine a light, nudge me, and then let me use my free will based on the lessons I've learned. It's a kind of collegial professional relationship. They're like an oversight committee, a group of five or six, based on the energies I've sensed, that seems to guide by consensus. They will pull me in one direction or the other. I never hear a minority opinion.

I don't believe that the guides I have now are all the same as ten years ago, or twenty. Like everyone's guides, there have been some comings and goings, depending on what has been going on in my life and what lessons I need to learn. Some energies are brought in for some specific purpose— just as we seek out a specialist to perform surgery, prepare our taxes, or fix our cars. A psychic I've worked with, Mary Jo McCabe of Baton Rouge, Louisiana, says that I have to stop referring to my guides as "The Boys." She told me that a female energy was coming in. But I'm still calling them The Boys.

So what was this personal guidance committee making of the direction I was taking back in 1998, when book royalties and infomercials were in the atmosphere? This was the question I had been avoiding. Now it was time to deal with it.

The business side of the psychic life is tricky stuff. This is spiritual work, yet there's no denying that if you have an ability or talent, it's possible to earn a living at it. Some may even make a lot of money at it. Few actually do, but they are the ones who carry the burden of public perception for everyone else. When I made my decision to actually make a career out of this, I had to come to an arrangement with my guides. Call it an understanding: As long as I didn't make it *about* money, I would be okay. As long as the work stayed front and center, they would take care of me. People have always said to me, Wow, can they tell you what stocks to buy? How about the winning lottery number? Can they give you some of their famous guidance in Vegas? They could. But they won't. I learned from the get-go that if I came anywhere near trying to use my ability for that stuff, they'd slap me silly. They've told me over and over: If you do anything with your abilities specifically for money, we will bang you so hard your head will spin.

So here's my rule: It's okay to want to earn a living as a medium, even a good living—and okay to succeed. As my colleague Suzane Northrop says, "There's nothing spiritual about poverty." What's not okay is stepping over the fine line between simple human desire and simple human greed. For me, if I cross it, I'm toast. That's not to say I can't do things that will bring me financial rewards. I just can't use money as the measure of my success, as if I'm a contestant on *Who Wants to be a Millionaire*. I can't use a calculator as my moral compass. And I can't abuse my abilities by charging an obscene fee for a private reading just because that's what the market will bear. And really, it's not that my field is so special. In any career, if you make it about the work first, the money will take care of itself. You don't have to be a spiritual person to embrace this ethic. And you don't have to be a Wall Street shark to lose sight of it. Especially if you also allow yourself to fall prey to some of the other human impulses: competition with peers, resentment at being left behind, the desire for control and power.

I'm always saying it's not the spirits who are getting it wrong; it's more likely that I'm misinterpreting their messages. So now as I decompressed from my recent crash and burn, I began to consider whether I had misinterpreted my guides' messages all those years. Did I allow myself to become so seduced by the expectation of what they were showing me— really since the day Lydia Clar sat in my bedroom and told me I would be a famous psychic—that I began to think of it as some kind of entitlement?

I never stopped honoring the work. Bringing knowledge and comfort to a lot of people remained my goal. I also held to the principle that if I could earn my money via books, tapes, or a ticket to a seminar, I wouldn't even have to think about how much I earned from the one-on-one readings that I felt were important to keep doing, no matter how successful I became. Still, I had to acknowledge that humanity might have lost some ground lately to the impulse to cash in. That was never my intention or motivation. But it might have seemed that way to any spirit guides who happened to be looking in. So now The Boys were slapping me silly.

They were busting me. I'm not supposed to be out front, I finally decided. At least not now. I'm supposed to do the work—do my readings in my office, and my lectures at the Holiday Inns—and continue trying to raise the understanding of spirit communication. But it was time to slow down, breathe deep, and put some spirituality back into this hard-driving, turbo-medium thing I had going. I wasn't some Type A on Wall Street—whoever talks to the most dead people gets a big annual bonus. (Forgive the metaphors—they give me a million of them.) I had been operating under the assumption that I had to do it all *now*. Sort of the opposite of when I got dragged into radio kicking and screaming.

Of course I didn't have to do it all at once. First, I had a lesson to learn: If I was going to climb onto a big stage, I had to get a peek behind the curtains. I needed to go through the experience of losing perspective and screwing up. And I needed to learn how to recognize and cope with people who might not necessarily put the work first. I'd never be able to control the actions of people I dealt with—and definitely not their motives and attitudes—but I could damn well control my own.

That said, I wasn't ready to own this insight. I still needed some time to let it sink into the wound and clean it out. "I think," I told Sandra, "that my expectations for the book were unrealistic."

WE WENT TO THE CARIBBEAN, Sandra and I, with her family and some friends. We rented a rustic cottage on a gorgeous seaside cliff with a pool and a gazebo—and spread out before us, the sea. The water was a dazzling aqua, but rough. Four-foot waves crashed against the sea wall beneath us. There's an energy to the islands that seems to recharge me every time I go there. There's a spot we like to go, and I don't know if it was my home in some past life, but something about the place is magic to me.

The others couldn't get down until Sunday, so I went with my friend Steve Guddat a couple of days before everyone else. And almost immediately after I arrived, I knew things were going to be okay. Late in the afternoon that first day, I was lying on a float in the pool. The sun was already starting to set, and I could see the silhouette of the palm trees against the sky. My mind started to drift . . . *I wonder about the aura of a tree. What would that look like?* I took a deep breath and felt the tension of the previous year leave my body. The disappointments and frustrations; the book signing in ladies' underwear; the disaster in Dallas, Yosemite Sam, and Elmer; the people who didn't like their readings; the attacks on Amazon—none of it mattered anymore.

Floating in the pool, I almost felt as if *I* had crossed over, in a sense. Spirits are always saying that they've left all their problems behind. Their physical pain is gone and all their worldly worries disappear. They don't care who got the house, they don't care that you weren't there when they passed, none of it matters anymore. They're okay now. And that's how I felt. The only way I can describe it is that I felt purified. Like I had finally released and surrendered this cloak of negative energy that I alone was holding onto. It just peeled away and fell into the water and dissolved.

There was something about the moment that was familiar to me. I realized what it was. Years ago, when I was a teenager doing psychic seminars on weekends, I would be in a room with other psychics, a different venue each week, and realized that there was competition among the psychics: Why is she doing twenty readings a day and I'm only doing ten? Why is he getting more clients than I am? It was human nature to feel competitive, and even then I remember being conscious of that trap. Instead, I adopted a Zenlike philosophy: Those who were supposed to see me were going to see me. If on one Sunday I read only three people, then I was supposed to read only those three people. If that other person is supposed to read fifteen people, she will read fifteen people, and it has nothing to do with me. Money? Whatever. Just do the work the best you can.

Only the scale was different now—the principle was the same. Whomever I was supposed to reach with my books—or seminars and lectures, for that matter—I was supposed to reach. If only 100 people read my book, then those were the ones who were supposed to read it. As soon as I reconnected with that value, I was back on track.

I have no idea why it happened so suddenly or at that moment. Maybe it was my guides' way of saying, Okay, you learned your lesson, you can come out of your room now. Go to the Carribean. Get some rest. Then go home and get back to work.

REVA AND THE PRINCESS

SOON AFTER MY MOTHER'S DEATH IN 1989, I had begun a grand quest for The Three Signs. It was exactly the kind of narrow-minded and mis-guided search that I'm always scolding my audiences and clients about. Never mind that over the next few years I would have two amazing visits from my mother in dreams, or that several times colleagues would pass on messages that I knew were from her. They weren't the messages I wanted to hear. The white bird at the wake, which wasn't technically one of them, only fueled my desire for The Big Three. When I tell people to come into a reading without any expectations, I know how wickedly hard it can be. For a long time, I couldn't do it.

I started making appointments with other mediums I knew or had heard of. But the first sign came during a reading my cousin Joey had with a medium in my area. Joey wanted to connect with his father, my Uncle Carmine. But during the reading, it was an aunt with a "P" name that came through. Joey, who was close to my mother, was skeptical, and basically challenged the medium to come up with the whole name. "She's telling me to say ... Prin ... *Princess*?" the medium said, apparently think-ing this couldn't be it. But Joey laughed and said, "Yes! She was Aunt Princess." She wanted Joey to know that she and his father were together, and fine.

Joey came over and brought me a present: a tape of the session. I was slightly disappointed that the first message had come through my cousin and not more directly to me, but I wasn't going to argue. I figured that my mother wanted Joey to know his father was with her, and he was fine. I was sure she would give the other two signs to me—and before too long. I figured that any decent medium would get at least one of the two.

Being in the business, if only a junior member of the fraternity, I had no trouble finding my way to mediums. Some I knew, such as Shelley Peck; some I didn't. I must have seen eight or ten in my pursuit of confirmation, visiting some of them two or three times. I went to the same medium Joey had been to. Nothing. Others got good, validating information, but not The Signs. I wanted The Signs.

A year passed, then two, then three . . . my mother was really starting to annoy and frustrate me. I mean, between private readings by my colleagues and events where I shared a stage with them, she had more than ample opportunity to put me out of my misery. I began working on *One Last Time,* and assumed I would have the signs by the time it was finished. I really wanted to be able to write in the book that I'd gotten all three. But all I was able to say in the book was: Check your expectations at the door. Because these spirits ain't giving you what you want to hear. Even I get what they give me—and I have connections. Nine years had now passed. Obviously, my mother had her reasons for making me wait. She taught me a lot about life. And this was a lesson, too. Still, I knew she would come through eventually, when she felt the time was right. I made sure to continue protecting the integrity of our pact. I did not reveal the missing signs in the book. Rick, my collaborator, asked, but I wouldn't tell him. I didn't tell Sandra. I didn't tell anyone.

IN SEPTEMBER OF 1998, I happened onto a new book by a medium I hadn't heard of before. It was called *Contacting the Spirit World,* and it was a guide for people who want to develop their own abilities to connect with that world. This book knocked me out. It was written in a very straightforward, matter-of-fact, useful way. No fluffy psychic babble about love and peace and someone standing behind you playing with your hair. I was so impressed with the book that when I finished it, I was probably like everybody else. I wanted a reading with the author.

Her name was Linda Williamson, and apparently she was from Britain. I read the book on a flight to Puerto Rico, and when I got home and went to a meeting at my publisher's office, I asked Denise Silvestro, my editor, if she could help me. "Can you find out who this woman is and how I can get to her?" I asked.

Denise started laughing.

"I know, it's funny. I'm a psychic looking for a reading."

"No, it's not that," she said. "Did you happen to notice who published her book?" She got up and went to her shelf. She picked out a copy of *Contacting the Spirit World.* "I published this book."

"Get out."

"It was published in England. I read it and liked it. I bought the U.S. rights."

Denise got me Linda Williamson's phone number, and I couldn't wait to call her. It was ten at night—in New York. That would be—well, very late in England. "Hello?" I heard in a very sleepy English accent. Uh-oh. She politely let me know what time it was in her part of the world. But she didn't seem to mind that much. She was excited that one of her fellow mediums was calling from America to say how much he liked her book. She, of course, was no more aware of me than I was of her.

"Would you be ever so kind and ring me up in the morning?" she requested.

"Well, I was just wondering if you might give me a phone reading sometime."

"I don't really do that. But if you're ever in England, I'd love to see you."

"Well, if you're a medium and you've done it a number of years, I'm sure you can do it over the phone. I do it on the radio all the time. It's the same thing." I'm usually not this pushy—I of all people should know what it's like to be on the receiving end—but I just had to have a reading with this woman. I was not getting off the phone without an appointment.

"Okay," she said finally, just to get back to sleep. "We can talk tomorrow. I can't promise anything."

The next morning, I got up all excited. Linda was going to give me a phenomenal reading. I knew it, felt it. I had such a strong feeling that this was going to be what I had waited nine years for that I just about thought she was going to get on the phone and say, "Hello, John, I have your mother Perinda here. She died of lung cancer on October 5th, and she wants to tell you Princess and Springfield and thanks for putting the Pooh bear in the coffin." There I go again. Easy, boy. Take a chill on those expectations.

I call her, ready to go. I have my phone headset on that I use when I do radio shows or phone readings. I've got my pen and my legal pad. I'm ready to throttle up the speedwriting I learned in high school.

"I'm very excited to be doing this," Linda says. " . . . I have a lovely woman here, and she's standing behind you . . ." Oh, no. "And she's sending much love and . . ."

I'm crushed. She can't be one of *those*. That's not what her book was about. I totally shut down. Instead of listening to what she's saying, thinking about it, I just write it down, for lack of anything better to do. She keeps talking, and in return, I offer only an occasional grunt of indifference. She tosses out some stuff and asks me to validate it. *Uh-huh. Yeah. No. Okay.* I've already sold my stock in her; she's not going to be the IPO who's going to make me millions. She's a gypsy fortune teller on the streets of Lower Manhattan.

But she gives you your money's worth, I'll give her that. I'm already on page six of my pad. "Your mum is telling me to tell you that she was your *guiding light*," she says.

"Not really," I reply dismissively. "She gave me a lot of direction, but I don't know if I'd call her that."

"Oh, dear."

"What?"

"Your mum is quite a forceful woman."

"She could be." I'm not giving her an inch.

Now Linda changes her tone, slows down, lowers her voice as if something momentous is coming. "She wants me to tell you . . ."

"Yeah?" Okay, what's my big message?

A pause. "Guiding . . . *Light.*"

Silence on my end. Then . . . *Ka-BOOM!* That's it—gone. Done. Case Closed. Can't speak. Tears pouring out. Nine years of anticipation erupt in a spectacle of pent-up emotion.

Sandra walks in, sees I'm a mess. *Oh, God. Who died?*

I try to pull myself together. I still haven't been able to say a word, so Linda has no idea that she's just become my new best friend. "You're a very difficult young lad to read," she says. "You don't really offer up much validation. I don't know if what I said to you made any sense."

"Linda," I said, finally able to say more than a word at a time, "it made more sense than I could possibly tell you." I told her the whole story, and she said in her understated British way, "Well, I'm glad I was able to help you."

And then I thought about how amazing my mother is. It was so obvious what the last nine years had been about. By holding back all that time, she was making a point that she wanted me to drive home in my work: the problem of expectations. She wanted me to teach through my own experience. Here I was, a professional medium who knows all the pitfalls, and I was doing the very human thing of holding out for that one nugget that I just had to hear, as if it contained the secrets of the universe, or at least the meaning of life. As if hearing the name of a soap opera would really change anything. I already knew my mother was around, leading an active afterlife. Look at all the stuff I let pass right by me because I didn't want to miss the Big One. Stuff I can't even remember—that's how much I ignored it. Great gifts of validation from mediums who just weren't delivering the packages I ordered. So I returned them. It was a ridiculous thing to do.

Still, I know why I did it, and I know why everybody does it. If you get the one thing you're asking for, it seems like a slightly higher level of validation. It's as if your mother or your husband or your daughter is answering you directly. And if that's happening, it really means they are there, as if they got a phone call through from a constellation so far away it hasn't been discovered. On an emotional level, that's incredibly powerful. And it's wonderful if you get it—witness the sentimental wreck I became when a woman I'd never met said two words to me over the phone from across an ocean. But what if you *don't* get it? Does that mean they're not there? Does it mean there's no afterlife? What if a medium can't get *that*, but instead can get *this*? If it's a solid, specific, factual validation, does that make it any less valuable? This is the inevitable trap of the Great Expectation.

I wrote in my book that after nine years, I still had not received the signs from my mother that she had agreed to send. I said I was okay with that. And by the time the book was finished, I was. She had come through to me many times, in many wonderful ways. I'd love to get the signs, I said, and still looked forward to the day when they came. In my weaker moments, I could even fall back into the trap. But I offered myself as Exhibit A: Don't lose the big picture. Appreciate the messages you get.

I said all of that in *One Last Time.* The book was edited, printed, and ready to ship by September. A few weeks later, I was on the phone to England in the middle of the night, my nine-year wait about to come to an end. It was a much-appreciated gift from my Guiding Light.

THE AMAZING DONNA

IN JANUARY OF 1997, when I was just starting to become known around New York, at least among the psychic cogniscenti, *Newsday,* the large Long Island newspaper, published a very unusual story in its Sunday feature section. "Is John Edward Communicating with the Dead?" the headline asked. What made the story unusual was that it wasn't about poking fun or taking easy shots or dismissing what I and others do as "cold reading," lucky guessing, or executing some absurdly elaborate con game. It was the most objective, open-minded, and genuinely inquisitive article I had ever read about spirit communication in a mainstream publication. It was also the first major story about me. Beginner's luck, I guess.

The writer, Bill Falk, had called and said he had heard about me from a colleague who knew someone who'd had a reading with me. He was intrigued and wanted to spend some time exploring what I do. Already wary of the press—I knew my elder colleagues weren't always treated with respect, and I myself had been mocked in a couple of small news articles—I called a journalist friend and asked him what he knew about Falk. He told me he was a serious journalist with an investigative bent and a solid reputation. "He won't do a hatchet job," my friend said. "He's exactly the kind of guy you want to write about you."

Falk took the time to interview me in depth and independently explore the phenomenon. One of the things he did was to bring someone to me for a reading. Not an original idea, but I was impressed he didn't just want a reading for himself. The person he brought was a middle-aged woman named Joan Cheever. I assumed she was a friend or relative of his, but she turned out to be an attorney who, besides being the former managing editor of the *National Law Journal,* had spent nine years trying to save a convicted murderer named Walter Key Williams from being executed in Texas. Along with another attorney, she had argued passionately that this man was emotionally disturbed and had received an incompetent defense. He had been convicted after a trial that lasted only a day and a half. The appeal failed, and at Williams's request, Joan was present when the man was strapped to a gurney and injected with lethal poison.

"Cheever is not a personal friend, nor anyone Edward could trace to me through any private detective work," Falk wrote, addressing one of the usual speculations people come up with when they can't explain how legitimate mediums do what they do. "I found her through an extended chain of personal and professional contacts. She hasn't appeared on TV or in newspapers here in the New York area. I am as sure as I can be that he knows nothing about her—not even her last name."

As Falk later reported in his story, several of Joan Cheever's relatives came through with the standard initials and sketchy details that are close enough to excite a believer, but too general for a skeptic. And then another spirit stepped forward, one who was not related to her. "Is there someone around you who had a sudden passing?" I asked, with Falk's tape recorder running. "I'm getting a very sudden feeling. Is there someone whose actions led to their passing? It wasn't a suicide, but their actions brought about their own passing."

I got a stabbing feeling, or maybe an impaling. Joan gave me a noncommittal look, as if to say, well, sort of . . .

"Did that make headlines? Because he's showing me headlines. But it's not just the passing that put him in headlines."

I got only two initials: "M" and "L." Walter Williams's parents were Melba and Lucian.

"Did you do any work for this person, did you have a connection with work for him or with him?" I asked.

"Yes."

"You worked together on a project, on a team. It's not like you just worked for the same company."

Joan was acknowledging almost everything I said, but I still felt it wasn't a great reading. This spirit had a lot more he could tell me, but he wasn't. There was someone else getting in the way, confusing things, but more than that, I felt that the main spirit was not communicating clearly because he was not that spiritually evolved. Falk later wrote that he felt that here I was hedging. But then the spirit quickly acknowledged a Bob who worked in television, and for the first time, Bill and Joan registered a strong reaction. As I later learned, Joan's partner on the case was a lawyer named Bob Hirschorn. He worked part-time as a commentator and legal analyst for a Texas TV station.

I got an "H."

"Yes, there's an 'H.'"

"Does it sound like Hirsh?"

Joan paused, obviously stunned. "Yes," she said finally.

The spirit told me that Joan was writing something about him. Yes, she told me, she was writing a book based on her experience with Williams.

"He says, 'Make sure you get it right.'"

Again, Joan was taken aback. Before the execution, she had asked Williams if it would be all right if she wrote about him. "Make sure you get it right," he had said.

"Did this gentleman have feelings for you?"

"No."

"Yes, he did."

"No.

"I'm sorry, but he had a crush on you. Maybe you didn't know."

Joan looked a little embarrassed, then fessed up. "I never told this to anyone," she said. It was true, Walter Williams did have a little crush on her. But it was a prison thing, she said. He was isolated, dependent on her. She just ignored it and did her work.

"He's very lighthearted about it," I said.

Afterwards, Joan Cheever said she was "100 percent convinced that was Walter." As for Bill Falk, he said he was still a tiny fraction short of 100 percent, "perhaps only because I'm afflicted with the occupational hazard of not being completely sure of anything."

Falk interviewed others, and observed Shelley Peck. He also did the obligatory interview with James Randi, who has the distinction of being the only person in America who lists his occupation as "skeptic" and uses the preferred first name "The Amazing." I've never met Mr. Amazing, but he seems to know all about me. He must be psychic. Falk concluded his five thousand-word story with an amazingly bold statement for a serious journalist to make in a major publication: "Either Edward and Peck are getting these details from conversations with the spirit world. Or they conjured up all this information through some unimaginably clever form of guesswork. Given all the evidence, I'm left with the strange conclusion that it makes more sense to believe they're communicating with the dead."

I heard from my friend later that the story caused a big debate in the paper's newsroom. A lot of people, including the editor, couldn't believe that their Pulitzer Prize–winning newspaper had actually run a serious story saying some local guy sits around chatting with dead people. My friend thought that if you really thought about it, this was the biggest story any journalist could ever hope to have. Headline: THERE IS NO DEATH. Subheadline: ONLY TAXES INEVITABLE. But Bill Falk's story was not only a brave piece of journalism. It was also a key link in a chain of events that ultimately gave me a gift I couldn't have predicted. Bill never knew how powerful his story really was. Now he will.

DONNA MARIE (a pseudonym) was a slender, pretty woman who talked fast and smiled sweetly as the words came tumbling out. She was about my age and taught high school biology. I had no trouble imagining she was a popular teacher.

Donna's father had died in November of 1995, and after seeing Bill Falk's story in *Newsday*, she called my office for an appointment. When I saw her, the first thing she said to me was that she had almost had a reading with me more than ten years before, when I was just seventeen. "I was sixteen," she said, "and I was with my friends. We decided to go to a psychic fair they were having at the Holiday Inn, just for fun. And you were there. They were trying to get me to go to your table. 'You've got to go see this guy. He's your age.' But I was too shy." She went to a more traditional psychic instead, one of the older women.

"I still do a mean card reading," I said.

Almost as soon as we began the reading, Donna's father came through. "He's telling me he already knows your children," I said. "He's talking about Anthony, who will come down and be your son. He's telling me specifically Anthony, not Tony." Donna said she had just gotten married and had no children yet. But she had always known that someday she would have a son named Anthony. In fact, her father used to tease her that he would call his grandson Tony. "And I'd say, 'No Tony. Anthony.'"

Her father's message now was a powerful solace to Donna. His death, from a heart attack in his sleep at age fifty-three, hit her very hard. She was so sad that he would never see her children. I can't remember a time when a spirit came through with such a significant message. It was also intriguing that he was saying he knew her unborn children. It seemed to mean their souls were still in spirit, getting ready to return to earth. When I was twenty, a year after my mother's passing, I had a dream in which my mother, dressed in a linen business suit and looking tanned, came to me holding a chubby-cheeked little girl with curly blonde hair. "Look what I'm bringing you," she said.

At the end of the reading, I told Donna how much I had enjoyed meeting her. It turned out that I knew her husband's cousin. We were from the same world. "I feel like I know you," I said. "I feel like I know your father."

Donna came to a group reading a couple of months later, and she and a friend, a fellow teacher, signed up for another one I was having at a Holiday Inn in November. But the timing was bad, or so it seemed. That night, her grandfather, who had been in a nursing home with Alzheimer's disease, was slipping away. "He was near the end, and all the family was there," Donna told me later. "A nurse said, 'He'll probably go tonight,' and people were telling him, 'It's okay, you can go,' even though he wasn't hearing them."

Donna wanted to stay with her relatives at her grandfather's bedside, but she also felt she had an obligation to her friend. "I felt terrible because her husband and her son had died six months apart, and she was a mess. She didn't believe in an afterlife, but she wanted to. We had waited six months to go to the lecture. At the nursing home, everyone said, 'Donna, go. It's okay.' So I decided to go. I bent down and whispered, 'Grandpa, please wait till I get back.' I felt so bad leaving."

Donna drove to the hotel and met her friend. I gave Donna a kiss hello, and they took their seats with the other twenty people. I read about half the people—Donna wasn't among them—and then we took a ten-minute bathroom break. During that time, I saw Donna in the hallway, crying. My first thought, to be honest, was annoyance. *I can't believe that,* I said to myself. I thought she wanted to hear again from her dad, and was upset when he didn't come through.

We went back into the room, and I resumed the readings. I read one woman, and then felt pulled in Donna's direction. By now, she was composed. "Your dad's here," I said. "Oh. He's got people with him. Did your grandfather pass?"

Donna nodded and began to cry again. "Wait a minute," I said. "Did he *just* pass? He's like really new."

"A half hour ago," she managed to say.

That's what Donna had been crying about in the hallway. She had gotten a call from her mother on her cell phone, saying her grandfather had just crossed over. And now he was coming through. But he was in the background. Donna's father was doing the talking.

"You just came from a hospital," I said to Donna. "You were having a party. There were *two* parties." Donna said she and her family had celebrated her grandfather's 80th birthday in the dining room of the nursing home the week before, and the balloons were still up. And tonight, they had ordered food in for all the family. "Your grandfather is here, but your father's speaking for him because he's so new. He wants to tell everyone he heard everything they said, and he says thank you, because it made it easier."

Although he wasn't saying much, Donna's grandfather was coming through with great energy. "He feels like Superman, he's just zooming around, he's so happy to be here. Like he's liberated. Like he's been asleep for sixty days. There's a lot of energy over there. It's like he went from one party to another. There's a crowd with him." I was getting showered with names and sounds. Rose. Gregory. "There are a lot of people who greeted him. They wanted him to come, and they wanted you to come here to get the message. That was the reason everybody told you to come. So don't be upset that you weren't there. You had a much more important job to do."

Donna's grandfather seemed to be really loving this. He was making me feel his personality. "He's like a politician working the room."

"That's so him," Donna said. "He was the president of the Ladies Garment Workers local; he helped people from Italy get work in the textile industry. The Italian-American Businessmen's Association named him Man of the Year."

"Who's the singer?" I asked.

"Oh, God. He played the organ and sang all the time. He made a record of a song he wrote. '*Baci, Baci.*' It means 'Kiss, kiss.' It's about someone going to Italy and falling in love with the country. He'd play the organ and lead us in singing it at every party. Everyone in the family knew the words. '*Kiss, kiss, kiss like this.*'"

When I talked to Donna about that night many months later, she still couldn't believe it. "This was so surreal," she said. "My grandfather had *just* passed. And he was checking in."

Donna became captivated by spirit communication for the same reason I did. "My father died so suddenly," she explained. "It was such a shock. One day he was here, the next—boom. Ever since then, I've wanted to know where he is. What is he doing, what is it like over there? I had this quest of wanting to know what the other side *looked* like. I would go to Borders and get stacks and stacks of books about people's experiences. I would read them straight through in one night. I didn't even know who wrote them. I was obsessed."

But she wasn't content to read about other people's experiences, or even to come to readings and lectures and hear someone else tell what it was like. She wanted a more direct connection. She wanted to see if she could develop her own abilities. That's something I try to encourage people to do, so from time to time I present a workshop called "Building Bridges." Donna attended one I gave the summer after I first met her, in the summer of 1997. She and the others in the group began with a meditation. Then I led them through a series of visualization exercises to bring them to a place in their consciousness where they could greet and communicate with spirits. Start on a beach, I instructed them. Breathe deeply, close your eyes. . . .

Donna remembers:

> I'm sitting there doing the exercises. John says to let the white light flow around us and through us. . . . I get a woman in her sixties or seventies with frizzy auburn hair. She has a pear-shaped body. She's carrying an old-fashioned black doctor's bag, and with this I'm getting that this represented that she was taken care of at home. She's smiling. And then I see, written across her chest, "Jean." She looks old, but I'm getting that she is the mother of someone my age. This is the very first time I'm doing this, so I think I'm just making this up,

imagining it. After a few minutes, John asks those who felt they got anything to stand. I stand, even though I don't know what I'm doing and I have no idea if what just happened was really a spirit communication. I really didn't think so.

I told everyone what I saw and felt, but I didn't say "Jean," because that's my sister-in-law, who I was with, so I didn't think that meant anything. But then somebody said, "I think that may be my mother." She described a woman who had that body shape. Her hair was auburn, but she dyed it black. She had hospice care. But that's pretty general. And then she said her mother's name was Jean.

"Oh my God, I swear to God that's the name I got!" I said. "I didn't say it because my sister-in-law is Jean."

The girl who stood up was about my age. She said, "The reason you were confused is because she had me when she was in her forties. That's why she looks like my grandmother. But that's my mother."

"You've got to be kidding me," I said.

She said, "Would you like to see a picture of her?" She took out a photograph, and this was the woman I had seen—same head shape exactly, same body shape. Her face was kind of average. Everything was the same except her hair was black. If I described the person I saw to a sketch artist, this is what he would draw. I could not believe I did this.

After the workshop, Donna began to dabble at home. She would practice with her sister-in-law. "I tried getting things on Jean's brother," Donna said. "And she validated them. Things about his personality, about her wedding. He was a high-functioning Down's syndrome, and I totally got his personality. I said, 'Wow, maybe I'm really doing this.' I got a great feeling from it, because I was giving Jean such a tremendous thing."

I talked to Donna from time to time and always told her I thought she should keep working on her abilities. Over the next couple of years, she would occasionally practice on Jean. She wasn't bold enough to ask anyone else, so there was a limit to how much she could develop. Besides that, she had gotten busy. She'd had her first child—not a son named Anthony, but a daughter she and her husband, Tommy, named Julia.

One night in October 1999, Donna was sitting in the rocking chair in her baby's nursery, just watching her sleep. She wondered if anything would come through if there wasn't anyone in the house except Julia.

All of a sudden, I get this woman who comes forward. She looks like she has dyed blond hair. She comes toward me, and I get two names written across her. I'm realizing that this is how I get names. I don't hear them. I see them, in big letters. The two names are Carol, and either Annette or Antoinette. It flashed very fast. Then she showed me a puppy, a cross, and then a sunset. I immediately connected this woman. It was John's mother. I had seen a picture of her in the *One Last Time* video. I said, "If you're really John's mother, tell me something really important to validate that this is you." She looked at me and said, "Tell him 'Pooh.'" It was like a movie in my head. I was seeing her say this, but I heard my own voice. I grabbed a pad and wrote down what had just happened. The next morning when I woke up, the first thing I felt was John's mother. She said, "Tell him bear."

"John, you're going to think I'm crazy," Donna said on the phone. "I don't know if this was your mom. It looked just like her from the picture in the video. She told me Carol and Annette. Or maybe Antoinette." A friend of mine named Carol was starting to spend some of her free time helping me organize my office. And Antoinette was a woman who had just been hired to do publicity for a tour I was doing through the Learning Annex, a nationwide adult education organization.

"And then I asked her for a stronger validation. And she said, 'Pooh,' and then this morning, 'bear.'"

"Oh my God," I said. "Do you know what you just did? That was my third symbol."

I was more composed this time. After the *Guiding Light* message, this was just icing on the cake. I was thrilled to get it, but by now I had come to understand that I shouldn't get much more excited by the Pooh bear than by any other validation.

Since *One Last Time* was published, I'd had dozens of letters and contacts from people claiming to have gotten a visit from my mother, delivering messages that made absolutely no sense. Is that one of the signs? they'd ask. People have stopped me in public to tell me they "got a sign." I found this hilarious because there was no way my mother would be talking to all these people. She was not a very sociable person over here. I don't think she became everybody's pal over there. I stopped paying any attention to everyone but professional mediums such as Shelley Peck and

Suzane Northrop, who I know have relayed messages from my mother. But she seemed to take quite a liking to Donna Marie.

After the Pooh bear message, I told Donna not to expect to hear from my mother anytime soon, if ever. But two weeks later, she had another visit. When she first started trying to build bridges to the spirit world, Donna had gotten a marble notebook to write down everything that happened. But after a while, the only thing inside were records and notes of encounters with my mother. The first one was October 10, 1999. The next was only fifteen days later, on October 25. Then another one a week later, on November 2. Ten visits in all, the last one on July 11, 2000.

Some of the information she got was incredibly detailed, as accurate as any I've gotten in my own work. Early in June 2000, Donna came to see me and said she'd had what she thought was another visit from my mother a few days before. "I've got to ask you this," she said. "I've just got to ask. In your bedroom, do you have a large, dark wood bureau with a hutch with a mirror? Because your mother showed me your bedroom. The furniture is light wood, and if you pull out the top right-hand drawer, there's a little box with a letter in it from your mom, or a piece of paper with writing on it. I'm seeing this like a movie. She's making me the camera. She's wearing a blue dress. She shows me a shiny gold steering wheel."

Donna's description of my bedroom and the furniture in it was dead-on accurate. And in the bureau she described, there is only one drawer that's mine. All the others are Sandra's. And in that one drawer is my mother's old red jewelry box, which has some of her old jewelry, along with some of mine. And with the jewelry is a folded-up letter my mother wrote, specifying who should get what jewelry.

The gold steering wheel? I had just gotten a new car.

Donna continued relating the latest visit. "I said to her, 'Tell me something you used to say to John all the time.' She gave me the song 'C'est La Vie.' It was one of those one-hit wonders in the '80s. I heard it on the radio all the time. I heard it in my head now."

"My mother said that all the time!" I said when Donna told me this. "I would ask her if it was Italian."

Donna says it wasn't until my mother gave her the Pooh image that she believed she might actually be able to do spirit communication. "I wasn't even trying to get her," she said. "Why did she choose me? That's when I started feeling maybe there was something to this."

I began encouraging Donna to work on her abilities, just as Lydia Clar and Sandi Anastasi and Shelley Peck urged me to do years ago. Most important, I told Donna, she had to do readings. "Who am I going to read?" she asked doubtfully. She had a point. She couldn't do friends and relatives for the same reason I don't do them. What was she supposed to do, set up a table at the Sunrise Mall? So I started having her come to my office to do readings, using a little room off the dance floor I installed in the middle of the office so I could still teach a few students ballroom dancing.

I started bringing in anonymous friends of mine for Donna to read, just as journalists have done when they're trying to test me. I have her sit in a chair facing the wall, then I bring in the subject to sit behind her. Because she can't see them, and because I instruct them to give only yes and no answers, she's forced to focus on the energies, with only my coaching as a guide. Since I'm often tapping in to the same energies, I can tell what she's getting, what she's not, and sometimes why.

One night, I brought two friends in. She tried to read the first one, my writing collaborator, Rick, but not a single thing registered. A virtual zero. But as I listened to the details that Donna was imparting, something clicked. I went outside to the office and asked for Joanne, a friend who was in the office that evening, to come into the room. When she came in, *everything* made sense to her. The second person was my good friend Ernie, whose grandmother came in loud and clear for Donna. Like anyone with marvelous natural talent but virtually no experience, Donna needs to just *do* it. As she gets more familiar with how spirits come through for *her*, and, through practice, hones her skills at interpreting the messages, she will become a superb medium. One day, she came to the *Crossing Over* studio, and was in my dressing room while my executive producer Paul was there. She looked at him and said, "I'm seeing 'MARTY, MARTY, MARTY' right in front of you." Paul smiled. "My father," he said. "He passed a few years ago."

Just as my guides summoned Lydia Clar to my house to get me going when I was fifteen, I believe I'm supposed to put Donna on her own path. Three times in my life, I've had people tell me that I was going to meet someone named Donna, who had a baby, and that I was going to help her. Two of them were fellow psychics. The other was the very same Ernie, who looked at me a few years ago and said, "John, who's Donna?" It's also no accident that my mother chose Donna to relay the third and final sign, or that she has come to her so often.

How does Donna feel about all this? It's a lot of pressure to put on someone who just wants to raise her family and teach high school biology. "If God really wants me to do this, He will put things in my path," she says. "Why did your mom come to me? She could have come to anyone. It's more than a coincidence." She knows that there will be challenges to her personal life if she actively pursues this work that some people consider a cross between practicing witchcraft and selling swampland. "What will my family say? What will people at school say? I'll have to deal with it." She wasn't quite ready to let me use her last name here. Donna's husband, Tommy, a businessman with a law degree, started out as a skeptic, but he didn't stay that way for long. He's seen too much evidence firsthand, much more than most people. He has always supported Donna's need to explore this world. And he knows how good it makes her feel.

"I've read nine people now," Donna said one day in the spring. "When these spirits come into my mind, it's almost like meeting new people. They make me feel them so powerfully. Ernie's grandmother— her warmth literally made me smile. It washed over me. She left such an impression that I thought about her for days. This has changed the way I look at life and death. It's been a great help in the grieving process over my father. So if I can help someone, I have to do that. I feel very humbled. If God wants me to do this, who am I to say no?"

— CHAPTER 3 —

THE
PRODUCERS

THE TUBE

As you may have guessed, I'm a recovering TV junkie. Well, maybe not quite recovering. Nobody knows this better than my friends in the spirit world. When I'm doing a reading, you never know when I might toss out the name of some secondary character in a show that got canceled after thirteen episodes in 1978 because somebody's father thinks that's the best way to get me to say that he was a plumber named Ed.

But liking TV and wanting to be *on* TV are two very different things. When I first signed the contract to write *One Last Time*, I told the publicity people that they would have to figure out how to promote the book without putting me on the TV circuit. I didn't want my face on television, and I hated the idea that someone would be telling me I had to do this show or that show—and maybe it was a show that might sensationalize or belittle the subject. Control, especially of my medium work, is paramount to me. There was also a part of me that didn't feel right about doing what amounted to commercials for myself, hawking spirit communication like Paul Reiser selling ten-cents-a-minute on AT&T. Not happening.

Happening. A year later, I was calling TV producers myself and asking them to put me on their shows. I'd had, shall we say, a change of heart. The publicity people had sat me down and said: John, listen very carefully. This is America. It's 1998. If you want to get your book into a lot of hands, you have to go on television. They were right, of course. If I wanted the book to be successful, I would have to get off my high horse and do what everybody else does. I mean, look how many books there are in Barnes & Noble. But that didn't mean I was willing to give up the big C. If I wanted to keep control of this, I would have to be my own publicist. In the back of my mind, I thought that if I made enough of my own contacts, I might be able to pick and choose which shows I went on. My guides gave me the green light, or maybe a blinking yellow. Proceed with caution.

When I started doing radio a few years before, I'd found that I didn't need a publicity person or agent to get me on shows. I was better off making contacts with producers myself and explaining who I was and what I did. It was pretty straightforward—call the station, get the producer, make my pitch, and usually, schedule a time. Or, better yet, get a call from a producer who had heard about me from a colleague at a sister station and wanted to have me on. TV was bigger, I knew, but producers are producers, right?

I began calling the main phone number of shows and finding out who was in charge. Being the anal-retentive person I am, I kept careful lists of contacts and phone numbers in a looseleaf binder, leaving a space to make notes of what people said when I called and how and when I should follow up. I began cold-calling producers on two coasts, hoping to talk my way into somebody's studio. I wasn't in any position to be that particular, but I hoped if I made enough contacts, I could be. How hard could it be? I felt if I they just talked to me, they would get a real feel for the work, not some hyped, hocus-pocus mythology. I remember a national show in 1994 called *The Other Side* that kept trying to get me on to do topics like hauntings and poltergeists, evil spirits and spells. When I told them all I wanted to do was come on and do what I do, they told me no thanks—that was already being done.

Now, four years later, it seemed that if this was something already done, it was making a nice comeback. People who talked to dead people were positively trendy—and the ones with books were always getting on TV. So at least they would know what I was talking about, but of course there was always the risk that this time it really was already done. *Oh, no, not another medium.* As far as I could tell, though, there still were more TV shows with time to fill than mediums with books to sell.

One of the first shows I called was *Leeza.* I liked Leeza Gibbons. She seemed sincere and bright, and her show seemed a level above the usual daytime fare. You know, today's theme: "I slept with my mother's boyfriend and she got mad and hired a hit man and that's why she's in prison and I dress like a slut and have seventy-three body piercings."

I had a contact at *Leeza,* a producer named Joyce whom I had called sometime earlier. I knew she was a spiritual person but didn't think she was into psychic stuff. Still, she was a good place to start. When I called, though, someone else answered her phone and told me the producer I was trying to reach had left the show. Oh, I said, is there someone else I can talk to about an idea I have for a show? You can talk to me, the woman said pleasantly. Her name was Ramey, and she explained that she was a "special projects" producer. It was her job to find unusual ideas, "not your run-of-the-mill show with trailer-park guests and all that stuff."

"Well, I'm a psychic medium, and I have this book coming out. The publicity department for my publisher said I'm going to need to start getting on television and stuff, and I want to be selective with what I do. I want to know that the subject matter is going to be treated with integrity, which I know your show would."

"Great idea, lousy timing," Ramey said. "I just did a show with another medium not two weeks ago. The network won't let me do another one so soon." I guess I got the right person, if about two weeks late.

"I've got some stuff I could send you," I said. I'd put together a little kit of my *One Last Time* video, some galleys of the book, and the *Newsday* article. "Do you think you might be able to look at it sometime?" Sure, she said. I packed up a box, and put Ramey's name in my looseleaf binder—Ramey . . . Warren . . . Black—with a note to call her back in a few weeks. I knew she wouldn't call me. These people never call you back. You have to keep after them. I moved on to the next show on my list.

There was a morning program called *Fox After Breakfast* that I thought might be interested. I called the person in my contact book, Paul Shavelson, the executive producer. I started my spiel, but he seemed to be only half-listening. He said something polite like, "We're not really interested in doing that subject matter at this time," and passed me off to someone below him, who said, "Yeah, I don't think we're doing that kind of thing."

After a few more calls, I realized something. This isn't like radio. In radio, you speak to the producer of the show. That's it. In TV, it's like every show has twenty people, and all of them are producers. Executive producers, associate producers, just plain producers. You have to talk to four people before you get to anybody who can make a decision, and then you're still nowhere because their decision is: Sorry, not at this time. Some of them were cocky TV types I probably was best to steer clear of anyway.

A few days after I started making calls, the phone rang: "Hi, John? This is Ramey from the *Leeza* show."

"Really?" I said. "*Leeza*? You're calling me back? I didn't think you would. That's so cool."

Ramey laughed. She wasn't used to so shameless a display of gratitude. I don't think they do that in L.A. "So what did you think of the stuff
I sent?" I asked.

"Okay. Here's what I think. I think the tape doesn't represent you as
well as I think you need to be represented. But I think you're amazing,
and I would love to help get you out there. If we wait awhile, we'll have
another shot at getting you on the show."

I thought it was great of Ramey to call me back just to give me some
kind words. She was someone definitely worth keeping in touch with. I
called her a month or so later, and we wound up talking about. . . stuff.
Religion versus spirituality. Family. Television. After that, we started
speaking regularly and became phone friends. She told me that the *Leeza*
show was just the latest in a string of TV jobs she'd had going back twenty
years. She had started out as a talent coordinator for Johnny Carson on
the *Tonight* show. From there she went to *Hour* magazine, the *Late Show*
at Fox, the *Home Show*, *Will Shriner*, *Body by Jake*, and the show she had
the most fun with—the *Tammy Faye* show. But she was restless after producing for these syndicated shows day after day, year after year. It was like
feeding morsels to an insatiable beast. Grind it out, do it again tomorrow,
and five times next week. She was about ready to do something she'd
been thinking about and planning for years. She wanted to form her own
production and media-training company. It was a natural move. She had
friends all over town. She even had a name for the company: Media-
Savvy. And a partner: Adora English, an entertainment producer for the
morning news on KTLA who had worked on "every fabulous and terrible talk show in America," as she liked to say. "On both coasts." Now all
they needed was the nerve to do it.

Ramey came to New York in May for the Daytime Emmys, but we
couldn't get our schedules to match, so it wasn't until October that we
finally had a chance to meet in person. I was coming to Los Angeles with
Rick Korn to meet with an old friend of his named Marc Gurvitz, who
was a talent manager and television producer.

Rick, Marc, and their friend Alan had grown up together in Plainview, Long Island. One night a few weeks after graduating from college in
1978, Rick ran into Alan in their old hangout on Long Island. Alan said
he was leaving the next morning for California, chasing his girlfriend and

figuring he'd find a job when he got there. Their old buddy Marc was already out there, and he could crash with him for a while. "Hey, man, why don't you come with me?" Alan said to Rick, who had a good first job in marketing but was living with his parents and open to suggestions. It was the third beer that did it. Alan went home to finish packing, and Rick went home to start. At five in the morning, he woke up his parents and said he was leaving for California. *What? When?* Right now. Alan's in the driveway. Rick loaded up his stuff in Alan's Toyota pickup, and they drove out of Plainview with Rick's distraught parents in the rearview mirror. They drove into the city and stopped in front of a building on Madison Avenue. Rick went upstairs and told his boss thanks for the opportunity, but he was moving to California. *What? When?* Right now. My friend's downstairs, and he's double-parked. And off they went, Rick, Alan, and Alan's dog, Goat.

Marc Gurvitz was already out in L.A. trying to break into show business. According to Rick, who loves to talk about Marc and his exploits, his friend was a ballsy, hilarious guy who would say or do just about anything to get into the game. By day, Marc ran the shipping department of Capitol Records, a job he cleverly used to make connections. If a tape had to be delivered to Jackson Browne, Marc would do the job himself and find a way to make it a personal delivery, which always came with a full introduction at no extra charge. At night, Marc made the rounds of the comedy clubs telling the standups he liked that they would go far if they let him manage them. Bill Maher and Sam Kinison, to name two, found that Marc had an uncanny knack for knowing what was funny and what was *really* funny. Marc used his savings to get an apartment in a building called the Oakwood where he knew the movie studios put actors up. He would come home at lunchtime and hit the phones, booking his clients and making deals. When Rick, Alan, and Goat arrived in the Toyota, they found a twenty-two-year-old kid with the words Gonna Make It Big practically stamped on his forehead.

The three Jewish kids from Long Island lived together for a while. Rick got another job in marketing, but eventually moved back east. Alan was really a California beach bum at heart, so New York was permanently in his rearview mirror. He had gone to school for marine biology but became a scuba instructor. A couple of years later, he moved to the

Cayman Islands. And Marc? Marc stayed in L.A. and Made It Big.

In 1998, he was a partner and head of the management division of Brillstein-Grey Entertainment, which Rick informed me was a very major Hollywood agency that manages talent and produces shows. They did *The Larry Sanders Show,* and now they were starting production on another show for HBO, some kind of series about mobsters they were calling *The Sopranos.* Marc was putting together *Just Shoot Me* and was an executive producer of *Politically Incorrect with Bill Maher,* which got him an Emmy nomination. Rick wanted me to meet Marc. He was convinced I should have my own TV show. A sitcom about a psychic, maybe?

Ever since we'd become friends, Rick had been trying to raise my profile. He was a marketing man, but he liked to spend at least some of his time on good things, benefits like World Hunger Year. He was in media marketing, but he could easily make the slight transition to medium marketing. It wasn't just the business opportunity that drove him. It was his genuine wish to introduce me to the world, and vice versa. But I didn't know about this TV stuff. I'm having trouble getting on *Leeza,* and Rick thinks I should have my own show. Not only that, it should be produced by one of the hottest, most cutting-edge companies in town. *You're* cutting age, Rick told me. Okay, whatever.

Marc Gurvitz was spending time in the Hamptons that summer, and Rick and I drove out to meet him. He was a nice guy and seemed interested in me, but I knew it was probably only because of Rick. We spent the afternoon together, I read him, and then we made plans to meet in California in October. In the meantime, Marc would bring the idea to Kevin Reilly, the head of the TV division of Brillstein-Grey.

The day before we were supposed to fly out, Rick phoned with some bad news. He'd gotten a call from Reilly, who said what Rick considers the four ugliest words in the English language: "We're going to pass." They didn't do much syndication, which is what they considered the type of show Rick was talking about. In fact, their very first one was in the pipeline. It was a show with Martin Short. They were going to start with that. They were interested in me, but their thing was really comedy. A show with a psychic medium didn't quite fit in.

We gave it a shot, Rick told me, trying not to sound too defeated. There will be other opportunities. And there's a lot of other stuff to be excited about—the book, of course, and the infomercial that came out of the Larry King video fiasco. The direct marketing company had hired a really good producer-director from Los Angeles, and we were starting to plan it out. Although it was technically being called an infomercial, I saw it in a much less crass way. Maybe I was being naïve, but I saw it more as educational television. Whatever I called it, Rick thought it couldn't miss.

Still, he was disappointed about Brillstein-Grey, much more than I was. But I told him not to cancel our flight. We were going to L.A. anyway.

Why? he wanted to know, not surprisingly. What's up?

Nothing, I said—we just need to go.

But the meeting's canceled.

I know—but we still need to go.

For *what?*

We just need to be there. We can see the infomercial guys. I'll call up this woman Ramey who's been so nice to me. All I know is, we've still gotta go.

Okay. Whatever.

So we flew out to California. With nothing much on the agenda, we drove up to Malibu. I had never been there, and Rick wanted to show me around. I wasn't impressed. In fact, Los Angeles in general didn't do a lot for me. New York and the Caribbean—that pretty much had me covered.

On the way back down Pacific Coast Highway, we pulled off to take a look at this other ocean. "John," Rick said finally, "why are we here?"

"I don't know," I said, adding with a laugh, "maybe we just need a vacation." We had called Chad Murdock, the infomercial producer, and made plans to get together. But I knew that wasn't why we had come. "You know, I think I need to meet this Ramey. I think that's why I'm here. Maybe she'll be able to help me with the book or something."

By that time, Ramey Warren Black's professional life had changed in a big way. Over the summer, Paramount Productions had hired a new executive producer for the following season of *Leeza,* and he wanted to bring in his own people. So even though she had another year on her contract, she made a decision. She said to her husband in the car one day, "You know what? I'm done. I've had twenty years of talk, and that's enough. It's time to do Media-Savvy." She worked out a settlement of her contract, called her partner-in-waiting, Adora English, and they decided it was time to jump off the cliff. Thelma and Louise were in business. They would start out doing media training, getting people booked on shows and preparing them for their 15 minutes of fame. Eventually they would move on to producing. On her card, Ramey identified herself as "President (Odd Days)." Adora had the even days. Their first office was Adora's dining room. A couple of months later, they got a desperate call from *TV Guide* saying the magazine needed a dozen celebrities right away to help launch the TV Guide Channel. "We asked for an extraordinary amount of money," Adora said, "and they came back and said yes." Adora had her dining room back.

When Ramey went out on her own, it meant that she was free to help me beyond her own show. Who better to explain me to producers than another producer? "You know what, John, I would love to do that," she said.

"Great, you're hired."

"No, don't hire me. Just send me some books and let me make my twelve calls. I'm not a publicist, but I know what doors to go into. Adora and I have worked with all these people; they're all our friends. I can call my friend who's the executive producer of *Sally*, our friend who's the executive producer of *ET*. So let us make our calls, and it's either going to go or it's not."

I couldn't believe it—my first Hollywood contact, and she turns out to be a total sweetheart. She just wanted to help me. How cool was *that*? So now in late October, I figured that had to be why I was pulled across country. I was supposed to meet Ramey, even though my original reason for going was called off.

Chad and his assistant, Nicole, came up to my hotel room in West Hollywood, and we spent a couple of hours talking about the upcoming infomercial. Then a call came from the front desk saying a Miss Black was on her way up. When I opened the door a few minutes later, I took a long look at the woman in front of me and said, "Yes?" She looked at me and said, "John?" "Umm . . . Ramey?" I looked at Rick, and we both started laughing. "What's the matter?" she asked.

"You're not black," I said.

"What?"

"Some psychic I am. I visualized you as a black woman on the phone.

When did you become white?" I don't know why—Ramey had no discernible dialect on the phone—but all these months I had a very strong image of a black woman.

"Nope," she said. "Only my name is Black."

We had a laugh about it, wondered what it meant that a psychic thought she was black, and said our nice-to-finally-meet-yous. Then all these producer types—Ramey, Chad, Rick—were chatting back and forth while I kind of zoned out. And then I was suddenly overpowered—really overpowered. "I'm sorry, but I need everybody to leave right now," I announced. "I need to read her."

Rick protested mildly. He reminded me that I said I would relax on this trip and not do any readings. "I know," I said. "But she's brought like an entourage." It was what I called a surprise-attack reading. Chad and Nicole headed out, and Rick went up to hang out at the pool.

Ramey sat on the couch and I took a chair. "I'm sorry to ambush you like this," I said, "but you didn't come alone. Do you want me to do this?"

"Oh, absolutely," she said.

"Have you ever done this before?"

"I've been read a few times by psychics."

I ran through the preliminaries, then took off my glasses and asked for her watch to hold. I breathed deeply and listened. If you asked me what happened over the next twenty minutes or so, I couldn't tell you very much. As is often the case, even for a great reading, I remember only a few highlights. I can summon the essence of it, the feelings and quality of it, but the details are like vapor. They're not my thoughts, so they pass through me without stopping to register in my brain. Fortunately, many people take careful notes; others are able to remember the dialogue so accurately it's as though they have a tape recorder in their heads. Ramey was in that group. She took out a notepad but didn't need it. She remembered everything, and later wrote an account for herself. That's what most of the following is based on.

One of the things I do remember is that the reading started strong, right out of the gate. There was a very pushy woman coming through pointing me toward Ramey's right hand. "That's my ring," she was telling me. She was really aggressive about this ring, which had a diamond in the middle of it. Ramey told me that this was obviously her grandmother on her father's side. "Pushy?" she told me later. "She was like Attila the Hun. As my mother says—and my mother's the nicest person in life—she was *mean.* The ring was indeed my grandmother's, and it has a very dramatic family story attached to it."

"Okay, who's Jim or Jimmy?" I asked, according to Ramey's account.

"My cousin," she gasped, clasping her hands over her mouth and starting to cry.

Suddenly, I knew the mystery was solved—Ramey was the reason I was here. "Your family is the reason I'm here," I said. "They got me on that plane." I assumed it was so they could get these messages to Ramey. What I didn't know was that it wasn't the only reason I was here. And Ramey's relatives weren't the only ones who wanted me to come to California and meet her.

Jimmy wanted me to get to the point. "He's saying not to worry about the separation between you. Let it go. He's telling me that there was something that came between you and a reason you couldn't get to him when he died. But he wants you to know that he's okay. He's with your father. Did your father not get to see you grow up?"

"No, he died when I was very young."

"Because he's here, too. And he wants you to know that he's very proud of you and he's always known what was going on in your life. Were you very young? Because he didn't raise you."

"I was eighteen months old."

"There's someone else here, too. The man who did raise you. He's showing me a pink rose with thorns on it. That means he was unable to express love."

"My stepfather."

"He's saying happy birthday to someone."

"Oh, my God. Today is my sister's birthday. She's his biological daughter."

This was one of those clear days when I could see (and hear) forever. Even the best readings have gaps, symbols that don't make sense, messages misinterpreted by me or misunderstood by the person I'm reading. But with Ramey's relatives, it was almost impossible to get it wrong.

"He's showing me blackness down here, like in the intestinal area," I said of Ramey's stepfather.

"He died of an aneurysm in the intestine."

Now it started getting really interesting. Here is the rest of Ramey's account, exactly as she wrote it. She put my words in italics.

There is another female above you who is coming in. It's an R-L sound.

Her name was Rilla and she was my other grandmother.
(John looked at me a little startled.)

Ramey, she was murdered.

True.

She was hit over the head.

True.

Was she killed in the kitchen?

No.

Well, they're showing me a room with food.

She was killed in the dining room.

And the person who killed her was a young man who couldn't talk right, like this. (He talks slowly, slurring his words.)

He was retarded. By this time, I had clapped my hands over my mouth and I was in tears.

She's saying "Estelle" or something like that. Does that mean anything to you?

Oh, my God. My middle name is Estelle, though I haven't used it for forty years. It's not on any documents, and even my husband didn't know this about me. And I was named after my grandfather, Estill.

Who had the problem? (He made a drinking gesture.)

My grandfather, Estil.

He then looked at me apprehensively. *There was another murder. Do you know that?*

I did.

This is a male above you, with a "D" initial. He was shot twice in the side. I feel the impact.

All true, except for the fact that this was my Uncle Cody. That would be a "C."

Write it down. I may be off on the name, but I'm never off by the initial.

I put a big "D" on my empty notepad.

He has a "K" attached to him. Katherine.

His daughter. We call her Kitty.

John went on to talk about my dog who was with my family. He mentioned details that no one could have known. My middle name being Estelle, which I haven't used in forty years. I hated it. There was nothing that didn't make sense, except for the "D." Finally, he said that they were pulling back and asked if I had any questions. I was so blown away that I couldn't even speak. And so the session ended. I looked down at the pad. The only thing I'd written down was a "D."

There was something great about that. I had been in the experience so completely that I couldn't possibly take notes.

Rick came back to the room, and we went downstairs and drove over to an Italian restaurant on Beverly Boulevard for dinner. Ramey had asked Adora to come, but she had another business dinner to go to. And as far as she was concerned, I was just another psychic looking for a little publicity.

We tried to have a friendly business dinner—talking about getting me on talk shows to promote the book, about the infomercial, Rick discussing his ideas for a TV show—but Ramey, sitting next to me and across from Rick, was someplace else. Finally, she said, "Wow. I can't talk about all that right now. I've got to talk about what just happened."

Ramey started telling Rick about the reading, filling in some blanks for me. "I was a good subject for you," she said. "I've had a lot of deaths around me." The two murders in her family were decades old. Her grandmother—the sweet one—was seventy-five years old when she was killed by a nineteen-year-old in her home in Kentucky in 1976. "He was retarded, this kid," Ramey said. "He was shoveling the snow at her house. My grandfather had died three weeks before from lung cancer, and she kept this kid on to help her, and he raped and murdered her in her own home."

I wondered what the deal was with the diamond ring Ramey was wearing. Her other grandmother—the tough one—was the first one through the gate when Ramey arrived at the hotel, and she really wanted it known that it was *her* ring. Ramey had mentioned that there was a story behind it.

"This ring has had a very long and strange life," Ramey said. "It was given to my grandmother by my grandfather on their tenth anniversary. That must have been around 1919. My grandfather was a law student when they got married, so they were too poor for a ring. She gave the ring back to him on their twenty-fifth anniversary. She had the center diamond set in a man's ring, surrounded by Pave diamonds set in platinum. When my grandfather died, my grandmother gave it to my father. When my father died, my mother kept it. When I was three, my mother and grandmother had a big fight because my mother had started dating the man who became my stepfather. My grandmother was a widow for fifty years. She didn't believe in marrying more than once. So she wanted the ring back. She was so mad that she threw her glasses against the wall and broke them. The next day she had to go to another town to get them fixed. And while she was out of the house, my mother packed up everything that would fit in the car and left town forever. We moved to her parents' home in another part of Kentucky. Before she left, she gave the ring to the preacher to give to my grandmother. Eighteen years later, it showed up set back in a woman's setting for my college graduation. I put it in a drawer and didn't wear it for five years. One day I decided I was over the whole thing and put it on. I've worn it every day since."

Ramey's grandmother seemed just as domineering as a spirit as she had been on earth. But even she wasn't as forceful as Ramey's cousin Jimmy. "He was like a surrogate father to me," she said. "He was older. Sixty-three when he died. And I adored him. He was a fabulous person with a great sense of humor. He was buried in his pajamas.

"You said, 'Jimmy is telling you that he knows that things were apart when he died.' It's true, I couldn't get to him. There was a jealousy issue with his wife, and I never got to say good-bye. He had been ill with emphysema, and he died right after my mother lost her husband, my stepfather. She had just talked to Jimmy, and he said she should go out to California. So my husband picked her up at the airport, and the next thing we know, we get a call that Jimmy died. For me to get my mother back to Kentucky for the funeral was very difficult. She had just gotten here. And I couldn't leave her. So I couldn't get to the funeral. But ever since he died, which was February 12th a year ago, I've talked to Jimmy all the time. I talk in the car. I say, 'If ever an opportunity presents itself, please come back, please say something.' So driving over tonight, I was excited. I kept going, 'Okay, Jim . . .' And then, he comes right through and you tell me he's the one who instigated the whole thing."

Rick listened attentively to Ramey's recap. He had heard and observed more than a few stories like this just from being around me—in fact, he had one of his own—but he was glad for Ramey. "That's pretty amazing," he said. "That's why I wanted to hook him up with my friend at Brillstein-Grey. To see if maybe there's something there."

"Oh, absolutely there's something there," Ramey said. "This is a *show*. I mean, if we could take what I just experienced and put it on the air, it would be so powerful."

I can't say that wasn't nice to hear, or that it took me completely by surprise. My guides had been giving me glimpses of a show for a while—and this was back when I was in my great expectations mode, before the crash. Still, my immediate concern was the book that was coming out in a matter of days and the publisher's determination to get me on TV. "I'm worried that they're going to book me on shows I don't want to do," I told Ramey. "I don't want someone telling me, 'You have to do this, you have to do that.'" I really liked Ramey, and now that she had her own personal experience, she could really sell me to her friends who ran all those shows.

"I'll talk to them, and I'm sure I'll be able to get you booked. But really, forget other people's shows. You should have your own show."

Which would mean, I guess, that Ramey's cousin Jimmy, this guy who was buried in his pajamas, hauled me out to California so I could square things with his little cousin, and while he was at it, get me my own television show.

"Can I do this?" Ramey asked. "Would you let us try to do something?"

"Sure," I said. "Go ahead."

Ramey called her partner, Adora English, from the car on her way home. "We're doing a show with John Edward," she told her. "The medium."

"Yeah, right."

"No, really.

"The guy with the book," Adora said. "This is a joke, right?"

"You're not going to believe what happened. I think it can be great television."

Adora began to laugh uncontrollably. "I can just see us in pitch meetings," she said. "Yeah, we got this guy, he talks to the dead! It'll be great!"

Ramey knew it sounded a little crazy, but she didn't really care. After she punched the end-call button, she started thinking again about her reading. The only thing that didn't make sense to her was why her murdered Uncle Cody kept insisting his name started with a "D." And then, driving through West Hollywood, it came to her. "Cody was all we ever called him," she told me the next day. "But that was his middle name. His first name was David."

THE TALE OF THE MANATEE

I GOT MY OWN SHOW RIGHT AWAY. Okay, it was the infomercial. Not exactly cutting-edge television. But it offered something I craved: control. Or so I thought.

One of the first things Chad Murdock and I discussed when he came to the hotel in Los Angeles was where we were going to shoot. The location was very important; we wanted a beautiful, idyllic setting. Say . . . the Caribbean.

So over the next few months, Chad started looking there. He found a place but couldn't work out a deal. He had a bunch of other possibilities, from Barbados to California. There were a couple of nice spots in Tampa, Florida. No, I said, I don't want to go to Florida. Too pedestrian. California? Too far. Back to the islands. Chad found another location in the Caribbean, and it looked like we were set. But then it turned out that the place wasn't available when we needed it. So what about Tampa? No—keep looking. A third possibility. A third snag. Tampa? Okay, okay. Tampa.

We arrived in Florida in the middle of February 1999, and any illusions I had about this being my show—any fantasy that all these TV people were here to carry out my every wish—were quickly demolished. I knew I was in trouble even before we shot a foot of tape. Our pal Elmer Fudd, the marketing company boss whose idea of television production was what went on at a Toshiba factory, wanted me to read the woman who would be the host. "I know you can't control the process," he said—and as soon as those words left his mouth I knew he thought I *could* control the process because deep down he thought this wasn't real—"but it would be really phenomenal if, on camera, you could wow her so that she could be visibly and emotionally reduced to tears. You know, so she can know firsthand what it feels like when she's selling these products."

And I was surprised when The Boys got pissed?

"First," I said, "you're right. I can't control this. Second, I can't make someone cry. And I wouldn't try, even if I could. Sometimes people hear the information and get emotional, but no medium's intention is to make someone cry. Third, I already know this woman's mother has passed. She died when she was very young. She told me that. So I can't read her. I can't be objective."

And fourth, I might have said, Who on earth would watch the host of an *infomercial* collapsing in tears and not think it was the lamest setup? I know a sucker is born every minute, but that's not the demographic I'm going for. This guy says he "understands the process," but just in case this is really just a scam, maybe a harmless gimmick to make people feel better, he wants to cover all the bases and make sure I know some things in advance. Just in case. He wants me to do an attack reading on this woman—hit her hard, hit her fast, get the reaction. That's the money shot. He's thinking about how he's going to *sell these products*.

By this point, Ramey and Adora had come through and gotten me on a few shows—Sally, Maury, *Entertainment Tonight*—but this was my first foray into what Rick Korn had in mind: a television production built around me. This was a pretty big operation, fifteen or twenty people, and it hit me that I was putting my credibility in their hands. Did they really get what I do and want to help me get my message out, or was this just another sell job to them? I trusted Chad, but those guys from the marketing company were scary.

We were shooting the infomercial at the waterfront house Chad had rented. And it was like he said, beautiful, a mansion right on Tampa Bay. A thread of the show was going to be Judy Guggenheim, a leading lady of after-death communication and co-author of *Hello from Heaven!*, interviewing me about my work in the living room, a huge, sun-splashed room adorned with white columns that made it feel like the drawing room of a governor's mansion. Judy and I sat in formal chairs on a red Oriental rug, facing each other at an angle. There was a large vase of flowers on a table to our side; a grand piano off my shoulder; and an elegant, winding stairway in the background. The room opened out onto a large patio with a pool. A wooden stairway descended from the patio to the beach, and fifty yards beyond was a sort of pier. It was a jetty of wood planks sitting atop a column of rocks and boulders jutting about twenty yards into Tampa Bay.

Judy started with the basics, asking me to explain the difference between a psychic and a medium. I explained that all mediums are psychics, but not all psychics are mediums, and began a discourse on spirit communication. But then, maybe ten minutes into the interview, I started feeling a connection, and a pull. I was trying to focus on Judy's questions, trying to talk about how I get my information, when I started *getting* information. I knew the schedule was changing.

Judy asked me something, but I just cocked my head and stared off with my mouth half-open, the way I do when I'm in receiving mode. After a few seconds in freeze frame, I explained that someone was coming through and I had to stop. "I'm sorry, I can't even listen to you because this is coming in so loud," I said. "Let's just get this out of the way, and then we can go back to the interview." Chad, of course, didn't see this as an annoying interruption. "Do not stop rolling," he told the crew.

"Just keep going," Judy said to me. "Tell me what's going on."

"What's happening is I'm trying to conduct an interview with you and help explain the process, and something else has totally taken over. There's like a totally different program happening where someone's trying to get their message through. You know, they wait for no one."

The production crew was caught off guard. This was an infomercial—spontaneity wasn't exactly their specialty. I felt like I was being pulled to my right, but when I explained that the energies coming through could be for anyone in the house, there was chaos. All I remember is a lot of people with equipment scurrying around in every direction. Chad went to an adjoining room where he had parked the marketing people with a monitor so they could watch the taping. He told them to come into the living room. Now the entire production team was standing in front of me—camera operators, assistants, even Yosemite Sam and Elmer Fudd. "Who is it?" Chad asked.

"It's none of these guys," I said.

Now I was drawn toward the back wall of the house. "Who's over there?" I asked, pointing to my right. "I think I'm back over there."

Chad looked over and saw a wall with nobody near it. "Nobody's been there the whole time," he said.

"Yes, there was," I insisted. "It's right over there. There had to be someone standing right there. . . . Who's on the other side of that wall?"

Chad looked at me for a second, then took a breath, as if something had clicked. Two sets of sliding glass doors flanked the wall. They led out to the patio, where he had set up a production table. He slid one of the doors open, and leaned out. "Nicole, would you come in?" he said.

Chad's assistant producer, a woman in her twenties with a beautiful, round face framed by straight black hair, poked her head in tentatively. She saw everyone looking at her. "It's a male figure coming through," I said. "There's an impact to the body."

"Oh, my . . ." Chad said. He definitely knew something.

I looked at Nicole. "This is for you, isn't it," I said.

"Okay, clear the room," Chad said. Judy got up and gave Nicole her seat next to me. The sound man brought over a body mike. "Ed, we're still rolling?" Chad asked the cameraman, who nodded. "Still rolling."

Chad, it turned out, had suspected this might happen since the moment their plane from Los Angeles had touched down in Tampa. In fact, he had been hoping for it, although he had carefully avoided saying anything to me. As they were landing, Chad told me later, he saw that Nicole was crying. He asked her what was wrong. "Remember the story I told you, about Roger?" she inquired softly. "This is the first time I've been back here since then." Oh my gosh, Chad said. He hadn't connected it when they were searching for a location for the shoot. The worst thing that had ever happened to Nicole happened in Tampa. She had told him the story, but he didn't register the place. And now he had brought her back here. He hugged her and apologized. "I'm going to get you through this," he said. "I promise."

Chad stood with Nicole as the sound guy attached her mike. She seemed to be bracing herself, nervously remarking that she had no shoes on. When she was ready, she looked at me uneasily. I stared away, focusing on the spirit who was so boldly barging in on our little infomercial shooting.

"Someone's coming through, and they're making me feel like they passed from some kind of head trauma. This would be something that was an impact. There's a very strong bond of love that's connected here; and there's a feeling of unresolved, unfinished, but continued business, which is really strange for me. Is this a male figure who's passed?"

Nicole nodded yes and wiped away a tear.

"Because it's either a brother of yours, or like a boyfriend. It's a male figure to the side. Do you understand that?"

She nodded again, and now her cheeks were glistening. Judy handed her a tissue.

"He's making me feel like you've had a continued kind of affinity with his energy since his passing." This brought a pained smile through her tears.

"His actions brought about how he passed. Are you aware of that? He put himself at the wrong place at the wrong time, that's how he's coming through. . . . He's showing me a ring. Were you guys talking about getting married, or talking about engagement?"

Nicole couldn't speak. Judy, sitting behind her, reached out and held her hand. "I know this is hard," I told Nicole. "He's telling me to talk to you about the ring. Now, this was a situation he should not have been in, correct? Just yes or no, if you can." Again, Nicole nodded through her tears. "He shows me that this is a fast passing. It's like one-two-three. What impacted his body?"

"He was out, uh, on his boat out here on the bay," Nicole said, barely above a whisper. "And, uh, shot."

I thought, wow, right here on this bay? I knew Nicole was from California. Now Roger showed me the boat and gave me a very warm feeling. "That boat was his baby," I told Nicole. She smiled. Roger practically lived on his boat, she explained later. To him, a perfect life would be spent on the water, fishing.

"He's showing me the number two."

"He died on the second. In May. A year and a half ago."

"He's showing me pink roses. When I see pink roses, that's their way of expressing their love. . . He's showing me that it was a struggle for you to be together. Like something pulled you guys apart. . . . Was he supposed to come out to you by June?"

"That's when he was supposed to move."

As Nicole later explained, her boyfriend, Roger, was from Tampa and was waiting for a job transfer to San Francisco, where she lived. They worked for the same San Francisco-based company and had met in the fall of 1996, when Roger came out for a business meeting. They clicked immediately, and when he went home to Florida, they began just about as long a long-distance relationship as you can have without leaving the continental United States. They talked three times a day, first thing in the morning, last thing at night, and once during the workday. They saw each other when Roger came to the West Coast on business, and twice when Nicole went to Tampa to visit him. In Florida, they spent almost all their time on Roger's boat. He loved being on the water. He told Nicole that he would be perfectly happy to quit his job and work as some captain's first mate. Roger was the company's national sales director, working out of his home. The head of the company had been talking about moving him to San Francisco. Roger didn't like the idea. He had grown up in the Southeast, played football at Florida State, and stayed put. He liked his life on Tampa Bay and wasn't a big-city boy. But when Nicole entered the picture, he really had a conflict.

Nicole and Roger's relationship was like something from *Guiding Light*. They'd had to keep their romance secret because the boss, a man in his fifties named Bert, had a thing for Nicole and made it known within the company that nobody could date her. He told people that she was "my girl," even though he was married, twice her age, and Nicole made it clear that she had zero interest in him. When Bert found out about Roger's relationship with Nicole, around Christmastime, he ordered him to stay away from her. And suddenly his plans to bring Roger to the home office were put on hold.

Now things started to get weird. When Roger came home with Nicole after a business meeting in Seattle, they found Bert the boss waiting for them outside Nicole's apartment. That's when Nicole started thinking about a sexual harassment case. But she couldn't convince Roger that she wasn't somehow encouraging Bert. After all, he was a rich, charming, powerful guy. "No man in his right mind would act this way toward a girl unless he thought there was a chance," Roger told Nicole. After that day, the air seemed to come out of the romance. It wasn't over—Nicole hoped this was just a bump in the road, that Roger would eventually move west and things would work out. She kept an eye out for an apartment for him.

One Tuesday night at the end of April 1997, Roger called Nicole in what struck her as a strangely serene mood. "He said, 'You know what? All I want to do is enjoy myself and be happy, because all the other stuff doesn't matter, the stuff at work, the confrontations. Just be a seaman somewhere and sail away.' And that's the last thing he said to me. And I think, wow, it's almost like he knew. You look back on things. I was flying to Orange County for my girlfriend's wedding two nights later, on Thursday at around eight o'clock. I had a very warm sensation, and I started crying on the plane. I looked out on the water as I was flying in, and there was this boat with all these lights, and I felt something and thought of him. I was upset about how things had gone the last few months, but this was different. I had a very strange feeling, one of those things you can't explain and don't think about until after the fact. I found out later this happened at just about the time they determined he died."

That night in May, Roger had gone out into the Gulf, a longer trip than his twice-daily jaunts around the bay. He never came back. The Coast Guard found his empty boat the next day. His body didn't surface for another eight days. There was a fatal bullet wound in Roger's temple, and the death was ruled a homicide. The FBI took over the investigation because the boat had been found in international waters, but the case hadn't been solved. Roger offered no clues from the other side, other than to say he had put himself in the wrong place at the wrong time. Nicole found this comforting, because it allayed some troubling suspicions she'd had about who might be responsible.

After Roger's death, Nicole was struck by the possibility that her boss might have been involved. He had fired her a few weeks after the death—they were making changes in the company, he said—and her family thought it was all too strange. But Nicole never shared her suspicions with investigators. "I was just a mess. I couldn't do anything," she said. She told me later that when I started reading her, all she wanted to know was: Did he do it? If he did, she would feel some responsibility, not just for what had happened, but also because she hadn't told the FBI investigators the whole story. So Nicole was more than happy to take Roger's message to mean that he had unwittingly gotten in the middle of something out on the water. Maybe he had stumbled onto someone's drug deal, or had some kind of confrontation with another boater. From

Nicole's description, though, the second possibility didn't seem likely. She described him as a sweet, easygoing guy, which is the way he came across to me.

While I was connecting with Roger, he gave me no clue who had murdered him, only that he had gotten himself into a wrong place-wrong time situation. I've gotten that kind of message countless times, for both murders and accidents, and it wasn't very specific. It could mean that the person had taken a foolish risk, or had simply walked into something. With Roger, my medium's interpretation was that it wasn't sinister or premeditated—more like an accident. But when Nicole told me the story, my human reaction was the same as a lot of people's. I didn't know the answer to this mystery. But I can't rule out the possibility that Roger simply didn't want to stir things up for Nicole. He knew she needed to find some peace and move on with her life. That would be consistent with the outlook of those on the other side. And one thing Roger was less ambiguous about was the one other thing Nicole needed to hear: that he now knew that she had been telling him the truth when she told him she considered Bert nothing but a nuisance. "He's coming across in a way to say to you he might not have appreciated who you were in his life, at the time," I had told her during the reading. "And that he can see that differently now." The whole tenor of the few minutes Roger, Nicole, and I spent together was one of comfort and reassurance. Of course, that's not unusual. Most readings are about comfort and reassurance. But this was not like most readings. Whether it was a case of truth withheld out of love, we'll probably never know. As far as I know, Roger's murder is in the FBI's cold-case file.

Nicole was a very professional young woman, a private person who kept control of her emotions and tended not to share her personal life with many people, especially those she worked with. So nobody on the set knew anything about all this except Chad. But now we all realized how hard this had to have been for her. One of the marketing guys told us that he had given Nicole a ride from the hotel to the set that day, and took a back route along an inland channel where they had come upon a sign saying manatees could be seen at that spot. He stopped the car and they went down to the water, where there was a big gathering of these funny-looking sea mammals splashing around.

Manatees, also known as sea cows, are an endangered species, adored around Tampa Bay, where "Save the Manatees" is a common battle cry. It's said that ancient sailors, including Christopher Columbus, thought manatees were mermaids—a mistake that could only be made by men who have been at sea for six months. Manatees can weight a ton, and they look like hippos with flippers. They're as gentle as puppies, and they like to play with people in the water, especially if those people scratch their enormous round bellies, for which they might get an actual sea cow kiss. You can't help but smile when you see a manatee. But when Nicole saw them in the channel that morning, the big, wet lugs seemed to turn her somber.

Nicole explained why. "The manatees were like our special animal," she said. "Roger was a really sweet, sensitive guy, and he had a thing for manatees. He would get mad at all the boats in the waterways because the manatees were so slow they couldn't get out of the way of the propellers. And so when I came to Tampa for the first time, he taught me about them. We went and looked at some, and I started to fall in love with them. After that they represented us being together. We would send each other manatee cards, manatee stuff. So whenever I see a manatee, of course I think of Roger."

We realized that Nicole must have been upset since the moment Chad had first mentioned shooting the infomercial in Tampa. "I didn't want to interfere with the shoot," she said. "I didn't say anything to Chad. But when it kept coming back to Tampa, I was thinking, *Why does it have to be there? Why can't it be someplace else?*"

Now we knew, of course, why it had to be Tampa. And why all those great Caribbean locations kept falling through. And it had to be that Nicole was out on the dock, looking out across the endless stretch of water where Roger slipped across to the other side, just as he was inside with me, breaking through the curtain.

"He's not in a bad spot, even though he had a horrendous passing," I told Nicole at the end of the reading. "He's making me feel like he had to interrupt what we were doing today to get me to do this, because this has been a very painful experience for you, being back here and having to do this. He recognizes that. You're trying to do this, be a trouper, be a professional, but he's aware and he appreciates it. He wants you to know your thoughts and feelings are being heard."

"Is that why you were pointing out that way, because I was sitting outside?" Nicole asked after Roger pulled back and she was finally able to speak.

"I was totally being pulled out there."

Nicole told me that when we had first met in California, she had hoped something like this might happen—her fears about who had murdered Roger were tearing her apart. But by the time we got to Tampa, she had changed her mind. She didn't want to bring her personal life so openly into work. And she was afraid of what she might hear. So she had made sure to stay outside during the taping. And when she heard the words "impact to the head," she thought, *Oh, shit.*

Nicole dabbed her tears. "I'm so embarrassed," she said.

"Oh, please don't be embarrassed," I told her.

"This is a special delivery," Judy assured her.

"Oh, major league special delivery," I agreed.

Chad suggested that we take a few minutes to break the tension of what had been a powerful experience for all of us. Nicole unhooked her mike and stood up, and without a second's hesitation started walking back toward the door through which she had come. She sat down and peered across the bay, completely lost in thought. And then she got back up and started walking toward the wood stairway to the beach, and then out to the pier. "I had this overwhelming feeling, a pull that brought me out to the dock," she would recall later that day. Nicole made her way slowly, barefoot, to the end of the dock. Chad saw her out there and had a cameraman film a long shot from the house. He couldn't resist capturing footage of this beautiful woman in this heartbreaking, contemplative moment at the water's edge. It might have seemed like an invasion, but there was a reason the cameraman made the shot.

When Nicole came back to the house, she had an amazed look on her face. It seemed that she was crying again. "You're not going to believe this," she said. "When I got to the end of the dock, I was standing there thinking about Roger, wishing there was some way he could give me a sign that it was all true. At that moment, I looked down into the water right in front of me, and there was a manatee. He lifted his lips out of the water and looked right at me. Then he swam away. I felt it was him saying good-bye, and I could have some peace. If there weren't all these people here, I swear I would have jumped in with him."

A skeptic might say, well, this *was* Tampa Bay. It's nothing special to see a manatee there. Yes, except for this: As a member of the endangered species list, the warm-water manatee is scarce enough in summer. This was February. It's a good winter if there are a couple of hundred of them in the entire four hundred-square-mile bay. And, as the owner of the house told us, those few will not be found anywhere near the cold waters where we were. They winter together in the only places they can survive, in the inland channels where Nicole had seen them earlier, and in the spa-like waters around factories and power plants way on the other side of the bay. No wonder Nicole's manatee just said a quick hello and turned around. He must have been freezing.

Now everybody needed a drink. We piled into a car—Chad driving, Nicole in front, Judy and me in the back The radio was on with the volume low, the music drowned out by our excited talk about what had just occurred. My ears, as you might imagine, are supersensitive, and I'm often saying to people I'm with, "Did you hear that?" As we were driving to the restaurant, I thought that there was something outside the car that we needed to hear. "Listen," I said. "Shh." Chad thought I was trying to hear something on the radio. So he cranked it up.

"What're you doing?" I blurted.

"I thought you wanted to hear it."

"No, it's outside . . ."

And then we all heard it. It was inside the car. A slow, sentimental '70s melody floating from the radio speakers, and the words from a high-pitched Motown man's voice: *I had to meet you here today . . . There's just so many things to say . . . Please darlin', don't you cry . . . Let's just kiss and say goodbye.*

Everybody in the car lost it. I'm leaking tears, Judy is speechless. Nicole is on her second box of tissues. We just sat there listening to the Manhattans singing the rest of "Kiss and Say Goodbye."

As the sun was going down that evening, I thought about how Elmer Fudd had tried to get me to make the host cry like I'm Barbara Walters. Now all I could do was laugh and shake my head at the spirits' superb sense of irony. Elmer couldn't have asked for a more emotional scene to *sell these products* if he had staged it himself. And that's exactly what he thought I had done with Nicole. "Was that a setup?" he asked me later. Yes, and she's Reva Shayne and I'm Otto Preminger. And the manatee was remote controlled. But he made my point for me: Souls in spirit are truly amazing. It's as if Roger wasn't just coming through for Nicole. He was bringing an even bigger message from the other side: Don't mess with this.

It's funny. I cringe at the slightest suggestion of manipulation on my end. But I never stop marveling at how often and how intricately the spirit world orchestrates things. Even as I was spurning this guy's shameless nudge to use his hired hand to stage manage reality, a spirit was working overtime to arrange a truly awesome One Last Time for someone else on the set. I can only smile when some cynic thinks I'm making it up. Our people on the other side come up with stuff I couldn't even dream of.

THAT WHOLE THING WITH NICOLE—that was really impressive. Even after sixteen years of hanging out in the intercosmic air space between the physical and spirit worlds, and after making a career of it for six, I'm neither blasé nor jaded. Hardly a week goes by when I'm not in awe of something that happens around me. And when it's one of those extraordinary, unforgettable experiences like that day on Tampa Bay, I feel honored to be a part of it. It's not a case of *Wow, look at what I just did. Sometimes I really amaze myself.* I don't see it as something *I* did. I see it as something *they* did. I'm just lucky they chose me as the conduit. After all, I've never been able to come up with a satisfying explanation of why I have this ability. And that's the only thing I call it. An ability—not a gift. As I see it, the only gift is the privilege of participating in a circle of energy from God Himself. I receive, interpret, and deliver messages from the *spirit* side to a recipient on *this* side. The recipient understands, accepts, and appreciates these messages. And that appreciation rebounds back to the other side. It's the completion of the energy circle that is the real gift.

When I have one of those rocking moments, I feel like an archaeologist who's made a big find. He's studied his field, he works hard at it, he knows where to look and what he's looking for. But in the end, it's pure blind luck that he's the one who discovers the 780,000-year-old elephant buried beneath the banks of the Jordan River. Everyone who watches the Discovery Channel gets to hear about it and see pictures, but he was there, he's the one who had the exhilaration of touching it first, of being the one who brought it up from the burial ground. He's the one who got to dust off the treasure and describe what it was and what it might mean. So that's me: Indiana Jones, wondering what I might happen onto when I start digging today. And thanking God for letting me do it.

It's even better than archaeology because it's not about ancient bones in the desert, but living spirits in the air. Spirit contact is an excavation of the soul of human experience. Not only that, I don't have to wait twenty years between great finds. They come on a regular basis. And the best ones can be the easiest to get. More often than not, the most specific validations—the big wallop or the quirky little detail that blows any shred of skepticism out of the water—just comes to me, without much work at all. There's no tug of war with a confusing energy, no sweet-talking a reticent spirit, no tortured game of twenty questions because I'm being shown an image that could be interpreted twenty ways. It's like a sneeze without the buildup. Boom—it passes through my brain and hits the air before I can even think about it. Sometimes I don't even know what I'm saying as I'm saying it. And then, after it's out, I think—and sometimes say out loud— *Oh, wow, I can't believe I got that. Where'd that come from?* I call it falling out of a reading. I hear the words when everyone else does, and I react just like them. For that moment, I'm sitting with them, detached from myself. *Wow, did you hear what that guy just said? That was so cool.*

It never gets old.

— CHAPTER 4 —

PROVING GROUNDS

20-60-20

Looking back on it now, the infomercial was a failure in every way but the most important one. It introduced me to the essence of television. It gave me a tremendous education in the marketing of a medium and the importance of protecting the integrity of the work in a world crawling with people whose main interest is exploiting it. Yes, a big, blinking yellow light from The Boys. Especially now that so many people were watching.

I can't prove this, but I feel safe in saying that more people than ever before are coming to believe in either the fact or the possibility of an accessible afterlife. And they're not just the people who have always been believers. When I first began doing group readings and lectures, the audience was almost all female, mostly middle-aged, and from working-class backgrounds. Now I see a much more diverse crowd. There are many more men—even if some of them are still there because their wives dragged them—more younger people, and more people who would have dismissed what I do as ridiculous not too long ago. They may still be skeptical, but they're willing to consider the possibilities. And that's good enough for me. I can work with an open mind.

When it comes to spirit communication, it's a 20-60-20 world. Twenty percent are True Believers. You don't have to convince them of anything. In fact, a percentage of this percentage can be so uncritical, so *un*skeptical, that they'll believe anything. And that's not good. For one thing, they can be taken in by a less-than-competent, less-than-scrupulous psychic. And they may be so consumed with grief and a need to hold on that they forget they're still living here—and their loved ones are living there. It's an important distinction. This subgroup can be as frustrating to me as people who believe nothing. Speaking of which—that's the second group of twenty percent. These are the True Nonbelievers. Whether it's fear of the unknown or just an ingrained, overly intellectualized belief system, they have no need to consider the phenomenon, let alone explore it. Ashes to ashes, dust to dust—they know *for a fact* that when you're dead you're dead. Skeptics, cynics—whatever you call them, their minds are closed for business. Don't even bother.

Then there is the great middle class—the 60 percent who aren't sure what they believe or don't believe. But they're interested, open, and more than likely would like to believe. They just need a good reason. Most people—probably even the confirmed cynics—would like to think that there *is* something more after this. The cynics won't find out there is until they get there—can you imagine their reactions the moment it happens? But for the majority of people, all it takes is a convincing personal experience to remove or at least chip away at the doubt that comes naturally. There's nothing wrong with that. Skepticism is healthy. So long as it doesn't keep people from at least poking their heads through the curtain for a look-see.

It's that 60 percent I think of most when I'm working—I'm trying to do as much as I can to raise the curtain. Not that it's my goal to convince or convert anyone, let alone *everyone*. But I would like people to have a meaningful experience, and to leave with as much information and understanding as possible, so they can make their own judgments. This doesn't necessarily mean delivering a jaw-dropping reading every time. First, I can't do that. Second, that might not even be enough for some people—even those who are open to the possibility of another existence after this one. People grieve in different ways, and even a great reading by a medium will not take the place of the process people have to go through to survive the pain of their physical loss. No matter how many validating facts I give them—even if they have absolutely no doubt that the person they loved was in the room with them, talking to them through me—they know they will never see that person again. Most people feel some comfort from a positive reading, and many are profoundly moved. But others find it confusing and upsetting.

I read a journalist named Lynn Darling one night in 1999 at the request of a documentary producer named Lisa Jackson, who wanted to use the reading in a TV special she was doing for HBO. It was a fun session for me because Lynn, a writer for *Esquire,* was a very intelligent, quick-witted, and intellectually demanding person. She seemed to enjoy the experience, in a very different way than most. Many people come to me ready with expectations and tissues, anxious for an emotional experience that will lead to comfort and closure. Lynn approached it more like the journalist that she is, even though she wasn't writing about it herself. She was intrigued by a good story, but part of what made it good was that it wasn't obvious. There was a lot to think about, a lot of questions to ask. A lot to challenge.

Lynn brought a lot of spirits with her, but the reading centered around the person I was sure Lynn was happy to connect with: her late husband, Lee. That assumption turned out to be wrong, but not for the reason you might suspect.

Lee Lescaze was also a journalist, and a well-known one. He was a top reporter and editor at the *Washington Post* and then at the *Wall Street Journal*. He had once reported from Vietnam. Now he was reporting from an even more distant place. His dispatches to me were filled with the kind of detail you would expect: that Lynn carried a small box that had been his, that he had died from lung cancer, that he was older than she was and had a prior family. And this nugget, the kind of specific, unknowable thing people tend to latch onto as proof: Lee was telling me that Lynn had been in a lingerie shop recently, and he had been there with her. "There's some kind of a bra issue," is how I put it to her, blushing the way I always do when spirits make me talk about their personal lives.

"Some kind of *bra* issue?" Lynn asked, giggling. Lee was telling me that Lynn had gone into a store thinking about buying some kind of underwear that was not really her style, but which he had once wanted her to wear. "Oh, how funny," she said, confirming that it was true, not nearly as embarrassed as I was.

Lynn seemed to appreciate the experience and was very gracious when she left. So I was puzzled when Lisa Jackson, the producer, sent me an advance tape of the program months later. In a post-reading interview, Lynn's primary reaction was annoyance. In fact, she seemed angry. She acknowledged being touched at first, wanting to believe that she could talk to this person she thought she could never talk to ever again. But she realized upon reflection that she was just suspending belief as you might when you go to see a movie. "The more I thought about it, the more the misses started entering into it," she told Lisa. "There were dates that meant nothing, anniversaries, and lots of relatives that don't exist, as far as I know. He has an answer to this, which is that Lee was passing a message onto somebody else. But the composite portrait was a very general one." She felt that whatever information I had gotten right was because she had unconsciously helped me, answering questions, giving me cues, leading me.

Watching the tape, and remembering the reading, I wondered how she could call all the specific validations I'd given her a "general" portrait, or how she had concluded that I was essentially interviewing her. But, of course, it wasn't a complaint I hadn't heard before. What really took me aback was her reaction to the whole idea of connecting with loved ones. Rather than bringing her some sense of comfort, or expanding her perceptions of life and death, it seemed to make her frustrated. It didn't ease her pain; it made it worse.

"He comes back and says he's okay?" Lynn said. "I mean, he's *dead*. How okay is *that*? I didn't find any consolation in the fact that Lee might be there. In fact, it's kind of disconcerting. If you think about it, it brings up more problems than it solves. My husband's around, and he's not talking to me, or at least he's only talking to me in the living room of this guy on Long Island. Now, does that mean I should be involved in some sort of post-mortem marital therapy? I mean, should I be dealing with the fact that he's not talking to me? And why isn't he talking to me—is it something I said? Maybe he didn't like the lingerie. Maybe he's mad that I go out with other people. And I'm not sure I wanted him in the lingerie shop."

Lynn was doing something I had never seen: She was rejecting this man she missed so much—even ridiculing him. That's how much this unnerved her. Of course, she would say she was ridiculing me and my work, not the memory of her husband or their relationship. But it seemed to me that the only reason she was so disturbed was that she did believe it on some level. Otherwise, she would have just laughed and started looking for the trick.

"Death is a very personal thing," Lynn said. "And it's an incredibly, incredibly hard process, the process of accepting someone's death, believing it, having closure with it, going on with your life and still keeping the memory of your loved one ever green in your mind. And the fact that he's here in the room watching me try on underwear doesn't do a whole lot for that process."

There was a time when this kind of indignant, seemingly glib reaction would have put me nearly into a rage, devastated me for days. Mediums do this work out of love, at least the ones I know and respect. We expend phenomenal amounts of energy to try to help people. So knowing we have given someone a negative experience instead is like kryptonite to us. I did take Lynn's rant personally at first. *Oh, my God. I didn't do my job right. I didn't explain something right. She didn't understand the process.* And, of course, I was mad. I e-mailed Lisa Jackson, saying I loved the program overall, that she did a great job with a difficult subject—but what was up with that wacko woman who didn't want her husband watching her buy underwear? Came Lisa's reply: Well, that wacko woman is my close friend.

Response to reply: Now that I'm taking my foot out of my mouth. . . . That I could laugh about it was actually a big step for me. It all went back to that day in the pool in the Caribbean when I told myself: *Get over it— get used to it; you'll never be able to satisfy everybody.* Some people won't be happy until I pull up a chair and sit their deceased relative right down in front of them. After I thought about it, I knew this was Lynn's thing, not mine. And I felt more sympathy than resentment. After all, here was someone who seemed to believe—or at least was open to the possibility—that her husband's spirit was alive and with her. And yet she found that much more upsetting than comforting. How could that make me anything but sad for her?

I also knew that there are people who feel the way she does. Maybe they wouldn't express it exactly the way an acerbic writer would, but not everybody embraces my work, even if they believe in the afterlife. For example, even though the afterlife is a key tenet of my own Catholic church, and many Catholics openly include spirit communication in their own lives, the church itself frowns on it. So rather than taking Lynn's words as a personal attack, I saw them as a dose of reality that people *should* see. It's part of the process—not just deciding whether you believe, but figuring out what it means if you do. Lynn's point of view was valid and poignant. I was glad the producer included them. Just as I want people to understand the process as I see it, I need to understand how it feels to them and appreciate their point of view.

Process. That's probably my favorite word in all this. It's why I wanted the infomercial people to show more readings—show what this is all about. Put in more raw footage of Nicole's reading, showing exactly how it unfolded. The vast majority of people have never been exposed to the unfiltered reality of a reading by a medium. Misconceptions and mythology are the grunge we in the field are constantly trying to scrub away.

That's why the mass media gets us excited—and gives us the willies. Whether it's journalism, entertainment, or that stuff all over TV that you can't identify as one or the other, you never know what you're going to get when you say yes. Unless, of course, you have your own show—but let's not talk about that right now. So when I got that first call from Lisa Jackson late in 1998, I was interested but wary.

Lisa was with Linda Ellerbee's Lucky Duck Productions—hmm— and she was producing a documentary on after-death communication (ADC). It wasn't the usual fare for Ellerbee's company. The veteran broadcast journalist and her staff had produced award-winning children's programs for Nickelodeon and public affairs specials about the Supreme Court, AIDS, and other weighty, mainstream topics. But the growing interest in ADC had gotten the attention of HBO. This was at a time when I was making my first tentative steps into television, planning the infomercial. Judy Guggenheim had recommended me to Lisa, and she wanted to see if I might be one of the mediums she could build a documentary around.

After a few phone conversations, I was pretty sure I didn't want to be on the program. I didn't know what kind of show they were planning— a debunking could almost be taken for granted, and a real hatchet job always had to be considered—and going on camera without having any control over how it came out made me very uncomfortable. The shows I was going on to promote the book were essentially unedited interview shows, not taped and neatly packaged programs that could be slanted in whatever direction the people making it wanted. And I still had no burning desire to see my face on television. If something that appealed to me came up, fine. If not, even better.

I had a counterproposal. I asked Lisa if she would be interested in using me as a behind-the-scenes consultant. I could help guide her over the pitfalls, serve as a technical expert, maybe help shape the program. Over the next few weeks, I spent a lot of time talking to Lisa about the work of a medium, explaining my ideas for how they might do the show. I must have done too good a job, because all I seemed to do was confirm Lisa's initial impulse that I should be in front of the camera. I felt much more positive, too. I was very impressed with Lisa and concluded that she was taking a serious, open-minded look at the subject. And since HBO was known for original programs that were fresh, smart, and often daring, I was satisfied that her documentary wouldn't be sensationalistic, or worse, an ambush.

What caught my imagination most was Lisa's ambition. She wanted to go beyond the standard approach—"Is (Your Medium Here) Speaking to the Dead?"—and break some new ground. Her enterprising idea was to have some of the leading mediums tested by a University of Arizona psychologist who had developed an interest in "survival of consciousness" research. Lisa said it hadn't been determined yet how we would be tested, but that this professor, along with his wife, a fellow psychologist, had some interesting ideas. And HBO was prepared to foot the bill.

I was intrigued by the idea. With my strong desire to increase knowledge about mediumship, and my affinity for health and medicine—not to mention my perennial curiosity about what exactly goes on in my brain—I was tantalized by the idea of a scientist being brave enough to open an area of research for spirit communication. But at the same time, I wanted to know what I was getting involved with. Who was this guy, and what was his point of view? What prejudices might he be bringing with him? Most important, what kinds of "tests" did he have in mind? Lisa sent me a twenty-five page proposal outlining his thoughts, and how he proposed to test the mediums who agreed to be in his study. I read through it and thought: *Huh?* It was a very esoteric description of a test this professor was calling "Whose Mind Is Being Read?" As far as I could tell, he was trying to determine where information came from. Did it come from our dearly departed? Or was the medium simply reading the thoughts and desires of the sitter? It would basically have us try to determine if both fictional characters and real people were dead, alive, fictional, or nonfictional. Confusing? For me, too.

"I'm not doing that," I told Lisa. "It's like some psychic parlor game. It has nothing to do with mediumship." Lisa thought I should talk to Suzane Northrop, who was also thinking about participating. Suzane is a wonderful medium from New York whose skill and integrity—and toughness—are beyond question. "Suzane's doing this?" I asked Lisa. I didn't know her all that well at the time, but I had a hard time believing Suzane would take part in this test.

But before I called Suzane, she called me. "Are you doing this?" she asked.

"Funny you should ask," I said. "Are you?"

"Oh, God, no way. It's bullshit. It's never going to prove anything about mediumship. I couldn't even understand half of it."

But even though both Suzane and I thought the psychologist's idea was totally off the mark, a funny thing happened. Talking about it made both us both want to pursue this further. We both felt that if a serious academic researcher wanted to study spirit communication in an honest and open-minded way, we shouldn't let the opportunity pass without even talking to the guy.

TESTING, TESTING

GARY SCHWARTZ IS A UNIQUE MAN. He's the kind of college professor who really takes the concept of academic freedom to heart. A bearded New York native in his fifties, he started out as an electrical engineering student at Cornell, but wound up with a doctorate in psychology from Harvard. He stayed on the faculty there for five years, then went to Yale for a dozen more. His specialty was "psychophysiology"—the study of the mind-body connection. As the director of a Yale center devoted to research in that field, he studied biofeedback, the mind-body relationship to emotion and pain, and the treatment of stress-related disorders. While at Harvard and Yale, he published six papers in *Science,* the official publication of the American Association for the Advancement of Science and one of the most prestigious research journals in the world.

But beneath all that respectability was a maverick waiting to break out. In the early 1980s, Gary became captivated by the research of a British biologist named Rupert Sheldrake. Sheldrake had come up with something called Morphogenic Resonance Hypothesis. Boiled down, it's all about how he thinks memory is stored in the universe. As his theory goes, anytime any form comes into existence—even words that are spoken—it leaves an imprint and joins the imprints of everything that has come before. And all of it becomes easier to create in the future because it's already there. Pretty far-out stuff, even for a professor of biofeedback.

Gary spent the next few years conducting experiments to test Sheldrake's theory. One of them explored how language evolves, and hypothesized that words repeated over and over through the centuries have an energy that becomes part of the universe's stored memory. Gary got a prestigious award for his work in 1986, which made the pages of *Time* magazine. But Ivy League academics being what they are, some of his fellow professors were less appreciative of his ingenuity than others. "Some of my colleagues at Yale thought it was terribly creative," he says, "and the other ones thought it was just terrible." And that's how Gary wound up in the desert. He loved the Southwest, but more important, he found the University of Arizona a more welcoming place for independent thinkers such as himself. He moved there in 1988, and since then, the university has created an internationally known Center for Consciousness Studies and a program in integrative medicine run by mind-body health guru Dr. Andrew Weil. They even gave Gary his own fancy-sounding lab. He named it the Human Systems Energy Laboratory.

That's Gary's baby. He and his colleagues began doing research in mind-body medicine, "energy medicine," and, eventually, the thing that really got his juices flowing: "spiritual medicine"—research into the possibility that there is survival of consciousness after physical death. "When people ask what I do, I say we work in three controversial areas," Gary says. "One is merely controversial; the second is very controversial. And the third is super-controversial." Survival of consciousness is not an issue considered by many serious scientists, but it's one Gary has been thinking about for nearly twenty years. He actually wanted to try to figure out the answer—and prove it scientifically.

Back at Yale in the early eighties, Gary had begun ruminating on the whole idea of universal memory—the theory that everything is alive, eternal, and evolving. He had theorized that anytime two things share energy and information, they become a "feedback system." Whether it's the hydrogen and oxygen that make up water, two strands of DNA, two heart cells, two people, the earth and the moon—these "systems" are exchanging information and energy that becomes a permanent part of the universe. It accumulates over time and turns into memory. To Gary, this theory predicts everything from cell memory—for instance, the confirmed cases of heart-transplant recipients experiencing personality changes that match their donors—to near-death, out-of-body experiences, and ultimately, the survival of consciousness after death. The essence of the theory is that there's no such thing as true death—of anything. Only transition.

"This would be terribly controversial, to put it mildly," Gary says. "So I didn't touch it with a ten-foot pole. In fact, I didn't tell anybody about it." He wasn't even sure if he believed it himself. It was an elegant theory, but it didn't fit with the assumption he'd grown up with: that death is The End. He wasn't sure he would ever take this idea out of its box in the basement. At least not as long as he wanted to keep his career. And then this private, purely professional interest converged with something very personal.

In 1993, Gary went to a conference and found his soulmate. Her name was Linda Russek, and she was a fellow psychologist, living in Boca Raton, Florida. A few weeks later, Gary went to Florida to visit Linda. Gary recalled that at four in the morning as she drove him to the airport, she asked him a question that nobody had ever asked him before. She said, "Gary, do you believe in the possibility of survival of consciousness after death?" The reason she was asking was that her father had died three years earlier. "Do you believe that my father can still be here?"

Linda's father had been a very well-known cardiologist—he had run the annual meetings of the American College of Cardiologists for twenty-three years, published two hundred papers, and edited seven books. And he did clinical work with his daughter. "Linda had a very, very close relationship with her father," Gary says. "When he died in 1990, Linda went on a scientific and metaphysical quest to see if she could prove whether he was still here."

When Linda asked Gary if he believed this could be possible, he asked her if it mattered what he thought. "Yes," she said, "because you're a serious scientist. And if you believe it, then you have to have a reason, and probably a good one." Gary told Linda that it so happened that he had thought about this a lot, but for reasons of self-preservation had kept it to himself. "I don't know if my logic is correct," he said, speaking these words to a colleague for the very first time. "I don't know if nature works this way. But based on what I know about physics, chemistry, and biology, I think it's very plausible that survival of consciousness can exist." Linda wanted to know more. Gary promised that when he came back in a couple of weeks, he would tell her the whole story.

Part of the reason Gary didn't tell anyone about his theory was that he wasn't sure he believed it himself. He could imagine people's reactions, because he was coming from the same place. "The way I was raised, there was Santa Claus, the Easter Bunny, and life after death. It was a fantasy, it was stupid. I was raised to believe ashes to ashes, dust to dust. My parents both died when I was at Yale in the 1980s. I never thought twice about whether their 'soul' would continue. Even though the theory says it would. So as a scientist, the theory led me to believe it was plausible. As a person, I was educated to believe it was impossible. So I guess I was an agnostic. I didn't know."

When Gary went back to Boca Raton two weeks later and explained his theory, Linda got all excited. But on this she wasn't exactly a dispassionate researcher. She wanted to believe. She told Gary he had to start working on this—it was too important to hide away like some horrible family secret, simply out of professional trepidation. Linda was like a lot of people in her need to know what had really become of her dad, and to stay connected. But the scientific investigator in her wasn't content to hope he was still around, or even to see if she could connect with him herself, or through a medium. She wanted Gary to change the focus of his work. In essence, she wanted him to scientifically prove to her that her father had not disappeared from the universe. And she would help him.

"So put yourself in my shoes," Gary says. "You've just met this very special person who's asking you to do research in an area you know is very controversial. You've never done any work on it. You know your colleagues would prefer you do this research somewhere else, preferably on another planet. She says, 'Gary, you've got to help me.' " Gary didn't only fall in love with Linda. "I fell in love with Linda's love for her father. And her dream to know scientifically one way or the other if her father was still here. So I looked in her eyes and I said, 'Okay, Linda, I'll help you, but under one condition: We don't tell anyone.'"

Linda moved to Arizona, and over the next few years, they began quietly exploring the big question. Gary recorded Linda's brain waves while she tried to contact her father. He put special high-frequency microphones around her, capable of recording sounds that vibrate four times higher than anything the human ear can hear. "To see if there was anything in a high-frequency range that might occur when a deceased person was in the area." No wonder he made Linda promise they wouldn't talk about it with anyone. As a scientist, Gary feels uncomfortable talking about these early, informal experiments, but says they were "suggestive enough to lead us to continue."

In 1995, Gary and Linda met a woman named Susy Smith, a prolific writer of books about parapsychology and the creator of a foundation for survival-of-consciousness research. She is said to have had a forty-year connection to her deceased mother. Then Gary and Linda met their first medium, Laurie Campbell, a homemaker from Irvine, California, who volunteered to participate in their research. Gary and Linda were also finishing a book, *The Living Energy Universe.* They were finally coming above ground.

One day in late 1998, Gary got a call from Lisa Jackson in New York. She told him she was working on a documentary for HBO called "Life After Life," and that it was going to be a serious examination of spirit communication. Gary is no fool. The only thing that had held back his research in survival of consciousness was money. The National Institutes of Health were not going to be writing him a check anytime soon so he could do experiments with people who talk to dead people. To get funding to research that, you'd pretty much have to be a psychiatrist studying schizophrenia. So Gary saw an opportunity. If you're really interested in the science of spirit communication, he told Lisa Jackson, if you really want to do something serious and special, then you should fund what would be the first-ever laboratory investigation of psychic mediumship. All we would need are the mediums. Lisa's response: What if I could deliver the top mediums to your lab?

When I called Gary Schwartz, I expected a short conversation that would most likely be followed by a call to Lisa politely declining her invitation to participate. If his proposed dead-or-alive test was any indication, he was probably a little too academic for my tastes. And I wasn't sure he wasn't just out to discredit us—although, why would he bother? That wouldn't exactly be seen as bold, groundbreaking work. But what happened was that we wound up spending two hours on the phone, in a very intense discussion and debate about the afterlife, our connection to it, and what might be provable. Gary later said that both Suzane and I really grilled him to make sure he didn't have some hidden agenda. He survived very nicely—he was just as passionate about exploring our world as we were about living it. Gary was very open, very receptive to ideas. And I felt that he was coming from the right place. He was extremely sympathetic to what it's like to be challenged in your work at every turn, accused by some of being a fraud. He said he wanted to assemble a "Dream Team" of mediums for the first-ever scientific peek at the other side.

"Here's the metaphor," he said. "Michael Jordan is one of the all-time great basketball players. Do you know what his average accuracy is shooting from the floor?" I had no idea. "Around 45 percent. In a good game, he might get 60 to 70 percent. So how can somebody who's on the average missing more that 50 percent of his shots be a superstar? The answer is that he's got to be better than everybody else. And just because he misses a lot of his shots doesn't mean you don't count all the ones he's made. It doesn't mean you chalk up his dazzling plays to luck. So the first thing is if we're going to look for a Michael Jordan in the mediumship world, we're not expecting you to be perfect. In fact, you can miss more than 50 percent of your shots. More than that, we know that on some days you can be good, and other days not so good. So we aren't going to pick on your errors."

Suzane had the same conversation with Gary, and the same reaction. We both called Lisa Jackson and said we would go to Tucson. We wouldn't do the dead-or-alive test, but Gary seemed eager to hear our ideas. Great, Lisa said, go out there and figure it out. Just make sure that whatever you decide, it's for HBO.

When Suzane and I flew out and met with Gary and Linda, they seemed overjoyed to see us. "Most professional mediums are afraid of scientists," he explained. "They think we're out to debunk them." Suzane and I wanted to start with the basics. Gary wasn't going to prove any Morphogenic Resonance Hypothesis with us, but he could set up a controlled experiment and document in a systematic way that we were getting accurate information about someone we had never met. And that wasn't a bad place to start.

The test didn't have to be that complicated: Just bring us into a room, one at a time, and have us read the same person—the "sitter." Gary and Linda would take careful notes on the information, then debrief the sitter later and see how accurate we were. It would be up to them to come up with a way of collating, interpreting, and presenting the data. As one of the suppliers of the data, that made me a little nervous. Sort of like a hesitant sperm donor—I didn't mind making the donation, I just wondered what they were going to do with it.

I liked the simplicity of the experiment, but tossed out one more idea. It came from my medical background. "Why don't we do EKGs and EEGs? Maybe we'll find out something about our hearts and brains when we're reading. We could put them on the sitter, too."

Gary and Linda looked at each other. "You guys would do that?" Linda asked.

Lisa Jackson found the idea of measuring our heart and brain waves very exciting. She knew hooking up electrical leads to the brains of mediums would look great on film. Maybe they would discover something interesting. But even if they wound up being just bells and whistles for the camera, we were going to be part of a landmark event. Gary had a completely open field.

Suzane wasn't so sure about the high-tech gizmos. She hadn't signed up to be poked and prodded like an alien in a secret Army lab after a UFO crash. When the TV producers had initially approached her about getting involved in the project, her first instinct was to turn and run. She didn't feel that she had to submit to the indignity of testing to prove what she did. But they kept coming back, and eventually, after talking to Gary, she realized that this was a rare opportunity for our field. None of us likes to admit that we lose any sleep over the professional cynics who go on Larry King and say we're ridiculous and so is anyone who believes us. But the truth is if *we* could go on Larry King and hold up a serious research paper documenting why *they're* the ridiculous ones for being afraid to even take a peek, we'd all sleep better. It wouldn't change how we feel about our work. But it wouldn't hurt our cause. "For twenty-five years, I'm traveling around the country constantly asking people to trust their own information, trust their messages," Suzane said. "How can I ask people to do that if I'm turning down an opportunity to do something that's never been done before?"

Suzane and I weren't afraid to be put to the test, but filming the research for television did raise the stakes. We wouldn't have any control over editing and presentation. And what if we had a bad day, or the sitter was uncooperative or was uninformed about the family tree? It could be a disaster—and not just for us but for the whole field. But the best-case scenario was exciting to think about. If it went well, millions of people would see, up close and for the first time, a legitimate university researcher delivering evidence of communication with the spirit world. I couldn't help but think of Darth Vader, the lady in black at the Barnes & Noble in Santa Monica. *Where's the proof? You can't prove this scientifically! You're all stupid fools!*

The only thing left for Lisa to do was recruit a few more mediums, and a sitter or two. She called George Anderson. He quickly agreed. So did another medium, Anne Gehman. Gary also asked Laurie Campbell, the homemaker from California who had participated in his earlier studies. Suzane had only one point she wanted Gary to pay careful attention to. "All mediums work differently," she told him. "I know you want a controlled experiment, but you have to give us license to work the way we work."

"We'll let you play it your way," Gary assured her. "We're going to do everything in our power to make it possible for a phenomenon, if it's real, to emerge."

I FLEW TO TUCSON straight from shooting the infomercial in Florida. Gary and Linda told us the plan for the next day: The five mediums would be brought into a room one by one to read the sitter the producers had recruited. The others would wait in a courtyard behind the lab. Inside the reading room, we would sit side-by-side with the sitter, a few feet apart and with a screen between us. We wouldn't see the sitter before or during the reading. We would get only yes and no answers to the messages we relayed. Both medium and sitter would be wired up to see if there was any correlation between our hearts during the reading. The mediums would also have electrodes attached to their heads to record brain waves. The cameras would record it all, and Gary and Linda would keep a careful list of every piece of information we generated. Eventually, the sitter would evaluate transcripts of the readings, and our performances would be compared to controls: sixty-eight people taking guesses. We all took a vow of secrecy during the experiment. We promised we would not say anything about our reading to the others.

"Tomorrow, we are going to do something that has never been done in the history of science," Gary told us in his most momentous-sounding voice as the HBO cameras rolled. "It's never been the case before that a group of pioneer mediums are teaming together with a group of scientists in a university that really believes that any important question could be asked in an open fashion."

The next morning, we trouped into Gary's little lab building to read our first sitter. Lisa Jackson had recruited someone from north of Tucson—as we found out later, a forty-six-year-old woman named Pat Price who had suffered through the deaths of six people close to her in the past ten years. Prior to our arrival, Gary and Linda had her fill out a detailed questionnaire about her losses. And that morning they had her sign a statement affirming that she'd had no contact with any of the mediums before the experiment.

Suzane went in first, and Gary told me later he wasn't prepared for the sheer force of her style. "You'll have to wait your turn," she said when she entered the room; she wasn't talking either to Gary or to the woman on the other side of the screen. Suzane is no wallflower to begin with, but when she's connecting, she kicks into a whole different mode. She's all over the place, her hands are going, and if this is possible, she speaks even faster than I do. She's just alive with information. With Pat Price, I learned later, Suzane really got in a zone, talking without seeming to stop for a breath, pouring out fact after fact that Pat had to keep up with to validate.

"My jaw was on the floor," Gary said later. "She was talking nonstop like a cab driver from New York, and getting all this highly specific information. Pat was looking at me, nodding and crying." The most emotional piece of information was that Pat had lost her son.

I went next, and probably seemed like Ben Stein in comparison. The electrodes were attached—not two or three as I thought, but nineteen, kept together on my head with a kind of shower cap. The first and strongest energy that came through was a male figure to Pat's side. It seemed to be her husband. I asked her if she understood that, and she said yes. A younger male figure also came through, connected to Pat's husband. I believed it was their son, and he had shot himself to death. Under normal circumstances, I would have just said it. But I was concerned about telling Pat something so sensitive in front of the cameras. I thought quickly, and just said, "I feel like it's boom! They go out, boom! There's like a big explosion or some type of big boom that happens. Does that make sense?"

"Yes."

Others came through, but it was Pat's husband who remained the strongest energy. I told her that I was being shown a bouquet of pink roses, his way of expressing his love. Then I got a sequence of information, all of which she validated.

"You did not have the opportunity to talk to him in the way that you wanted to talk to him prior to his passing, correct?"

"Right."

"Okay. Now he's making me feel that either his mother passed very young in his life, or that he was absent or distant from her in life, that there might have been some type of emotional disconnect somehow. And I feel like on the other side they were able to reconnect that. Okay? That's what's being shown. Do you understand that?

"Yeah."

"He's telling me it's okay. He wants you to know that it's okay. He's making me feel like that's why he's made it so important for you to know that he's here. Okay? He wants me to also confirm to you that he's made a visit to you, and what I classify as being a visit is where somebody comes through to you without a psychic, and he's telling me to confirm for you where he came to you, where he was standing in what looks like to me to be the bedroom, where there was a closet door that's open and you had just been smelling his clothes or you were smelling something that's connected to him. Does that make sense?"

"Oh, yes."

There was just one thing strange about this reading: Pat Price's husband was not dead. In fact, he was sitting outside the room. I was very unnerved when she introduced us later—so much so that I didn't ask her why she kept validating that he had died, or so it had seemed. I was glad her husband was alive, but I thought I had completely misinterpreted the messages and really blown the session—while being tested in a university laboratory on national television. The whole thing was very confusing—both how I had gotten something so wrong, and why the sitter kept saying I was right when I was wrong. One possible explanation for both these unusual circumstances would emerge months later.

George, Laurie, and Anne followed to complete this grueling day for Pat, who must have felt overpowered for days afterward. I found out later that she heard some of the information over and over again—including her son Mike's death, which all of us got, although not everyone got it as a suicide. When I told Gary at the end of the day that I had gotten the suicide but awkwardly tried to protect Pat by describing it as a "boom," he was skeptical. He wondered if I had heard from Pat or one of the other mediums after my session that it was suicide, and was now trying to claim I had known it all along. He didn't know me, and he had to maintain his scientific objectivity, entertaining all possibilities until he could eliminate them. He never told me this until much later, after we had gotten to know one another.

A few months after the test, Pat Price was brought back into the lab to carefully score transcripts of each of the sessions. Every utterance by all five mediums was put in one of six categories—name, initial, historical fact, personal description, temperament, and "opinion"—and Pat then evaluated each statement and assigned it one of seven ratings—everything from possibly correct to definitely an error. Gary and his colleagues sat with Pat and made her justify every rating. Then they put the data into an Excel computer file.

When Gary tabulated the data, he wouldn't tell us who had the highest score because he didn't want it to be a competition—or at least he wanted to minimize our natural instincts. He saw this as a team effort. The important result for him was our cumulative performance. He found that our accuracy rates ranged from 77 to 93 percent, with our total average score as a group, 83 percent. The control subjects, the non-mediums, were 36 percent accurate in their guesses—and those were answers to questions, many of which they had a 50 percent chance of getting right. They filled out questionnaires asking whether they thought nine of Pat's relatives and two of her pets were alive or dead, along with questions ranging from "Was the sitter's child happy?" to "Who called the sitter 'Patsy?'" For many questions, less than 5 percent of the controls got correct answers.

A few months later, I had a chance to watch an unedited tape of Suzane's reading. The information came fast, even faster than at other times I'd seen her, and it didn't stop. When the data were tallied, they showed that Suzane had generated 136 pieces of specific information—and more than 80 percent of it was accurate. That means that in one twelve-minute reading, she made more than *100 correct statements* about someone she had never met and could not even see. But it doesn't stop there. She did this with almost no conversation with this woman. Suzane asked only five incidental questions during the entire reading. For lack of an explanation they like better, some entrenched skeptics like to call what we do "cold readings"—ask a lot of questions and skillfully figure out facts from the answers you get, read body language and facial cues. What would they call what Suzane did in Tucson? Probably their latest rationalization: a "hot reading." Otherwise known as fraud. Spy, do research, go through the garbage—whatever.

The results of the heart and brain tests were interesting. Gary's hypothesis was that if a medium was reading the energy of the sitter, and you measured the brain waves and heart rates of both, you might find that their hearts or brains were in some way synchronized, or coupled—like one of Gary's feedback systems. Maybe our two hearts would beat in coordination. But we as mediums believe the opposite is happening. We *disconnect* from the sitter because we're not really reading *them,* we're reading the spirits they came with. So Gary measured each of us at rest, with our eyes closed, and then during our readings. He found that on average, over the course of the readings, our hearts became not more synchronized but less so—which would be consistent with our claim that we are not connecting with them, but with another entity. This happened with all five of us. As for brain waves, our EEG patterns revealed no connection between the sitter's heart and our brains.

When we were done and Gary gave us the numbers, Suzane and I were thrilled. "Now we can say it's been proven," Suzane said, just about ready to call Larry King herself. But Gary said, well, not exactly. "It's not a perfect study," he said. The flaw? He had not kept us apart after our readings. We hung out in the courtyard, and even though he had someone with us, and even though the only conversation was between the mediums who had already done their readings, Gary said he could not say with 100 percent certainty that we did not trade information.

Suzane is the archetype of the straight-ahead-no-time-for-niceties

New Yorker. And she was incensed, to use a nicety. The idea that we had cheated was absurd, not to mention insulting. Gary said he knew we hadn't cheated, hadn't broken the secrecy pledge, but this was science. If he was going to write this up for publication, present it as a landmark study and the foundation for the future, then he had to be able to say that cribbing had been eliminated as a possibility. Then why didn't you think of that *before* the experiment? Suzane wanted to know. "So we come all the way out here and do this and now we can't even say it's documented? That's bullshit."

Gary wanted to do additional experiments, not for HBO but for his own research, and Suzane and I agreed to come back to Arizona twice more over the next ten months. Anne Gehman and Laurie Campbell joined us in the second experiment, at a resort called Miraval. This time, each of us stayed in our own room and the sitters were brought to us, and besides not being able to see the sitter, who would be brought in behind us, we were not allowed to have any verbal communication for the first ten minutes. This was called the Silent Sitter Experiment, and Linda and Gary devised it after arranging at the last minute to make one of the sitters Pat Price from the Tucson test. He wanted to see if any of us would realize it was the same person during the ten-minute silent period. None of us did. But later, when he told us the reason he had asked her to come back for a second experiment, I was bowled over. Only days before, Pat's husband had been killed in a car accident. When I read her this time, he *didn't* come through. Gary and I tried to sort through this irony, one layer at a time.

After the first reading in Tucson, I assumed that I had just been wrong, that I had not clearly discerned the energy and was connecting with someone else. But after the second reading at Miraval, I realized that it was Pat's son Mike, who had committed suicide, who was giving me the information about his dad's imminent crossing over—as a preparation for his mom. At Miraval I also learned that Pat had some psychic ability of her own, and unknown to anyone, had a premonition of her husband's death before the Tucson test. That was why she had answered yes to everything I had said about her husband having passed when he was sitting right outside the room. She was literally answering the question I asked: "Do you understand that?" What she meant was that she understood the information in the context of her own premonition. Had I asked more straightforwardly, "I'm getting that your husband has passed. Is that true?" she would have answered differently. It also turned out that she was a little confused during the session. When I described her going into a bedroom and smelling an article of clothing, I felt it was coming from her husband. But this was something that she had done in her son's room after he passed.

This was a perfect example of my personal adage: "Sometimes I get it right, sometimes I get it wrong. But I get it." In this case, I just assumed that the events had already happened. I thought the information was coming from Pat's husband when it was actually coming from her son *about* her husband. It's also important to note that every medium is also a psychic, which means we do have the ability to project future events. So there's always the potential for confusion. That's why it's important to understand the process, and know that sometimes it's the things that make no sense at all at the time of the reading that turn out to be the greatest validations.

When Pat came back to Miraval—before I knew it was her sitting behind me—it was her son who did the talking. He told me, "This is a validation of the validation." I didn't understand who this spirit was or what he was talking about until I turned around afterward and saw that it was Pat. And then I realized it was young Mike's way of saying, "You screwed up last time. That was me trying to prepare my mom. So let's get it right this time. Now tell my mom I'm with Dad and we're okay."

I FOUND THE FIRST TEN MINUTES of each reading at Miraval strange and intriguing. Without any verbal communication between medium and sitter, we wouldn't even know, as Suzane put it, whether the sitter was "man, woman, or dog." And in fact, I thought one of the sitters, a man, was a woman. At least he wasn't a dog. Later, when another sitter came in, one of the first things I got was the movie *Pretty in Pink*. I didn't know what I was supposed to do with it—was it a reference to a character in the movie, an actor, something in the plot? Then I just said what I got. "You look pretty in pink." The man behind me was wearing a hot pink fluorescent jogging suit.

The idea of not being able to ask any questions was interesting to me, because one of the most common accusations against mediums is that a reading is basically an interview in which the subject doesn't realize he's being interviewed. It's a "cold reading"—a mix of skilled questioning, clever deductions, and of course, lucky guesses. Yes, there are people who do cold readings. They call themselves "mentalists," and they are essentially mental magicians. Meanwhile, a good medium will hit on highly specific and obscure details that could not possibly be elicited through a cold reading. But, of course, perception is everything. A medium who has question marks at the end of a lot of his statements—as most will—might be confused with someone who's just doing an interview. But are these really questions? Or are they simply requests to confirm information?.

There's a big difference between saying, "What is your middle name?" and "Who's Carl?" The latter is the natural way a medium would work: You get information, it's information that's not yours, you don't completely understand it, and you want to know if you got it right. Many times if a medium does have to ask a question, it's really just a way of facilitating the information so he can move on to the next thing. But after the experiments in Tucson and then Miraval, I realized that this was a form of lazy mediumship. It's just as easy to make statements and allow them to be confirmed: "He's telling me your middle name is Carl. Is that true?"

It was at Miraval that I saw the tape of Suzane's reading in Tucson, in which she asked only five questions during a reading that elicited more than 100 pieces of specific, accurate information. And then, when I was not permitted to ask the sitter any questions for ten minutes, I realized how unnecessary feedback from the client really is. It's helpful to validate information, but in the end, what the person says has little impact on what I say. Robert Brown, a medium and colleague from London, refers to me as a "psychic terrier." I stay with what I'm getting, like a dog with a bone, even if the person is emphatically saying no.

Of course, Pat Price saying yes when the answer was no was a new wrinkle. What would I have done if she had said her husband was not dead? Would I have had the confidence—not to mention the rudeness—to insist that her husband, who was sitting outside the room, *was* dead? Not likely. I might have stayed with the information and let her identify who it was coming from. If I was certain it was her husband I was getting, I might have found a way to give her a gentle heads up. Or I would have dropped the entire line, too unsure and uncomfortable to pursue it. I always say whatever I get I put out there, usually without even thinking about it. But once in a while, it's not a bad idea to think twice.

A few months after the Miraval tests, Gary brought the sitters to Tucson for the same kind of detailed scoring session that he'd had with the sitter in the first experiment. Our cumulative accuracy rate was 82 percent. There was a relatively small difference between the silent period and the questioning period. We were 77 percent accurate when we could neither see the sitter nor verbally communicate with him. When we could speak, our accuracy rate rose to 85 percent.

THE 90-MINUTE HBO SPECIAL, *Life After Life,* aired on October 5, 1999, and featured more of me than I expected . . . or would have liked. The part showing me doing readings or being interviewed was fine, but the rest was embarrassing. Me with Sandra, me with my dogs, me working out in the gym, me dancing. I also thought the program didn't do justice to Suzane Northrop. Very little of her phenomenal reading of Pat the sitter survived the editing. But Lisa Jackson did a fine job treating the material seriously and exploring it more openly and thoroughly than anyone before. She didn't take a position in our favor, as I had hoped she might. But she didn't try to debunk us either. She played it down the middle, showing us in good moments in Gary's lab and in private readings, along with interviews with skeptics—intelligent and reasonably dispassionate academics, as well as volunteer subject Lynn Darling—not show-business cynics who don't have the intellectual curiosity to really explore what this is all about.

Gary and Linda did the last of the three tests a month after the HBO special aired, then went on to write up their findings in a twenty-nine-page paper for the *Journal of the Society for Psychical Research,* a publication devoted to the exploration of psychic phenomena. Not exactly *Science,* but as Gary says, none of the big scientific journals will touch this stuff, so you publish where you can, where there are open minds. But it didn't keep him from presenting his work and data with the highest scientific integrity—and in careful language. "It appears that highly skilled mediums, in laboratory-controlled yet supportive conditions, can receive specific categories of information that can be rated accurately by trained research sitters . . . ," he wrote. "These two experiments provide quantitative data that are consistent with the hypothesis that some form of anomalous information retrieval was occurring in these skilled mediums." He also got to work writing a book, *The Afterlife Experiments: Breakthrough Scientific Evidence of Life after Death,* which was scheduled to be published in 2002.

While the findings didn't speak to the question of how we were doing this, Gary suggested that further research with brain-wave measurements might offer some clues. And anticipating the skeptics, he noted: "Traditional hypotheses of fraud, subtle cueing, and statistical coincidence are improbable explanations of the total set of observations reported here." Conscious of the concept of scientific certainty, Gary said he could not definitively rule out that HBO cooked up the whole thing, with or without the complicity of the sitter or the mediums. "Private detectives were not employed to attempt to independently verify confidentiality. However, it seems highly improbable that Lisa Jackson, an Emmy Award–winning producer who works for a multiple Emmy Award–winning production company, would risk her professional and personal reputation to engage in fraud at the University of Arizona."

No surprise, though, that after the HBO special aired late in 1999, Gary found himself being cut in half by James (The Amazing) Randi, a magician by trade who likes to pull barbs out of his hat and hurl them at the nearest medium. Since he first surfaced years ago, Randi's refrain has been that psychics and mediums are just clumsy pretenders, at best magicians adept at sleight-of-mind tricks. As America's debunker laureate, he's written two fire-breathing exposés, one title as pointed as his eyebrows—*Flim-Flam!*—and the other as long as his white beard: *An Encyclopedia of Claims, Frauds, and Hoaxes of the Occult and Supernatural: James Randi's Decidedly Skeptical Definitions of Alternate Realities.* His most famous stunt is a standing offer of a million dollars to anyone who can prove after-death communication.

The Amazing Randi's assault on the Merely Unusual Schwartz started on Randi's website and continued in an article in the *Times* of London before ending up in letters back and forth. Randi trotted out his usual assertions about mediums, then launched into his newest target. "Schwartz's method of edging up on doing real science has one big advantage for him," Randi wrote. "It allows others to get excited and to assume conclusions that are not supported by the half-research he conducts. And can attract funding and attention." Gary, loving a good fight, answered back that Randi was "a living example of someone who seems incapable of learning," and thanked him for instigating the creation of the first scientifically documented evidence of mediumship. "You are the prime inspiration for creating the Mediumship Science Aptitude Test."

"So this is science, Dr. Schwartz?" Randi responded. "You really need more experience of the world, sir."

Like any scientist, Gary was always eager for more experience of the world, and was already at work designing his next big test: an elaborate experiment involving five research sites in the United States and Europe, in which neither the mediums nor the sitters would speak to each other, and only a third person would hear the reading.

When Gary first started his research a few years ago, people would ask him whose side he was on—the mediums or the skeptics. "Well, I'm not on either side," he would say. "I'm on the side of the data. If the data takes me to the mediums, I go to the mediums. If the data takes me to the skeptics, I go to the skeptics. Now, if you ask me whose world view I prefer, there's no question that the mediums' is much more beautiful and special. But my job is not to test my beliefs. It's to follow the data. Are we trying to prove the survival of consciousness? No. What we're trying to do is *allow* survival of consciousness to prove itself. If mediums are willing to stand up and be counted, scientists should be willing to stand up and count them."

— CHAPTER 5 —

SIX LIES
AND VIDEOTAPE

HITS AND MISSES

If we were 83 percent accurate in the Arizona experiment, what about the other 17 percent? Among skeptics and believers alike, there's a catchphrase to describe what's become a popular way to evaluate a medium: *hits and misses.*

I hate those three words.

To think spirit communication is about hits and misses is a miss itself. That implies that the misses are just wrong. But they're not—even the 17 percent that Gary Schwartz counted as inaccurate. I believe that all the information I'm given is accurate. It's what happens next that counts. Any number of factors—the skill of the medium is a big one, but not the only one—will determine whether the information will be considered a hit or a miss. We may not always understand how spirits choose their messages, or why they convey them with this symbol and not that one, but spirits don't play games or misstate. If I pass on twenty-five pieces of information and nineteen are validated, it doesn't mean I've gotten six "wrong," any more than it means that they've told six lies. What makes a piece of information a perceived "miss" is either a simple short-out some-where in the medium-spirit-recipient circuit, or a delay in the validation. This may sound like a cop-out, but this really is a three-way partnership that requires positive, open, and strong energy from everyone involved—on both sides of the great divide.

If I bring through information that someone being read does not acknowledge, one of five things is happening. I have control over just one of them.

1. I'm misinterpreting the symbols I'm being shown. That's a biggie.
2. The information is meant for someone else in the room, and we're not connecting strongly enough to get me to go there.
3. The sitter doesn't know whether the information is true or not because of an unfamiliarity with the family tree, or because this is simply something that he or she is not aware of—yet.

4. The person does not want to acknowledge something for personal reasons.

5. The person is suffering from "psychic amnesia," a temporary affliction that has been known to render people incapable of remembering their spouse's name or their child's birthday.

Take it from me: There are a thousand ways for a medium to misinterpret a message from the other side. The most common problem I have is receiving a symbol, often a fleeting one that fades as soon as the next one appears, and describing it incorrectly. The spirits will use my references, things I will recognize and relate to, to get me to say something. But as in a game of charades, I might see the symbol from the wrong angle and pass on the wrong information. Or be too literal—or not literal enough. During one reading at a lecture, I was shown the image of a woman I recognized as Jennifer Valope, a TV news anchor in Miami. I threw out everything I could: News reporter, TV, Miami. Nothing. Finally, I just said what I saw: Jennifer Valope. The person in front of me said her name was Jennifer. That could have gone another way and been considered a "miss" with a lot of fishing around—a cold reading. Wouldn't it have been easier for the spirit to just give me the name audibly? Why use such a roundabout symbol? The answer: Who knows? Sometimes spirits can be very clever. Other times, obscure. Ultimately, though, it's hopeless to ask why they give one symbol and not another. Does everyone who plays charades use the same clues? They give me what they give me. I pass it on the best I can.

Misinterpretation of a fleeting symbol or sound is only one of the two most common obstacles to the mythical perfect reading. Just as common is the delayed validation. Most often it's a piece of information that a person doesn't know about and has to check out—anything from a detail about an event from the past to the name of a neighbor's grandmother. So many times I've been directed to deliver information to someone who seems to have no connection to the spirit, so of course can't validate the information. In many cases, it's because they actually do have some connection, but it's not obvious and they may not even know it. I might be reading someone who's a distant or even unknown relative of a spirit that's trying to get a message through to another relative. Or the person being read is a friend or acquaintance of the intended recipient. Trying to connect mutual acquaintances like this can lead to a lot of blank expressions and denials, which can be frustrating for all three of us.

People often wonder why spirits use these indirect, unlikely connections. The answer is simple: It's their best chance to get a message through. I have an analogy for this: If you were stuck in some remote, foreign land without a phone and ran into someone from your hometown who was on his way home, wouldn't you want that person to get a message to your family that you were all right?

A MURDER IN MICHIGAN

THERE'S ONE OTHER KIND OF MESSAGE that comes through and either seems like information that's ten miles off the mark, or makes people stretch in every direction to try to make it fit. And that's a message about something that hasn't happened yet. I don't know if I was foreshadowing Pat Price's husband's death when I interpreted him as being already crossed over. But it's not unusual for me to receive and pass on information that seems wrong at the time it's delivered but later turns out to have meaning. It doesn't have to be earth-shattering. Often it's a forgettable, mundane event.

The first time I met Carol Maywood, I told her in the course of a reading that someone was putting up new wallpaper. It didn't mean anything to her, but a few months later, somebody in her family, maybe it was her sister-in-law, changed the wallpaper in the bathroom, or maybe just the top part, I think they call that the border. It might have been the bedroom. See what I mean about mundane and forgettable? Which makes what happened later in that reading all the more extraordinary.

Carol is a radiologist and medical administrator from Phoenix. In May of 1998, she lost her sister Louise, who died as suddenly as it is possible to die of cancer. It came out of nowhere, and her devastated family, a close-knit group, was left reeling and terribly wounded, each trying to help the others cope. Flipping channels one day later that year, Carol saw me on one of the afternoon shows and was curious enough to go out and buy the first book she had ever read on spirit communication. Carol had always believed that when we die, our energies merge with a universal force and we cease to exist as individuals. Our personalities go on only in the memories of those we leave behind. What I and others were saying was very different. She liked the way it sounded.

One day in the spring of 1999, Carol's brother, Dan, called from his home in Michigan to say he had seen me on *The Crier Report*. They had discussed the subject, and Carol had thought about what it might be like to connect with her sister. Was it possible?

"John Edward is going to be in Phoenix," Dan told her on the phone. "You've got to call and get tickets. I'll give you the number. You *have* to go." Carol was taken aback by the force of Dan's demand. She didn't mind—they were extremely close and it was hard for them to offend each other, but still, it was not at all like Dan to tell her what to do about anything.

Carol made the call and went with her mother to the event I was having in downtown Phoenix. Carol was like most people in that room or any other room I've ever appeared in. She hoped she would be read, and if she was lucky enough, to hear from someone in particular. But it didn't look like it was going to happen. Two hours in, and nothing for Carol and her mother. But then—and I'm telling this from her perspective, of course, based on what she told me later—I asked if anyone had "a Holland connection." I was feeling an older male figure and being shown wooden shoes. Nobody acknowledged it. But when she saw that I was slowly walking in their direction, Carol whispered in her mother's ear and then raised her hand, tentatively, as people usually do when they're not sure if it's for them but since nobody else is claiming it . . . . Carol's Uncle Steven, her mother's brother, had married a wartime bride from Holland. Both of them had passed.

The next sequence of information confirmed that I was in the right place—Uncle Steven's jovial, ladies'-man personality, and the presence of a "D-N" name with him, which Carol's mother immediately connected to her cousin Don, who was very much like Steven in personality. The feeling they gave me was that although they were not close on earth—they were far apart in age—they *were* close now that they were together on the other side. "Who had the stage background?" I asked, seeing a theater stage. Carol's mother said her mother was a stage actress.

It was the typical family gathering, except that, to her disappointment, Carol's sister was not among them. Then, toward the end of the reading, they were telling me that the family would be getting together soon. "My sister's birthday is in July," Carol said, almost desperate to make her sister a part of this.

"Nope," I said. "Sooner than that. It's in about a week. They're telling me they're all going to be there." It was nothing that they knew of, Carol said. I wondered if I was blowing someone's surprise party. This was one of those times when the people I saw in front of me were saying no and the ones I couldn't see were saying, *oh yes*. In cases like this, my money is *always* on the ones who got in for free.

When Carol got home, she called Dan in Michigan. She was glad her brother had told her to go—although Louise didn't come through, Carol and her mother got to be one of the chosen. She recounted the reading, and then they tried to figure out what that family gathering thing was all about. What could be happening in just a week? Dan took out his palm calendar, which had all kinds of offbeat occasions on it. "Hey, what about Bugs Bunny's birthday?" he said kiddingly as he scrolled. "Louise loved Bugs." They couldn't figure it out, but Carol and Dan talked twice more that week, about the reading, about Louise, and about Dan's upcoming visit to Carol in Arizona. Could that be the "gathering"?

Early on Saturday morning, the phone rang in Carol's house and she heard these words in her sister-in-law's voice: "Dan is dead."

He had been found in his car, in the parking lot of the factory plant where he worked the overnight shift. He had been shot in the head with his own gun. In a year's time, Carol had lost both her sister and brother without warning—at least none that she had been able to perceive.

When she regained a semblance of equilibrium, Carol thought about the imminent "family gathering" her relatives had talked about. She didn't think they meant Dan's funeral. He was cremated, and there wouldn't be a memorial service until his birthday, months later. Then Carol realized what it was. She calculated that Dan had died exactly seven days and four hours after our spirit contact. The family gathering they were talking about was on the other side. *They* were the ones who would be getting together. Helping Dan cross over.

Now the question became, What happened to Dan? Remember the

unsolved mystery of the murder of Nicole's boyfriend Roger in Tampa Bay? Here's another one. It happened less than four months after Roger interrupted our infomercial to get a vital message to his girlfriend, apparently to allay her fears about his murder. But this one took a slightly different turn.

The police in Michigan immediately ruled Dan's death a suicide and closed their "investigation" without conducting standard crime-scene tests or questioning people connected to him. Carol, her sister-in-law, and others close to Dan could not believe he had killed himself. But for the first few days, they couldn't focus on anything but breathing. Dan had been divorced, and had remarried just three years before. His wife was devastated, totally out of it. And Carol had all she could do to stand up herself. Besides her own grief, she had to deal with telling her parents that now two of their children were dead.

It was a week before Carol was able to begin thinking about the investigation of her brother's death. She was sure he had been murdered, and so was everyone else in Dan's circle of family and friends. He had not been depressed, and he been making all kinds of plans. He had bought train tickets for a trip to the Grand Canyon he and his wife were going to take during a visit to Carol in Arizona a month later. They were planning to move to Texas after his retirement in two years, and he was trying to convince Carol to move there, too. He had arranged to leave work in time to go to his friend's wedding reception on Saturday, and he had taken chicken and ribs out of the freezer to defrost and marinate for the weekend.

Once she was sure he had not committed suicide, Carol began to think about who might have killed him. Dan had no enemies, she thought. But then, she realized that he did. Dan had been in a legal dispute with someone he had hired to restore a 1965 Thunderbird. The man did a terrible job and cheated him, leading to an angry confrontation in the parking lot outside Dan's apartment. Dan had recently won a $30,000 court judgment against him. Carol learned that the man thought he wouldn't have to pay because he was declaring bankruptcy, but believed that Dan informed him that bankruptcy rules didn't apply to frauds. He would still have to pay him the money. Not long after the judgment, Dan was dead.

When Dan's family tried to bring this and other information to the police, they were rebuffed. "They told us, not very nicely, 'You just let us do the detecting,'" Carol said. But apparently they detected nothing. They returned the gun, still covered with blood, to Dan's wife. She cleaned it, assuming the police had gotten fingerprints off it. They hadn't bothered. They said the case was closed. Carol hired an independent coroner, and his opinion was that based on his wounds and the positioning of his body, Dan could have been killed, most likely during a losing struggle for the gun.

Carol thought the obvious suspect had to be the man Dan was having problems with, a young guy named Baxter. She theorized that Baxter wanted to meet with Dan, maybe telling him that he wanted to pay him some of the money he owed. But Dan would not have wanted Baxter to come to his apartment again. Maybe he told him to come to his work, where there would be people around. He brought his gun because he was afraid. Carol believed the case wasn't investigated because the town where it happened was virtually owned by Dan's employer. There had been three previous murders on the property in the past five years. They didn't want this in the papers.

One night soon after Dan's death, Carol decided to sit down at her computer and put down everything she knew and everyone she had talked to—an organized chronology of the events leading up to that night in the parking lot. And while she was doing that, she became aware that she was seeing the events playing out in her head in great detail: Dan driving his heavy equipment "Hi-Lo" from the factory to his car hoping to attract the attention of plant security. Positioning his car so that he could see Baxter coming. Loading his gun and taking a spare magazine clip from his fanny pack and placing it upright in the console between the bucket seats, leaving the console lid flipped open. Holding his gun and rehearsing the actions he might have to take to defend himself.

"It was like a videotape running in my head," Carol recalled. "As if I were watching a mystery movie. There was a distinction between my own thoughts when I started typing, and when this started taking over."

Without missing a beat, Carol kept typing, only now she was transcribing what she was seeing in her head:

Baxter pulls up, walks over to Dan's car, then opens the passenger door to come in as Dan demands that he show him the money. But Baxter grabs for Dan's jacket and holds the door open, and Dan immediately cocks his gun and points it at Baxter, telling him to stop, put the jacket down, and leave. But Baxter angrily grabs for the gun, dropping Dan's jacket, the keys in the pocket jingling as they hit the blacktop. Quickly Baxter leans into the car and overpowers the much smaller Dan, twisting Dan's arthritic hands so that the cocked gun is now pointed at Dan's head. Now Baxter begins to laugh, gloating at the situation. Dan uses his left hand to try to force the gun upward and away from him, but Baxter uses *his* other hand to keep it down. As they struggle, Baxter shoves the gun hard against Dan's head, and it fires. The bullet casing ricochets off the ceiling, hits Baxter, and lands on the passenger seat near the door. Shocked, Baxter releases his grip and lowers Dan's hands to his lap, still holding the gun. He backs out of the car, picks up the jacket and keys, hastily replaces them on the seat, leaving a bloody smudge on the jacket lining. He looks around and sees no one has responded to the gunshot, and drives carefully away.

Carol said the scene flowed seamlessly from one moment to the next, but seemed to be in response to her questions. She didn't think they came from her imagination because the details—Dan's elaborate preparations, the sound of the jangling keys dropping to the pavement—were too vivid and came too quickly. She contrasted it to the way she worked as a radiologist to come up with a likely diagnosis: In her mind, she would put together all the circumstantial evidence—what she knew about a patient's history, symptoms, and physical examination, as well as the sometimes subtle indications she detected on an x-ray or MRI—to try to come up with a probable scenario.

"This didn't feel at all like that," Carol said. "Of course, you wonder if this is just your mind at work, but it didn't feel as if it was coming from me." She entertained the stunning possibility that this "videotape" had been sent to her by Dan, but she didn't dwell on it because it was just too strange and unsettling. And she was careful whom she talked to about it. She tried to have the case reopened—or really, opened—but got nowhere. All she had, in the view of the police, was speculation.

Over the next two years, Carol became a regular at events I had in the West. She came to five more after the first one in Phoenix—in Salt

Lake City, San Diego, Las Vegas, Scottsdale, and Detroit—traveling hundreds of miles in the hopes of connecting with her siblings. Not just her sister Louise, of course, but now also her brother, Dan, the one who had practically ordered her to come to that first event in Phoenix. I really don't remember much about our first encounter, but Carol and her mother approached me after the next one, in San Diego, and told me the story. It was very upsetting to hear, but Carol's mother said, "I just wanted to thank you. Knowing that everyone was there to greet Daniel was the only thing that got me through this."

Carol went to San Diego, and all the other places, wanting more than the comfort of that knowledge. She wanted to know the truth. She hoped Dan would give it to me to relay. But these were events with a few hundred people, and she was disappointed each time. Most of the time I didn't even know she was there. But her story has stayed with me. When I think of Dan's apparent desire to literally show his sister what happened and compare it to the way Roger only wanted to ease Nicole's mind in Tampa Bay, I can't help but feel sure that spirits really do give us what we need. We're all different, those of us here on earth, and those on the other side. If Carol still had any strands of belief that our individual personalities dissolve into some great universal abyss when we die, she could let them go now, into the wind.

In the midst of all these trips to see me, Carol did go to see another medium in Arizona. The medium told Carol that she that her brother had died in a car accident. That wasn't far off. And the medium did detect that there was a mystery surrounding the death. She told Carol, "What you feel in your gut happened, did happen."

When she heard this, Carol took it as a validation, if something short of a definitive one. She had tried not to think too much about the videotape that had rolled through her head, but now she allowed herself to believe that she really hadn't made it all up. For the second time, it seemed, her brother had put a thought in her head and told her to go with it.

It's impossible to know the true intent of that thought. Maybe Dan wanted his family to know that he did not commit suicide. Did he want something more than that? Spirits have will. Sometimes their purpose is clear, sometimes not. Sometimes I get it wrong, sometimes I get it right.

I remember once reading a woman at a lecture in Boston who had lost her five-year-old daughter. When her little girl came through, she gave me one detail after another—her name, the name of the doll she was buried with—and her poor mom was terribly shaken and crying. It was one of those times when everyone in the room was affected by one person's pain. And then the spirit of this little girl gave me a feeling of intense concern for her mother.

"I'm going to give you this in my interpretation," I told the mother, "and I'm sorry for having to ask you this, but were you planning to kill yourself?" The woman seemed as if she was going to pass out. The person next to her had to hold her up.

And she acknowledged it. "Yes, I was planning to," she said, crying. I told her that her daughter wanted her to know that they were still connected, and that she should allow herself to move on. "She's telling me you have to stay here, you have more to do. She says, 'You've got to take care of my little sister.'" She was literally talking her mother out of suicide from the other side. A friend who was with me that night told me it was the most intense reading he had ever seen. I can't know for sure; I only hope I'm right. But I think the spirit of this little girl managed to pull her mother in from the ledge.

It would be understandable for Carol Maywood to take her brother Dan's "videotape" as a push from him to pursue an investigation and, hopefully, justice. But as a medium, I prefer to see Dan's message more simply and purely: that even though his death was horrible and it remained a mystery, her family should accept it, and know that it was all right for them to move on. I'm constantly getting a "let it go" feeling from the other side. A tragic death, a mystery, doesn't alter that desire. Dan and Carol were still connected. And she didn't need a medium to know that.

— CHAPTER 6 —

LEGENDS OF ROCK

Debbie's Daddy

One day during the winter of 1998, I got an e-mail from a friend of mine, Stephen Reed, wondering if I might do him a favor. He hated to ask, he knew I was busy, but would I be able to squeeze in a reading for someone? She had just lost her dad, and it would really mean a lot. Like most of my friends, Stephen knew I don't like to do readings as favors because it's not fair to the people who are waiting and don't have a back way in. So for him to ask, I figured it must be pretty important. And I was getting a "do it" feeling from The Boys, so I said sure, no problem. But I was on the road a lot, so I wasn't sure when I could do it. I was about to go to New Orleans. *Hey, she's in Tennessee,* Stephen e-mailed back—maybe you can stop there on your way down. *Don't push it, Stephen.* I told him I would do it by phone when I got to my hotel in New Orleans.

The woman's name was Debbie, and she sure was from Tennessee. I told her I knew she had just lost her dad but that I had to be honest with her. I had no control who came through. Sometimes it's the person we least expect or want to hear from.

Two women came through first. Debbie identified the first as an aunt of hers who had died of breast cancer. The second was a black woman with a beautiful smile. She was bringing in a tall man wearing creased blue jeans, a blue shirt, and white tennis shoes. "He's telling me he's your dad. He says this lady was the one who greeted him on the other side."

"That's Gracie!" Debbie said. "She helped raise me. She came to work for my family when I was very young, and she was like a second mother to me. My dad used to drink, and when he got rowdy, we always called Gracie. She was the only one who could calm him down."

I thought it was a little odd that Debbie was trying to connect with her dad, and here he was, but the one she was excited about was the maid. She said later she didn't acknowledge her father at first because she wanted more evidence, even though everything I said made sense to her. Her dad never wore a pair of blue jeans that weren't starched with a permanent leg crease, he loved white tennis shoes, and in her hands as we spoke was his favorite blue shirt. She was ready to acknowledge Gracie with far less. But Daddy was special. She was holding out for more. She didn't validate anything. But just in case, she had a friend listening in on an extension, taking notes.

"This man is acknowledging a marble statue. Does this mean anything to you?"

"Yes, it does."

"Okay. There's some guy coming through now with dark hair and dark glasses. He's standing beside your dad."

"That would be Roy Orbison."

"He's saying he's hanging out with the guy that always wore the dark glasses and dark hair. There's someone else. He's telling me he's with the guy who had the belt that's hanging on the wall."

"Elvis."

"*Elvis*? Who is this guy, anyway? Who am I talking to—who's your dad?"

"My dad was Carl Perkins."

I was clueless. "I'm sorry, but I don't know who that is."

"He wrote 'Blue Suede Shoes.' It was Elvis's first big hit."

"Holy shit," I said, unable to restrain my shock. I'd gotten Andy Warhol once, but *Elvis?* I know how ridiculous this might seem. I mean, Elvis? *Puleeeze.* But it's not like I was reading one of those Elvis impersonators from Las Vegas. Debbie really did have a connection. And I really didn't know that. And her father's name really did mean nothing to me, having been born two months after Woodstock.

"Okay, now he's telling me there was some kind of incident with a dog the night after his funeral. He wants you to know he was there. Do you understand?"

"Yes." Carl's dog's name was Suede Blue, and they were very tight. They had a trick they did together, Carl getting down on his hands and knees, and Suede jumping over him. It was a trick Suede would do only with Carl. After the funeral, Debbie and her mother looked out the window and saw Suede in the backyard, jumping as if Carl were there. Debbie had remarked to her mother that she felt her dad *was* there. Now he wanted her to know that he was.

Debbie was trying to take all this in when I told her, "Your dad says you don't have to cling so tightly to the shirt you're holding." Remember, this was a phone reading, and she hadn't validated any of the earlier information, so I didn't know she was holding the shirt.

I smelled something. It was musty, dank. Like a basement with a moisture problem. Debbie said I seemed to be describing her father's studio. It was next to the pool. "Elvis keeps coming in," I told her. "He and your father had drifted apart in this life, but they are well connected on the other side. Your dad is acknowledging some special picture of Elvis."

"Oh, yes, the famous Elvis picture. When Daddy built his recording studio, the first picture he put up was one of Elvis. I asked him if he was ever going to let Elvis die. He told me Elvis would live forever."

"He wants you to know, Debbie, he knows you did everything to save him. He was so tired. His body was just shutting down. He made the decision to go. He wants you to know that. He realized his work here was done, and he was ready to go. He says he arranged this phone call himself. He's smiling. Something about roses? He still works in the rose bed, but these have no thorns."

Debbie said her parents raised beautiful roses, and every morning when they were in bloom, her dad would have a fresh bouquet waiting for her mom when she got up. He always fussed about the thorns. He described his funeral—"He compares it to Princess Diana's. He liked the butterfly wreath Dolly Parton sent. He wants you to thank Billy Ray for the beautiful song." I swear I'm not making this up. I was blown away by the amount and detail of the information Debbie's dad was giving me. I told her he must have been a very spiritual man. Debbie said he was.

"Did you at some point ask your dad if you were doing the right thing or what should you do?"

"I sure did. Those were exactly my last words to him before they closed the casket."

"Well, he wants you to know you are doing the right thing, and he will always be with you to help you. Now he's holding up a coffee cup. An empty coffee cup."

"He'd be sitting in his chair in the den. Mama would be in the kitchen. The den and kitchen are basically one big room divided by a bar. When his coffee cup got empty, he didn't say a word. He just held it up and Mama would bring him more. One day I was there and I told him he was so spoiled. And he just smiled. He loved it, and so did she."

"He's saying he wants you to be sure she's always treated like a queen.

He's so proud of her and knows she is very strong. He wants you to tell her he will let her know he's around. He will meet her on the other side when it's time. . . . Something about biscuits, and he keeps saying 'hatch.' "

"Mama is a great cook. She's known for her biscuits and what Daddy called 'hatched-up meals.' He loved those meals she just whipped up on the spur of the moment more than the big feast at Thanksgiving."

"Is there a river behind your house? Did someone pull someone out of it?"

"No, but Daddy and I, along with a good friend, Randy Moore, started a song about someone saving a friend from drowning."

"That's it. He says to finish it. It's important. He keeps referring to the word *spirit*. He says it's important as it relates to you." It would be a year before Debbie realized that this reference had a double meaning. Her father's last business partner introduced her to a music publisher in New York named Mark Fried, who signed her as a songwriter. The name of his company was Spirit Publishing.

WHEN I GOT HOME FROM MY TRIP to New Orleans, I got a call from Stephen Reed, thanking me for doing the reading. Debbie had never had an experience like this, he said, and it really helped her. Her father had died only three weeks before. I told Stephen that Debbie's father's energy was amazing for someone so new to the other side.

Stephen said that now he could tell me more. The person who had actually asked him to set this up was not Debbie, but a friend of Debbie's father's named Rick Korn (whom I've mentioned earlier in this book). He was a younger guy, about Debbie's age, who had met Carl only three years before he died, but became extremely close to him. It was Rick who set Debbie up with Spirit Publishing.

Rick Korn was one of those guys who always seemed to be onto some new idea or project, always networking and introducing his contacts to his other contacts. He was in media marketing, to describe his career loosely. After growing up on Long Island and then living with his high school buddy Marc Gurvitz during Marc's fledgling years as a comedy manager in Hollywood, Rick headed back east. He worked everywhere from the Home Shopping Network in Florida to Whittle Communications in Tennessee. Now he and his wife, A.J., and their three kids were up north again, on the Jersey shore, where Rick had started a company called Television Production Partners. He put together ten of the world's biggest advertisers—AT&T, Sears, McDonald's—and got them to put forty million dollars into a pot to create quality TV programs that they, rather than the TV networks, would own.

One day in 1995, A.J. answered the phone and found an older-sounding man with a major country twang on the other end asking for Rick. "Do we owe one of the gardeners from Tennessee some money?" she asked Rick with a laugh, handing him the phone. But when Rick got on the phone, the man introduced himself as Carl Perkins. When Rick didn't immediately recognize the name, the man said, "I wrote 'Blue Suede Shoes.'" The song was literally his calling card. As mentioned earlier, Carl had a dog named Suede Blue and his daughter's restaurant was named Suede's. The phone number ended in 1956—the year Elvis recorded the song that made them both a little more famous.

Elvis Presley was the first singer hired by Sun Records, and Carl Perkins was the second. In 1956, Presley, Perkins, Johnny Cash, and Jerry Lee Lewis *were* rock 'n' roll. They were known as the "Million Dollar Quartet" because each had recorded a hit song. Carl's was "Blue Suede Shoes," and it's been called the first true rock 'n' roll hit. Carl wrote it in 1955, after Johnny Cash joined him for a show in Mississippi and suggested he write a song based on a saying he'd heard on line in the mess hall in the service: "Don't step on my blue suede shoes." A few nights later, Carl was playing in Jackson, Tennessee, and saw a guy dancing in the crowd trying to keep his girlfriend away from his new blue suede shoes. He woke up with the song in his head in the middle of the night, went downstairs, and wrote out the lyrics in pencil on a potato bag.

Carl's recording of the song sold more than a million copies, for which Sam Phillips, the owner of Sun Records, gave him a pink Cadillac. Carl had a band with his brothers, and they got into a horrible car accident that broke practically every bone in Carl's body. Elvis came to the hospital and told Carl he was going to sing "Blue Suede Shoes" for him on the *Perry Como Show*. It became a mega-hit, but Carl didn't get any money from it and had to sue the owner of Sun Records to get the rights back in 1975.

Carl's life was like that. He was always trying to overcome setbacks and obstacles. While touring with Johnny Cash in the early 1960s, a ceiling fan fell on him and crippled two of his fingers. He figured out how to get by with three fingers and kept on playing his guitar. But his bad luck with money continued. People always seemed to be stealing his songs or screwing him on royalties, although the Beatles were good to him and recorded four of his songs: "Everybody's Trying to Be My Baby," "Honey Don't," "Restless," and, of course, "Blue Suede Shoes." But money wasn't important to Carl. He didn't need a big house or any of that stuff like most of the people he knew in the record business. He just cared about his family and writing songs and singing and playing the guitar. He was completely devoted to Valda, his wife since before "Blue Suede Shoes." She was a seamstress by trade.

"Do you know the reason Elvis used to wear the high collar?" Rick Korn once asked me. "He had acne on the back of his neck when he was younger. So Valda designed that and also the big, fat belts that he used to wear. She designed the first studded belt for him. Years later, Elvis gave the belt back to Valda, and she and Carl framed it and put it up in their bedroom."

In 1991, Carl, a heavy smoker, was diagnosed with throat cancer and had to have surgery that the doctors said would probably leave him without a voice. Before the surgery, he offered a deal to God: Give me my voice, and I will use it to do good. He came out of the surgery singing better than he ever had, with more range. And he kept his end of the bargain. He started the Carl Perkins Center for the Prevention of Child Abuse, which eventually became the second largest center in the country for abused children. In newspaper interviews, when he was asked why he had picked child abuse as his cause, he always said he had been moved and inspired by a horrible picture of an abused little boy he saw in a local newspaper. He said the boy looked like one of his own sons. But the truth was that the little boy reminded him of himself.

When he was a young boy in west Tennessee, Carl, like more than a few children growing up poor in cotton country in the early 1940s, was sold by his family to a farmer who wanted the use of his big hands in the fields. Many large families who had boys with big hands would sell their sons for a piece of the profits. It was a way of life. Through his youth living with a family that wasn't his, Carl had been beaten and abused, but like many people, he tried to lock it away when he became an adult. It wasn't until he was almost sixty and facing cancer that he unbolted the door to his past and let it tumble out. When he saw the picture of the little boy in the paper, he told those close to him that he knew that this was the work that God intended for him as his part of the deal to let him keep his voice. Carl was of a time and place in which there weren't lines out the door of psychiatrists' offices. The center for abused children became his therapy.

After his surgery, Carl began writing more spiritual music—long, poetic songs that he felt came from a different place in the universe from the rock ditties he had written before. He said that while in the hospital, God gave him a tiny glimpse, a feeling, of heaven. And when he got home, Debbie helped him write a song whose lyrics were drawn from the sense of the afterlife that he felt had been given to him by God. The song was called "Beyond the Blue," and as he was writing it, Carl realized for the first time that he wasn't afraid to die.

Beyond the blue,
No one ever dies, no broken hearts, no hungry eyes,
Streets paved with gold, frightening winds don't blow.
Beyond the blue we all have a home
No one's left to grow old alone,
No fear of the night, no doubt what's right,
Beyond the blue . . .

When he called Rick Korn that day in 1995, four years after his cancer, Carl said he was looking for someone—not necessarily someone in the music business—to help him relaunch his career. He was working on some new music and had some ideas about what he wanted to do with it. A mutual friend had given him Rick's name. They hooked up and began working on projects. They did an album together called "Go, Cat, Go"— a line from "Blue Suede Shoes"—with contributions from Carl's old friends, the three surviving Beatles. Carl had performed on Paul McCartney's 1982 album "Tug of War," the one on which Paul sang "Ebony and Ivory" with Stevie Wonder.

Although they were of different generations and from very different backgrounds, Carl and Rick had a rare connection. "We had similar creative frustrations," is the way Rick puts it. "We were brothers in arms." The kid from Long Island loved to listen to the slow, tobacco-stained drawl of this Legend of Rock from Tennessee. His singing was one thing. But it was his talking that captivated Rick.

"Carl told so many great stories, and every story had a kind of spirituality to it," Rick said. "He didn't just tell you a story about him and Elvis drinking in some bar and flirting with women. He would tell you a story that had a meaning. He was almost preachy, but in a good way. There was a kind of aura about him, and it just made you feel so comfortable and warm. One day I said, 'Carl, I could put you in front of a wall and you would talk for twenty-four hours straight. It would be great if we could get a camera and you just telling these stories. They should be preserved.'"

Rick called Dominic Ambrosio, a friend of his who worked for HBO and was living in Nashville at the time, and asked if he'd be interested in coming to Memphis with a camera and a sound man and spending a weekend with Carl. They could figure out what to do with the footage later. Dominic drove through a rare Tennessee snowstorm to get there— despite Carl's urgings to stay home and come a week later— and he and his sound man set up in Carl's musty studio. True to form, Carl just talked and talked, one great story after another about Elvis, Roy Orbison, Johnny Cash, the Beatles, his wife Valda, his brothers, and his kids. And before long, he got around to the best story of all, the story that had given Rick the idea of asking Dominic to do this in the first place.

It happened in 1981, and it began with a phone call that Valda answered. "He *says* he's Paul McCartney," she had told Carl, handing him the phone.

Carl got on and said, "Whatcha doin', boy?"

"I'm sitting here at the house," Paul said. "What are *you* doing? I'm down here in the West Indies recording an album. I've got a song I've written that's perfect for you. Can you come down to Montserrat?"

"Well, if I knew where it was, it would help," Carl said.

"Somewhere in the Caribbean. Just head down this way; we'll find you."

So Paul sent Carl a ticket, and he flew down and sang lead vocals and played guitar on a song called "Get It" for Paul's album "Tug of War." He spent eight great days with Paul and Linda, along with George and Ringo, Stevie Wonder, and the legendary Beatles producer George Martin, with whom Paul owned a studio on the island. The studio was in Paul's house, while Martin had his own house elsewhere on the property. Carl described Martin's house as a castle. That's where he stayed for the week.

"As the time was drawing near for me to go home, I was sitting out on the patio," Carl told Dominic Ambrosio and his camera, his guitar sitting on his lap and looking like a part of him. "And I was thinking how lucky Carl Perkins was. And I'm kind of sentimental. Sometimes I can sing it but I can't say it, and that night before, I wrote a song. And in the morning, I went down to the studio and said to Paul and Linda, 'I'm not good at saying good-bye, but I wrote this song last night, and I want to play it for you.' It was called 'My Old Friend' . . ." Carl sang it now for Dominic with the extra emotional emphais on the refrain: *My old friend, won't you think about me every now and then . . .*

"Well, halfway through the song, I see Paul is really crying, tears flowing down his face," Carl said. "And he stepped outside. I said to Linda, 'Linda, I didn't mean to upset him.' She says, 'Carl Perkins, how did you know?' I said, 'Darlin', I don't know what yer talkin' about. How did I know what?' "

John Lennon had been killed only months before outside his apartment building, the Dakota in New York. Linda explained that, although it wasn't publicly known, only days before his death, she and Paul had visited John and Yoko at the Dakota. At the end of the visit, as they were saying good-bye, John said to Paul, "Think of me every now and then, my old friend."

"Linda put her arms around me," Carl said now on a cold January day in Tennessee sixteen years later, "and she said, 'Thank you, Carl, he needed that.' It was a touching moment and it was a frightful moment for me." The song had just come to him out of the blue that night as he sat alone on the deck off his room in George Martin's castle. And the strange thing, he later told Rick, was that he didn't write the song down—something he always did. Whenever he thought of a lyric, let alone an entire song, he had to write it down right away or he would lose it. "Rick," Carl said, "that song was with me. I couldn't get it out of my head." He was sure John had written the song from beyond and given it to him for Paul.

Now, with the camera rolling, Carl wanted to finish the story by singing the refrain once more for posterity: *My old friend won't you think about me every now and then. . . .*

And just as he hit the last chord and it began to dissolve into the dank studio air and Dominic hit the fade button on his camera, the intercom in Carl's studio sounded.

"Carl?" It was Valda.

"And that was the little girl that answered the original phone call," Carl said with a laugh as he reached over the soundboard to the intercom. "Hello."

"Paul McCartney just called."

Carl looked at Dominic. "Val, are you kidding me?"

"I didn't answer the phone, I was in the washroom . . ."

"*What? Paul McCartney?*" Dominic asked in disbelief from behind the camera.

"Paul McCartney," Carl answered, as if he needed to say it to believe it.

"Hear me?" Val said asked obliviously.

Carl turned to the camera: "Now, listen. I'm tellin' you guys," Carl said. "If you think this boy has not got a connection to the spirit world . . ."

Carl told Val they were coming right up to listen to the tape. He hit the Play button and heard the voice of Paul McCartney: "Carl, Val, this is Paul and Linda. We're on holiday here in the Caribbean and our minds wandered over to you. We just want to say hello and send our love and wish you a Happy New Year. Call us back when you get home."

The footage Dominic shot that weekend didn't find its way out of the can, but Rick knew it had to have some purpose. He had never been very religious or particularly spiritual, but after hanging around Carl the last couple of years, he wasn't chalking up Paul McCartney's phone call to coincidence. In time, he would understand the connections.

BEYOND THE BLUE

TEN MONTHS LATER, in November of 1997, Carl had a pair of strokes, the second more serious than the first. He came out of the hospital, but he was weak and partially paralyzed. He fell into a coma, and on January 19, 1998, at the age of 65, Carl Perkins passed away. It was exactly a year to the day Carl had sat in his studio telling stories, and Paul McCartney had made the phone call that nearly knocked him out of his chair.

When Carl died, Valda and Debbie asked Rick Korn to come to Tennessee and help arrange the funeral, which meant dealing with a lot of celebrities and a lot of press. It was a Who's Who of rock 'n' roll descending on Jackson, Tennessee, from all over the world. Rick was honored to do it for Carl. He would never forget driving to the airport in Carl's tan Lincoln Continental, with the license plate that said SUEDE, and picking up George Harrison the morning of the funeral. Driving to the chapel, this child of the sixties, who was a second grader at Parkway Elementary School when the Beatles took Ed Sullivan's stage, thought, *I'm sitting next to George Harrison.*

In his hotel room in Jackson the night he arrived, Rick, exhausted, turned on *Larry King Live*. The guest was James Van Praagh. Rick wasn't interested. "At first I'm thinking this guy's full of crap," Rick recalled. "But Larry's buying it, and I respect Larry. And the more I listened, I was saying, wow, this guy's pretty good. And I was thinking this is weird. Larry King's doing a show on life after death the day after one of my best friends dies."

He thought of calling Debbie and telling her to put the show on, thinking it might be comforting, but he stopped himself. He didn't know what her beliefs about this were, and didn't want to take a chance of upsetting her. After the show ended at ten o'clock, the phone rang in Rick's room. It was Debbie. "By any chance, did you watch Larry King tonight?" she asked.

"I want a reading with that guy," she said. She wanted Rick to call his brother, who was chief operating officer of CNN at the time. Rick wasn't sure he could get his brother to arrange a psychic reading for someone he didn't know with a guy who was on Larry King, but if Rick had words to live by, they were: It never hurts to ask. He told Debbie he would call his brother right after the funeral.

The next morning, Rick went to the airport to pick up Stephen Reed, a TV producer who had been working with Carl and Rick on a special for the Showtime network. Driving into town, Rick told Stephen about what had happened the night before, and how Debbie wanted him to connect her with a psychic medium. Stephen said it just so happened he knew a medium. He might be able to hook her up with him. "I don't know," Rick said, "she wants me to get this guy who was on Larry King." Stephen said, "Let me talk to my friend John."

I had met Stephen around 1994, when I was still working in the hospital but thinking about a career change. My cousin knew a woman whose daughter wanted a reading. In those days, that's how I got most of my clients—the source was always two or three people removed. The daughter's name was Victoria, and she had a radio and TV production company. Afterward, she said she liked the reading so much that she wanted to try to put some kind of radio show together. I can't always explain what makes me interested or not interested in something, other than to say that I usually get a little pull in one direction or another. So even though I was still a little media-shy, the pull in this case was in the direction of "check it out." Victoria arranged an introduction at a Japanese restaurant with a producer. That was Stephen Reed. Stephen had no belief whatsoever in what I do, but hey, this was business. He was glad to meet me at the "check it out" counter.

Driving through Central Park that night, I was thinking about whether some kind of show was really going to happen, and where it was going to wind up. Just then a bus passed with an ad across its side for the cable-TV Sci Fi Channel, and with it a flashed message of the psychic kind: *It's Sci Fi.* When I met Stephen and Victoria, I was all excited. "It's going to be a TV show, and it's going to be on Sci Fi," I said. They looked at me as if I was the goofy kid that I was. Slow down, cowboy. You haven't even been on the radio yet. We actually did get a meeting at Sci Fi, but they weren't interested.

Stephen and I became good friends anyway, so when he asked for a rare favor, I tried to say yes. When he e-mailed me and asked if I would read the woman in Tennessee, he did it with an urgency that my guides made me feel I should pay attention to. Stephen told me the woman's father had passed, although he knew enough not to tell me anything more about her. But he did give me the feeling that there was something unusual or important attached to this woman. It would be a good idea for me to read her.

154

As soon as she hung up the phone after our reading that day in January of 1998, Debbie Perkins Swift called Rick Korn, crying. *Oh, no,* he thought. *It must have been a disaster. The guy must have been a fake, and she's really pissed. I'm gonna kill Stephen.* But to his unspeakable relief, Debbie wasn't upset—she was overjoyed. She gave him the whole thing, beginning to end, reading from the pages of notes her friend had taken down while listening in on the extension. Rick couldn't believe it. He had never really thought much about life after death, although he'd had two experiences that he'd never forgotten. Once, when he was in his twenties, he thought that a friend who had died came to him in a dream. And then, when he and his wife and kids were living in Tennessee in the early nineties, something happened one night that was so unsettling that he had never been able to talk about it, or even acknowledge that it had happened—even to his wife, A.J. Now, after hearing about Debbie's reading, that night started coming back to him.

A.J. didn't believe anything Rick told her about Debbie's reading. And Rick is a pretty convincing guy. "Well, if it's true, set up one of these readings for me," A.J. challenged him. Rick had already asked Stephen for one favor. But he really wanted A.J. to have a reading. He found himself thinking a lot about that night in Tennessee. He couldn't shake this feeling that I might be able to unlock this secret he had lived with for eight years.

So Rick asked Stephen for another favor. And Stephen said he really didn't want to ask me again. "Well, can A.J. and I take John and his wife out to dinner?" Rick said. "Just to thank him for Debbie? He wouldn't even take any money from her." Stephen called me, and I said dinner would be fine. And that I really didn't mind reading his friend's wife when we got together. It wasn't a problem. We could do it at Stephen's apartment before dinner.

When Rick told A.J. about it, both started thinking the same thing. They didn't even have to say it out loud. *A.J.'s father.* It had been eight years now.

Driving toward New York on the New Jersey Turnpike, A.J. started getting really cold feet. "I'm not doing this," she said. "I can't do this. I mean, even it's true, my father's dead. I don't want to disturb him. There's something not right about that. It's against my religion." She's Catholic;

Rick is Jewish. "Anyway, I don't believe this."

"A.J.," Rick said, "do you remember the night when we were living in Tennessee and you woke up in the middle of the night? And you said there was someone standing over the bed?"

Of course she remembered.

"And you said you didn't know if the guy was going to kiss you or attack you? And I went around the house with my broken lacrosse stick, and there was nobody there? And then you said the guy had a hat and coat on, and you thought it looked like your father?"

A.J. didn't like where this was going.

"Well, what I never told you was that I saw him, too."

"You did not!" A.J. said.

"I did. I'll even tell you what he was wearing. He had the same kind of coat that your father wore, and he had the same hat that he's wearing in the picture on the dresser."

"You didn't see it," A.J. insisted.

"I didn't want to believe it. I was afraid to say it. And we never, ever talked about it from the minute it happened until right now."

"You didn't see it!" A.J. repeated, very upset now. "You just incorporated my dream into your own dream after I told you about it."

Rick and A.J. never fought, almost never disagreed about anything. But on this, they were diametrically opposed. A.J. was ready to jump out of the car right there on the New Jersey Turnpike. "Okay," Rick said. "All right. But this guy's doing us a big favor. He's got a waiting list. We're not going there and then not doing it."

They didn't say another word the rest of the way into the city.

WE MET AT STEPHEN'S APARTMENT. We said our hellos, and Rick and I did the "You're-from-Long-Island?-Hey-I'm-from-Long-Island-too" greeting. And then I went into a room with Rick and A.J. and gave them the family-tree rundown: Above you, below you, to your side. This was the opposite of the usual case of the wife dragging the husband. Rick was all ears. A.J. had her hands folded.

The first thing that came through was a male figure above A.J. with an "E" name. It's like my last name, Edward, I said.

"That was my father's name," A.J. said, glancing at Rick.

Another relative came through, a cousin A.J. didn't know very well, but who was very close to her father. "She's the one who greeted him when he crossed over," I said.

"Now, your father, he died, he had an impact. I feel like he was stabbed. No, not stabbed, shot. Was your father shot?"

"Yes." A.J. looked very jumpy; her mouth was open.

"Three bullets. But was he hit by a train at the same time, or . . . what's the train connection?"

They both started to answer, but I cut them off. I meant it as a question for A.J.'s father. "Just say yes or no. He wasn't hit by a train."

"No," Rick said.

"He was shot."

"Yes."

"Was he shot *on* a train?"

"Yes."

"But these guys stalked him. There were three of them, three guys. But he wasn't shot on the train."

"Yes, he was."

"No, he was shot between the cars of the train."

"Yes. That's right."

"Now, why is he showing me he didn't die from this?"

"He did."

"He's saying no, it's something circulatory. Like something with his blood."

"Well, actually, the gunshot wounds that he had enlarged his ribcage. In fact, he had the exact same wounds as Reagan when he was shot. So he got off the train, sat on a bench, and bled to death. Nobody came to help. They thought it was a guy sleeping on a bench. Had they gotten to him within an hour, two hours, he'd still be alive." It turned out that a conductor had actually seen A.J.'s father being stalked and then shot, but when he saw him get off the train, he thought he might have been mistaken. The conductor didn't call it in until the end of his shift. By then, A.J.'s father had bled to death on the bench in the station.

A.J.'s father was pulling his energy back now, and then he stopped, as if he had a parting comment. "Your father, he wants you to know . . . why is he pulling me down South?"

"My brother lives down South," Rick said.

"No, no. What's connected to the two of you down South?"

"Well, we used to live in Tennessee and Florida."

"Tennessee. I don't know what this means, often I get these things and they don't mean anything to me, but hopefully it means something to you. So I'm just going to throw it out. He wants me to tell you that the man with the hat and the coat over the bed was him, and he apologizes for scaring you."

Rick and A.J. gasped and looked at each other. Rick excused himself and went to the bathroom. A.J. sat there in shock. She was in a daze.

That same night, another energy came forward, and it was for Rick. I recognized it. "What's your relationship with Carl Perkins?" I asked him.

"Well, I was his business partner."

"Oh, okay. Right. Were you and Carl in Texas?"

"Yeah, we were."

"Austin?" I asked.

"Yes. Austin."

That's all Carl Perkins gave me this time. But it was enough for Rick.

He explained: "Carl and I were together in Austin, Texas, and it was monumental, a turning point in our relationship. In Austin every year they have something called South by Southwest, where the entire town turns into music industry city. Every record company, every record executive in the world comes to Austin, and in every bar and every place imaginable there are bands playing, and that's where bands are signed. I had convinced Carl to go there and be the keynote speaker, which he didn't want to do. He came up with every excuse under the sun not to go to this thing. I said, 'Carl you gotta go, you gotta go.' We had made an album—funny, it was called 'Go, Cat, Go'—and I'm telling him it's important for the album, you need to do it, you have so much to say to young artists, you've got to be there. And he did go, and it was probably, next to Martin Luther King, one of the greatest speeches I have ever heard. A spiritual speech about how money is not important, how you have to do things because they're right sometimes. Tony Bennett also gave a speech, but it was a real downer about how the music industry sucks, and Carl's was that it's not about the music *industry*, it's about the *music*. It's about the healing power of music, and if you happen to make a living along the way, great.

"The place was packed with like two thousand people, and everybody was mesmerized. He was supposed to talk for an hour, but because he didn't want to do this, he had said to me, 'I ain't going up there speaking for no hour. If I have to go out there and speak for an hour, you're introducing me and it better be at least a half-hour long. And I did. I went up there, and the headline in the paper the next day is: 'Perkins hits high note despite infomercial-like introduction.' I'm up there selling 'Go, Cat, Go,' saying, 'It's got Paul McCartney, George Harrison, Ringo Starr, Johnny Cash, Tom Petty, all these people. And how many people in this industry besides Carl Perkins could get those people together?'

"And what was so monumental about it was that up to that point, though we were getting close, it was still businesslike. He wasn't sure of all my intentions because he had been screwed so many times. So right after the speech, he wanted to go out to lunch, just the two of us. He told his band and his sons to go off and do whatever. And he said, 'I just wanted to spend this time with you, to thank you. I said, 'For what?' He said, 'This was a very important day for me. And it's a very important day for us. That's a great thing that you made me do.'"

Rick had said there was poetry in the songs that Carl wrote late in his life. I thought that simple message was poetic. He had so much to say to his daughter. But all he had to say to Rick was one thing: *Austin*. And for Rick, that was all he needed to hear.

That night was also important for Rick and me. Still sky-high from the reading, he asked me why I wasn't on TV. "You're like Opie does Dead People," he said. I laughed. Stephen thought that Rick should try to work with me. That sounded good to me. Rick and I were nearly fifteen years apart. He had the whole suburban dad, Little League thing going, while I had no kids and was flying around the country telling people their relatives may be dead but they're okay. But we had a great connection and became fast friends. He tried to steer me in the right direction, as he had done for Carl Perkins.

LATER THAT YEAR, Rick and I, along with Lydia Clar, went to Dallas for the event that was destined for disaster—remember the credit card fiasco? But there was one amazing thing about that trip, and if I had been able to step back and see the big picture, I would have realized that it made the whole thing worthwhile.

The three of us went out to dinner the night before the event, and afterward, with some time to kill, we decided to see what a mall in downtown Dallas looked like. Rick wasn't wild about the idea. "I am, I guess, a mall-a-phobic," he said. "I'm not the world's greatest shopper. I get antsy. Real antsy." But he was a trouper and came right in, glad to see that it was a pretty dinky mall. We'd be in and out.

After about a half hour, we agreed we'd seen what a mall in Dallas looked like and we could go, which thrilled Rick. I led the way down the escalator. When I got to the bottom, though, I stopped in my tracks and did one of those pirouettes that happen when I'm getting grabbed by the neck. Of course, there were people behind me, and if you stop at the bottom of an escalator and don't keep walking, people start to pile up. "What's this guy doing?" someone behind me said.

I pointed to my left and told Rick, "There's a Carl Perkins reference in that store. We have to go into that store." Normally Rick would have wanted to check for a Carl Perkins reference, but this being a mall, all he wanted to do was get out of there. But he knew that wasn't happening. Not after that pirouette. We headed for what Rick proclaimed to be the "world's biggest *tchochke* shop." It was what you might expect if a hundred families hauled their garage-sale leftovers over to the local mall and dumped them in one gigantic store.

Rick surveyed this department store of junk. "Okay," he said hopefully, "are you getting a feeling?"

"Nope," I said.

"*Nope?* So where do we start?"

"Right here." We were at the front of the store.

Rick tried a shortcut. He went to a person at the front register and said, "Say, do you have anything here that's Carl Perkins-related?"

The woman looked at him like, *who*-related? "Mister, we got everything here. You're gonna have to look for it."

That look of panic on Rick's face was the recognition that there was absolutely no organization to the store. So forget a Carl Perkins section. I helped look for five or ten minutes, but after leafing through some old *Life* magazines, I got bored and went off on my own. I realized that unless it was Elvis Presley's studded belt, I wouldn't know a Carl Perkins reference from a *Marlin* Perkins reference. This was for Rick to find. Lydia was no help, either. She went off to do some Christmas shopping.

Rick was searching the store, looking through stacks of old forty-five records. "Is it Elvis?" he asked me.

"Nope." He could tell from my face that we weren't leaving without finding whatever we were supposed to find. I wasn't doing it for him. I was doing it for Carl. There was no doubt in my mind that this was really important to him.

The woman who worked in the store asked, "Did someone send you here?" Oh, you could say that.

"Beatles?" Rick asked.

"Nope."

"Here's a book on Memphis."

"Look through it."

Rick looked for something remotely related. Nothing.

After about an hour, Rick said he couldn't do this anymore. He was sorry, he knew Carl wanted him to find this thing, he would really like to find it, he had given it a try, but now he had to go. "John, can we please leave now?"

I shot him my "no way" look and went back to my own shopping. At which point, Rick turned in frustration, like an impatient kid, and bumped his shin on the leg of a large round table behind him.

"Oh, man that hurt," he said, bending down to rub his leg. And as he came back up, his eyes landed on a glass snowball music box. And inside the snowball were a pair of little blue suede shoes. Rick picked it up, and turned the little lever. And heard The Song.

"That's it," I said.

I figured that the least I could do was buy the thing for Rick. I brought it up to the register. "Found what you were looking for?" the clerk asked. Suddenly it didn't seem so much like a junk store anymore. The price was $56—as in 1956, the year of "Blue Suede Shoes."

Rick didn't want me to pay for it, but I told him I wasn't really buying it for him. "We need to give this to Debbie," I said.

Rick wanted to call Debbie and give her the snowball, but her father's death was still fresh, only ten months removed, and he didn't want to upset her. So he waited until he got home after the weekend. He called her on Monday. "I started telling her what happened, and in the middle of the story, she started crying," Rick told me when he called me after talking to her.

Rick told me that he apologized to her, but she just said, "No, no, you don't understand. . . . After the second stroke, deep inside I knew Daddy's time was about up. A very dear friend came to visit him and brought him a very special gift:. A snowball music box. Inside were the familiar blue suede shoes and, of course, the song playing. Daddy sat there in his favorite chair with his guitar on one side, and I watched him as he watched the shoes go round and round. There was a sadness in his eyes, and I could also see a glimpse of pride as he set the snowball on the table beside him. He reached to get his coffee cup, and as he did, he knocked the snowball over, and it shattered into a million pieces. Daddy's left side had been left very weak by the second stroke. I rushed to his side to clean up the mess, and I looked into eyes, and neither of us said a word for a moment. Tears streamed down his face. In that moment, I knew he was very sick and that he knew it as well. How I wished I could have put those broken pieces of glass together as if the accident had never happened. Somehow I felt if I could, Daddy would get well."

"Debbie, this is just incredible," Rick said when she told him the story over the phone that day.

"No," she said. "What is really incredible is that today is my birthday."

Rick just let that sink in. "Well, then," he said, "I guess I have your birthday present from your father."

FOUR NIGHTS LATER, I had a long-scheduled event at Town Hall, the venerable concert hall in New York City. It was a benefit for World Hunger Year, organized by Rick. I did readings, and Todd Pettengill joined me onstage for a little comic relief byplay—"the Psychic and the Psychotic," as we called ourselves when we appeared together on the radio and at events. Rick invited Annie Haslam, the singer from Renaissance. He had signed her up to record four songs for the CD that was going to be included in the infomercial package, including Carl Perkins' "Beyond the Blue," and he wanted us to meet. Rick got her to go onstage and sing *a cappella* for the first time in her career, one of her songs about angels. She left with a copy of *One Last Time.*

I came back onstage at the end of the evening, wanting to end the benefit on a high emotional note. In my hands I held Debbie Perkins' snowball music box. "When something really wild happens, I just can't keep it to myself," I told the audience. I began telling the story of what had happened just days earlier in Dallas. Rick had asked Debbie to come to New York and tell the story herself, but she didn't think she could handle it. Instead, she wrote it down and sent it to us. I asked Todd to read it.

"When you lose someone so close to you, you look back at those moments and you realize you cannot do anything to change things," she wrote. "I celebrated my forty-fourth birthday Monday without my Daddy. I was so depressed all day. And then Rick called and told me that John had a gift for me that my father had led him to. So my daddy let me know again through John that he is alive and well on the other side. My Daddy never missed giving me a special birthday gift. He found a way to give me the greatest one of all this year.

"My father was bigger than life to me and to many. He penned many songs that were recorded by many people. But he was Daddy to me. Not only was he the greatest daddy a girl could ever have, he was my best friend. From the other side, my father sends me signs that he is alive and that he will always be with me. Death is only a separation in the flesh and not in the spirit. The past year has been difficult. I long to see my father one last time, and yet I feel closer to him in so many ways now that I can't physically see him every day. I know he watches over me and speaks to my heart."

Debbie said that the gift had inspired her to write a song for the occasion. She titled it, "One Last Time."

Carl had always been convinced that John Lennon gave him the song he wrote for Paul McCartney, "My Old Friend." In some way, he was doing that now for his daughter. They gave each other their One Last Time.

— CHAPTER 7 —

MEDIUM COOL

THE PITCH

Ramey Warren Black was in her car, flying through the clouds after her surprise attack reading that night in October of 1998. She got home and told her husband he wouldn't believe what had just happened to her. And how she was going to turn that experience into a syndicated television show. So what if Ramey's new business partner, Adora English, thought she was absolutely out of her mind for even saying the words "psychic medium" and "TV show" in the same sentence. No, not the way to get their business off the ground. Not when they've named the company Media-Savvy.

That her partner had greeted her first big idea with an enormous eruption of laughter did not faze Ramey in the least. All she had to do was wait until the next day, which would be the 25th—an odd day. Ramey would be president of Media-Savvy for the next twenty-four hours. If only she could get a deal done in a day. But as Ramey told me over dinner that night, I had to give her a year. Fine, I said. If it happens, it happens. For now, I just wanted to get on other people's shows so I could talk about my book. But I did have some ideas if she managed to get anyone interested in doing a show with me.

Ramey started by getting me on some of the shows where she had contacts—*Roseanne, Leeza, Maury*. That gave me both some exposure and some tape. When the time came to try to pitch a show, she and Adora would need to give the people in suits something they could pop into their Sonys. Ramey introduced me to her agent, Richard Lawrence, and he looked like an agent to me, so he became mine, too.

Meanwhile, Ramey put together a group reading, more or less for Adora's benefit. "When Ramey called that night, I thought it was the funniest thing I'd ever heard," Adora told me later. "Ramey has a tendency to be like a huge idea person, and I'm more the one that carries things out. And I just thought she was wacky and affected by the reading she'd had and she wasn't thinking clearly. I mean, we're starting this company. How on earth would anyone take us seriously if we're walking into pitch meetings talking about a show with a guy who talks to dead people? But in five minutes, I went from sitting there with all this crossed-arm body language, to a broken-down sobbing mess just like everybody else. I remember thinking, *Okay, how's this guy doing this? What's the trick?* I said to Ramey, 'You're absolutely right. This is a show.'"

Over the next few months, I put on paper how I saw the concept of the show—with a little help from my guides. By the spring of 1999, I had regained my footing and felt I was back in their good graces. I knew I was meant to do a show and that it was going to happen. This may sound a lot like my attitude about *One Last Time*—it was meant to be, so it *would* be. We know how that turned out. The difference now was a big one: I knew a show would happen, just not when.

Unlike before, I was now at peace with the idea that things would happen in the right place, at the right time, and under the right circumstances. If it happened now, great. If it happened five years from now, fine. I was in no hurry. Ramey and Adora liked that. "A lot of times we're taking people around and they feel they need to be a star right this minute," she said. I told her I didn't feel I needed to be a star this minute, the next minute, the next day, or ever. In fact, I didn't want to be a star. I realized having a TV show would raise my visibility a few notches, but I could care less about being recognized. I only cared if the work was. Adora asked me if I was ready for this. If the show happened, would I be able to handle the demands of doing spiritual work in the pressure cooker of the television industry? Would I be able to handle the grueling schedule, not to mention the stress that was sure to come from collaborating very closely with people whose work was entertainment. "You better know what you'd be getting into," Adora said. "You better have your eyes wide open."

My working title for the show we were trying to develop was "Soul-Mates." I sent Ramey a three-page outline describing it as "a thirty-minute talk show with a humorous, emotional, and real-life inspirational edge." The heart of the show would be readings. A few people from the audience would get picked to come up on the stage and be read, and we could do follow-ups with them to find out about the information that came through—what made sense and what didn't, maybe a little personal history so the viewers would get to know the people whose spirits came through. There would also be celebrities—if we could get them to come on. This part didn't mean a lot to me, but my guides were telling me that it would be a necessary ingredient of a successful show. They could discuss their beliefs and experiences, and maybe even tape a reading. We would give them control over what we aired. And since this would be a talk show of sorts, we could offer the standard inducement: They could come on and talk about their latest projects. I had a bunch of other ideas: interviews with authors of spiritual books, guest psychics, segments on mystical places, "everyday angels—ordinary people doing extraordinary things for others"—and "The Miracle Segment," a discussion of historical and modern-day miracles.

I was getting comfortable with the idea of *having* a television show, if not with actually *doing* one. At least not alone. My idea was to have a co-host, mainly so I wouldn't have to do all the TV stuff that I knew wouldn't come naturally and might even block the concentration I needed to do my readings. In fact, the way I saw it was that *I* should be the co-host—a psychic sidekick to someone else who could draw off at least half of the attention, if not more. I could come out, do the readings, and leave. My partner would do all the "we'll be right backs" and "coming up nexts," and do some commentary and banter to keep it moving and make it fun.

I had a few people in mind, but my first choice was Todd Pettengill, the radio comic from WPLJ in New York whom I'd worked closely with for three years. Todd had been one of my earliest patrons on radio and had helped force me to branch out. On the radio or at events, he was the comic relief between readings, specializing in making fun of stupid things I said trying to interpret information. His mock-the-medium routine was a big hit at the World Hunger Year benefit we did at Town Hall in New York. Most of the letters I got afterward were about how hilarious Todd was. I thought our chemistry would be great on TV, his humor playing off the emotions of the readings. What I didn't want was a love-peace-New Age show that would have narrow appeal. "We will be careful not to be too psychic, spiritual, or religious," I wrote in my proposal to Ramey. "We will want this to appeal to the general public."

Ramey, Adora, and I talked about the project a lot over those months, fully aware that we were proposing a very rare thing in the TV business: a show completely without precedent. There were no models. We were making it up. To Ramey, this was incredibly liberating, if also a little bit frightening. As Adora had suggested after falling out of her chair laughing when Ramey first told her about it, starting up a company with such a weird idea was either brave and shrewd . . . or really, really stupid.

Eventually Ramey and Adora put together an eight-page proposal—a treatment, they called it—that jettisoned most of my secondary ideas and focused the show on the stories of ordinary people and the loved ones they reconnected with. Ramey wanted to stay close to her initial instinct—to build the show around the kind of powerful experience she'd had in the hotel room in October. She liked the idea of a co-host—it was too soon to suggest Todd or anybody else—but got rid of the title I'd come up with. She put a cover page on her proposal that said, for lack of anything better, "The John Edward Show." Boy, did that look weird on paper. I'm, like, Ed Sullivan.

The first page was the hype. "John Edward is an internationally acclaimed psychic medium with a huge following. . . . The Larry King switchboard was blown out for hours. . . . John recently appeared on *The Howard Stern Show.*"

Page 2: movie-ad quotes from the stars. "You're amazing! This is awesome!" — Roseanne. "That can't have been a wild guess. That can't have been a wild guess!"— Larry King. Then a detailed description of a typical show: "Segment Four: With the co-host roaming the audience, John gives readings to audience members. 'Who ate at MacDonald's? Anyone get food to go at McDonald's?' One woman finally raises her hand. 'My name is Marion MacDonald.' 'Close enough. Has your husband passed?' This is the money segment. This is why people tune in. In this segment, we have emotion, hope and closure."

This being TV, Ramey and Adora knew they would be trying to sell this concept to men and women who would want to know exactly where all this emotion, hope, and closure would be coming from, and how we were going to make sure every episode had it. These were people who lived in a scripted, controlled, neatly packaged world. Ramey and Adora were of this world themselves, so they knew as well as anyone that "Reality TV" was an oxymoron. They didn't think there would be a lot of interest in doing this show if it meant filling an audience with random people and then hoping some of them had interesting dead friends and relatives, and that they happened to be the ones who got read. You're leaving this all up to *chance?* Thanks for coming in.

So they came up with a list of ideas to deal with that guaranteed issue before it even came up. Idea: "A group of friends come together to hear from their mutual friend who has died of AIDS. He cut them off toward the end of his life." Idea: "Parents of a young man killed in the TWA Flight 800 crash have come to find a reason why their son had to die." I didn't like the sound of this. Leaving it up to chance was exactly what I'd been doing for fifteen years, and it seemed to work out fine. Ramey assured me that this was just pitch stuff, things you had to say just to get them to let you in the door. It occurred to me that all those years I'd spent in front of the tube hadn't given me a clue to what was behind it. It's like what they say about how sausage is made—you don't want to know.

Ramey gave the whole pitch a catchy tag line—"Tune into a miracle with John Edward, the next dimension of talk"—and pronounced us ready for daytime. She said she would be sending out a package to half a dozen major syndicators, after which I would have to go out to L.A. to meet with the ones that were interested in making a pilot. Syndicators? I asked. Ramey explained that these were companies, or arms of companies, that produce and distribute the scores of daily shows —"strips," they're called—that fill most of the television day. Everything from *Jerry Springer* to *Judge Judy* to *Family Feud* to the same episodes of *I Love Lucy* that have been running for forty years. I'd heard of the bigger ones like Paramount and Columbia Tri-Star, whose logo I'd seen at the end of a thousand midnight reruns. But the other ones, Buena Vista, Studios USA, Twentieth Television, Telepictures, were names that meant nothing to me. "Those are the big shops to go to," Ramey explained. "After that you're going to the smaller syndicators, and we really don't want to do that."

First Ramey and Adora went around and talked to development executives without me. They wanted to get the yeah-sure-he-talks-to-dead-people stuff out of the way. Without me there, the programmers could say anything they wanted, and a number of them made the most of that opportunity. This was fine with me. The less time I had to spend in L.A., the better. I didn't like the energy of the place, and although I loved Ramey and adored Adora, I didn't like the vibe I got from a lot of people out there. Besides, as a nervous flyer, I could do without a lot of cross-country flights. So Ramey and Adora knew they were not going to get me out there every time some TV executive picked up the phone.

Which not all of them did. Or if they did, it was to laugh in Ramey's ear, just as Adora had predicted. "A couple of people didn't even want to let us in the door, and there were a couple that let us in, but only for curiosity's sake," Adora told me, but only much later, when it didn't matter. At the time, both she and Ramey were all sunshine and optimism. I was the dark cloud. All of this—syndicators, strips, treatments, pilots—was mysterious and complicated to me. It was hard to imagine how you got from here to there. Not a bad time to remember my grandmother's favorite saying: "Don't look at how far you have to go; look at how far you've already come."

Ramey narrowed down the list of people I should meet, and I flew out and started "taking" meetings. In L.A., you don't *have* meetings or *go to* meetings. You *take* them. It must have something to do with the aggressive nature of Hollywood. I'm not sure what you do with meetings after you've taken them. Anyway, we took a whole handful. Every time I turned around, I was shaking hands with another vice president of development. There must have been more than twenty meetings over the course of those months—big groups of TV people around conference tables, all of them grilling me as I'm sure they never had anyone who had sat at that table before me. And of course, with varying degrees of tact, everyone wanted me to, you know, "do it."

Ever since I was a teenager, people have been pointing their six-shooters at my feet: "*Dance!*" I was at a book signing in San Francisco once and a woman rushed over to me, screaming, "John Edward! Do it! Do it! *Is my mother here?*" So *proving it* has long been pretty much a daily activity for me, a test that's never over. I had been through a version of the let's-see-whatcha-got routine three years before, when I'd made the rounds of New York publishers, hoping that when I told an editor that her father was showing me all kinds of fishing stuff and she told me he was a professor of fisheries, she would then reach into her drawer and pull out a contract. The first part of that sentence happened. Not the last part.

Performing for television executives raised the stakes, but didn't change what it was. Jump through this hoop like a big wet seal and I'll pull a pilot deal from the bucket and toss it in your mouth. Still, even if that was my feeling on a purely personal, self-esteem level, I couldn't really fault anybody for cross-examining me and for wanting a personal experience before even considering what we were proposing. After all, book publishers wanted to make sure I was real, and how big a risk were *they* taking? I would hardly be the first medium to publish a book. But I *would* be the first one to have a syndicated television show, if any one of these people decided to pull the trigger on this idea of thirty minutes of daily television "full of emotion, humor and enlightenment."

I knew Ramey had her work cut out for her, so I told her I would do whatever I could to make her job easier. "If you need me to do strategic readings, I will," I said. All I asked for was a little dignity. I wouldn't read anybody during an introductory meeting, or as a prerequisite for a meeting. If they were truly interested in the show, we would arrange something later.

But Ramey and Adora were very protective and said I didn't even have to do that. "If somebody says, 'Hey, show us what you do,' we will never make you do that," Adora said. "We've made that clear to them. It's just not fair to put you in that position. You're not a dog-and-pony show."

But of course I was. We met with one guy with not an ounce of class—the Hollywood Creep incarnate. He flew into the room without even an attempt at social grace, or consideration that perhaps I was something other than a piece of meat. "Okay, take my secretary, go in another room, and do what you do. Let's go, I need you to go do this right away." I just looked at him and concentrated really hard on not saying, "Your mother is coming through, and she thinks you're an asshole, too."

Ramey and Adora looked worried—Oh, God, what's he gonna say?—so I decided to be a good boy and go along. "Fine, fine," I said, not bothering to hide how infuriated I was. "You want me to do this, fine." The secretary, who was barely out of her teens, had a major attitude. And I wasn't exactly in a zone of love and positive energy. A young male who died in an accident came through, but she would not validate it. I couldn't help myself. I leaned forward and told her, "Do you know that people wait months and sometimes even years for the opportunity that just fell in your lap? I suggest you appreciate it because it is happening, and there's a reason. And that reason is your friend's brother." Then she validated the information, and came out and reported to her boss that I was for real. At which point, he took me into a room with a guest who was in town for a meeting and told me to read him. This person validated some information, but Mr. Hollywood couldn't be bothered. I stopped, told him I was no longer interested in discussing any project with his company, and walked out. I told Ramey and Adora that no amount of money would get me to work with that guy. Don't think you need to worry about that, they might have said.

If there had been any more like this guy in L.A., I might have gotten right back on the plane and headed for the nearest radio studio. Fortunately, the others were polite and interested, if skeptical. Adora was impressed, anyway. "You've answered these questions a million times, but every time you make it sound like it's the first time," she said. Maybe I really could be on TV. I had it down to sound bites. And some people seemed to really get what we were talking about. Not that they were running out of their shoes to sign me up. "They're all intrigued and they're all scared," Ramey summed up over the phone after we'd made the rounds and I was back in New York. "I'm hearing 'too risky—do you have a judge?'"

TV is an industry that loves a brand-new idea as long as someone else has done it first. Dead Man Talking? You go. No, you go. No, you go. I'm sure they wished I was Judge John. I could walk into the soundstage courtroom wearing robes and carrying sage incense, overrule objections that only I could hear, and give my verdict without having to ask the witnesses any questions. Psychic judge—can't miss.

While we were waiting to hear back from the two or three studios that seemed interested, something very fortunate happened. During the summer of 1999, a movie starring Bruce Willis and a remarkable kid named Haley Joel Osment came out, and suddenly everybody in America was saying, "I see dead people." It was as if *Sixth Sense* dropped from the sky, and the people we were talking to looked up and went *Hmmm*. I went on *Larry King Live* with M. Night Shyamalan, who directed and wrote the film. I don't know if his movie made the difference, but it didn't hurt.

The first nibble came from Columbia Tri-Star. Ramey and Adora got all excited when I told them I was seeing a logo with feathers. "Oh, feathers!" Adora said. "The Pegasus in the Tri-Star logo! Okay, it's going to be Tri-Star!" But it wasn't. (Maybe I'd gotten my signals crossed. Could feathers have had something to do with Lucky Duck Productions, which was making the HBO documentary at the same time?)

Ramey thought the next best shot was Studios USA, producer and distributor of everything from the Sally-Maury-Jerry trio to *Law & Order*. She'd had some preliminary but promising conversations with people there. And some interesting things started happening, although they're really only interesting in retrospect. While Ramey was starting to woo Studios USA, I got a call at my office from a woman named Tahira Bhatti-McClure. She worked in the programming department at the Sci Fi Channel in New York, and one of her jobs was to find new talent and fresh ideas for the network. Tahira told me that her mother-in-law had gone for a private reading after hearing me on WPLJ, and had given Tahira one of my brochures. She wanted to talk to me about the possibility of doing a show for Sci Fi. She thought it was cool that I was so young and, to hear her mother-in-law tell it, someone she as a TV programming developer should meet. I thanked Tahira for calling and asked her to get in touch with Ramey.

Tahira's call took Ramey by surprise. She thought it was weird that someone from Sci Fi was trying to get in on the proposal. After all, things were starting to heat up with Studios USA—Sci Fi's sister company at USA Networks. Anyway, she was glad to send Tahira a demo tape and treatment, so long as Tahira understood that we were setting our sights a little higher than a single cable channel. "Got it," Tahira said. "Of course you're shopping the syndicators. But don't forget about us." Tahira discussed me with her boss, who was interested and wanted to investigate further.

When we later pieced this story together, the timing of things suggested maybe a little string-pulling from the other side, and I don't mean the West Coast. Here's what happened: A day or so after Ramey and Tahira talked on the phone, Bonnie Hammer, Tahira's boss, was at an event at the William Morris Agency in New York. In the course of mingling with her colleagues, Bonnie heard that Studios USA was going after a deal with a young psychic medium from New York. When a major entertainment company is said to be talking to one of *us* about a syndicated show, it tends to get talked about. And someone like Bonnie Hammer tends to listen. Whatever happens inside the head of the person who runs the Sci Fi Channel when she recognizes something she wants— that's what seems to have happened to Bonnie. She realized the psychic that Studios USA was pursuing was the same one Tahira had talked to.

First thing next morning, Tahira went to Bonnie's office—with the tape she'd just gotten from Ramey. They watched it together, and ten minutes later, Tahira was on the phone setting up a meeting. In the meantime, Bonnie and Tahira came out and sat in on a small group reading at the Holiday Inn on Long Island that was practically my home stage. During the reading, there were messages for Bonnie from members of her family that she validated and appreciated. I liked her right away—there was definitely something special about her. She seemed to really *get* what I was all about, without even knowing much about me.

Ramey flew to New York, and we met in Bonnie's office on the twentieth floor of USA Network's New York headquarters on Sixth Avenue. Bonnie had only recently taken over programming at Sci Fi and explained that she was on the hunt for alternative shows that would broaden the channel. "Anything outside of what we *know* to be true," is the way she described the genre she was trying to develop. "If it's speculative, if you can't quantify it with proof, then it fits. You can't really prove the afterlife. People either believe it or they don't believe it. Even if there are all kinds of affirmations and confirmations, in your gut you have to want to believe it."

Bonnie said later, "Nothing was popping until I saw this piece of tape." She told me at that first meeting that she wanted to take the next step, and get approval from her boss in L.A. to make a pilot. "I really would love to do something with you," she said. "I would love to just let you do what you do and just capture it with cameras."

Despite all the good feelings with Sci Fi, Ramey saw it as a backup. She was going hard for the channel's big sister. There was a woman at Studios USA named Libby Gill who was as gung-ho as Bonnie, and the exact opposite of the Hollywood Creep. She understood the idea from Day One and became its champion. That wasn't so easy a thing to be. One of the people Libby worked with came to our first meeting with body language that said "I don't think so." He was upfront about not being a believer, and he hammered us hard. "What's the show?" he asked, like the network guy in that famous *Seinfeld* episode. Ramey could have told him it was a show about nothing—nothing you've ever seen before. But she didn't want to scare him. So she told him it's a show like you *have* seen before— with a twist. "The show is stories," she said. "It's human stories. It's about love and loss and all the things that every talk show is about. Only there's another dimension." I walked out of that meeting thinking that was the last we would see of them.

But Ramey thought she had them hooked. The only thing holding them back, it seemed to her, was that they didn't want to make a commitment based mostly on a tape of me on *Leeza* and *Entertainment Tonight,* an eight-page treatment, and some meetings. They needed to see me do it. So she and Adora set up a "showcase" in a fancy room at the Bel Age Hotel and invited about thirty-five people. Half were from the studio; the other were half friends and acquaintances of Ramey and Adora's who might bring some interesting guests from the spirit world. One of them was a woman who ran an adoption agency and was going to be subletting her office space—Lucille Ball's office from the fifties—to the Media-Savvy madames. At the Bel Age, I did what I normally do with a group—some readings, some explanation, some stand-up philosophy. The first person I read was the adoption lady. She had lost two babies to crib death. Then I went right to a couple of guys I later found out were two of the biggest executives at Studios USA. And I got pulled over to the development guy who had been so skeptical at our earlier meeting. His father came through, and I got information, which he validated, that a former girlfriend had breast cancer and that he needed to call her.

Afterwards, Ramey was beaming. "You blew them away," she said. She was sure we'd closed the deal.

Two weeks later, I was getting off a plane in Tucson for the Miraval experiment with Gary Schwartz, when I got a cell-to-cell call from Ramey. "They want the show!" she screamed. "Studios USA! They want the show!"

Silence on my end. "It's not going to happen," I said.

"What do you mean it's not going to happen?"

"I don't know. Something's not right. I'm getting that it's not happening."

"John, they just called. They want the show. They want to make a deal."

"No, it's not going to happen."

"I can't believe you're saying that," Ramey said, crestfallen. "I mean, we already popped the champagne."

"Sorry. Better put the cork back in the bottle."

That was on a Friday. On Monday, Ramey called back. Well, about that champagne. It looks like we have to do one more meeting. There was someone new moving into a top job at Studios USA. We would need her support. We had the meeting in New York, and Adora came out thinking we'd sailed through.

"That was great," she said. "Piece of cake."

"Are you nuts?" I said. "That went really bad."

She looked at me like I was insane. "No, it didn't," she said. "It went really well."

"Did we go to the same meeting?" I asked.

"Yeah, but I don't do what you do."

"She's going to pass," I said.

Adora hoped this was a case of a psychic having an off-day. You read your people, we'll read ours.

A few days later, the new programming chief at Studios USA turned our green light red. "She thinks it's too risky for her first project," Ramey said. "So we're back to square one."

Ramey's call confirmed what I already knew, but it stirred up that old internal dialogue with The Boys. Once again, I had to wonder what the deal was, universally speaking. Why put me through all these meetings and hard work with these big syndication companies if you're only going to blow me out of the water in the end?

Unlike nine months before, though, I wasn't about to slip into a funk over this. I allowed myself one bad day, checked back in with my TV-show mantra—*Yeah, fine, whatever, if it happens now, it happens now*—and just said screw it, not my time. I remembered the lesson of Darth Vader, the lady at the Barnes & Noble in Santa Monica. My Boys had a plan. All I had to do was trust them and watch it happen. This time it was easy to turn the corner and focus on other things. Namely—ironically—*One Last Time*.

The book was out in paperback, a second chance at life, and this time I was taking some control of the process. A mutual colleague had intro-duced me to a woman named Debbie Luican, who was the executive director of the San Diego branch of the Learning Annex, a kind of national adult education organization. Debbie worked with the A-list spiritual speakers—Deepak Chopra, Wayne Dyer, Sylvia Browne—and agreed to work with me. She was a straight-ahead, no-nonsense type, supportive but very matter-of-fact about my work, as if to say, *I've spent a lot of time around psychics. You're not going to impress me.* She simply said: "You've got a really important message. Stay focused." I found that incredibly refreshing. It was exactly the kind of unadorned, straight-to-the-point support I needed to hear.

Debbie first organized events in San Francisco, Los Angeles, San Diego, and Phoenix, and then, starting in September 1999, a forty-city tour that would last nine months and help put the book on some regional bestseller lists—although nationally it would remain only a moderate success. But with my new and improved Zenlike attitude, and knowing that at least this time I was doing it my way, I didn't spend a lot of time worrying about numbers.

Having exhausted our possibilities with all the big TV syndication companies, square one for Ramey and Adora was the Sci Fi Network. Ramey called Bonnie Hammer, who was ready to pounce. All she had to do was get the support of her boss, Stephen Chao, president of USA Cable. Stephen had popped in for five minutes at my first meeting with Bonnie earlier in the summer. He joked around—*Hey, what am I thinking?*—which is his style, and talked about the potential for syndicating the show even if it started on Sci Fi. I didn't know if he was a believer or not, but as Bonnie says, that wasn't the point. "His only concern was that he didn't want to have an imposter, which is very different from does he believe or not believe," Bonnie said. "The thing that Stephen needed to believe was that we had the real enchilada—that if these things *are* true, then we have a true representative of what it is." The other things he wanted to make sure about, of course, were that Bonnie and her team understood what the show would be, and that I could do television.

If I had any concerns about doing the show for a channel with the word *fiction* in its name, Stephen moved quickly to diffuse that. "That's the name of the channel," he had said at that meeting. "And the truth is that to a lot of people this *is* science fiction. But there are a lot of people who believe it, and they're going to be watching this channel."

I had to believe Stephen knew something about breaking new ground in TV. So his support soothed the letdown Ramey felt about not making a deal with a big syndicator. It sounded like we might eventually get there anyway. I flashed back to the psychic billboard I saw on the bus in Central Park five years earlier: The answer is Sci Fi.

THE CATCH

HERE'S HOW IT WORKS IN TELEVISION: If the programmers at a network like an idea for a show on paper, they order a pilot to see if it translates onto the screen. If they like the pilot enough, they'll put the show into production for what amounts to a trial run. Usually it's thirteen weeks of episodes. That's the extent of the commitment. After that, it has almost nothing to do with whether they like it or not. The only people whose taste counts at that point is the viewers. Ratings.

Bonnie Hammer wanted a pilot in a hurry—six weeks—so we got right down to planning. One good thing about doing the show for Sci Fi was that we were in New York. We had a long list of things that had to be discussed and decided. The format of the show was the big issue, and within that were a million smaller ones. How much of the show would be readings? Who would be read? How many people would be in the audience? How would they be chosen? Would there be celebrity readings? What about a co-host? And then there was an equal number of technical TV questions. What would the set look like? How would it be shot? Would there be any scripted material? And, of course, what was the show going to be called? "SoulMates" was out. Everyone seemed to want my name in the title, but maybe as the second part, as in Something-or-Other with John Edward. One of the names on the list of candidates was "Crossing Over," and the consensus seemed to be *Yeah, okay, that's fine for now. We've got more pressing problems.* This was just a pilot. We'd come up with a title eventually.

It dawned on Bonnie that it was a blessing that we were starting at Sci Fi. This was Crossing Over in more ways than one. Nothing like this had ever been attempted in television. So syndicating it from scratch might have been the worst thing we could do. Instead, we could give the show what Ramey called a "soft launch"—a quiet, measured beginning on cable, like opening a Broadway show on the road to get the kinks out. Plus, as Stephen Chao had pointed out, we would be on a channel whose viewers would be predisposed to believing what they were seeing. We could build an audience from there. We could let the show evolve, make our mistakes, figure out what worked and what didn't—and then, if things went well and Stephen and his boss, the legendary Barry Diller, liked what they saw, we'd have a shot at a wider audience through syndication.

When we first saw how the deal broke—Studios USA backing out, its little sister Sci Fi waiting outside the door, eyes in the keyhole—Ramey wondered if it was all a setup by the parent company to manipulate a deal in their favor. Only later did we realize that this had not been planned. The head of Studios USA really didn't want to make this her very first project, and the head of Sci Fi really did see it as the perfect show for her up-and-coming channel. "It sort of organically happened that way," Ramey said. To me, it was happening the way it was supposed to happen. Fatalism was not necessarily the operating philosophy of people who work in the television industry, but Ramey seemed to be enjoying the ride. She wasn't going to be arguing with The Boys.

Ramey hired a director named Peter Kimball, who had worked on *Oprah,* and he arranged to borrow and redress the *Maury Povich* set, a Studios USA show that was shot at the Hotel Pennsylvania, across the street from Madison Square Garden. The first big decision Bonnie made was that I would be on my own. She didn't like the idea of a co-host, not after she came to the group reading on Long Island. "I want pure John," she said. *Uh-oh.* I really didn't think pure John was such a great idea.

"I've never done this before," I protested. "I've never had to talk to a camera." That wasn't completely true. I remembered being on a show in Boston once where they asked me to read something from a TelePrompTer. I was bad. Really, really bad. But Bonnie is an awfully persuasive person, especially when she believes in something. Ramey and Adora said don't worry, you'll be fine. "If you really can't do it, we'll have to revisit it and find another way of doing it. Maybe with voiceovers." In the back of my mind, I was thinking that this was just the pilot. Bonnie will let me have a co-host if and when we do the real show. She'll see how bad I am.

For now, my attitude about the whole thing was that all I knew about television was how to work the remote. Bonnie and Ramey were the TV people, and it would be up to them to figure out how to turn this idea we had been talking about for a year into something that Stephen Chao could pop into his VCR in L.A. and see what he needed to see to call up Bonnie in New York and say, "Let's do it." As long as they didn't interfere with my work, I wouldn't interfere with theirs.

Interference turned out to be a matter of interpretation. We taped the pilot on a Friday and Saturday in early December, and during one session on stage. I read a family for whom a spirit came through very forcefully. "It's like boom, boom, and he falls," I told them. Then I was shown the face of a friend of Sandra's and mine—a flight attendant for TWA. "Did he pass in a crash?" I asked. "It's Flight 800, isn't it." It was. Then, awhile later, I was pulled over to a woman in the audience. "You went to Mexico," I said. Yes. "There was a night when people got really smashed. Someone ended up face down in the sand." Yes. "Your sister wants you to know she saw the whole thing. . . . Wait a minute, did she die in a plane crash, too?" There were several more families that had lost relatives in the explosion of the New York-to-Paris TWA Flight 800 off the south shore of Long Island in 1996.

Knowing that our opportunities to gather strong material for the pilot would be limited, Ramey thought bringing in families of the TWA victims was a prudent idea. But I was uncomfortable with it, mostly because it represented a violation of one of my most basic guiding principles. These people no doubt came in expecting, or at least hoping, that I would connect with the person they lost in the accident. If I was preaching the gospel of "check your expectations at the door," it would be hypocritical of me to be actually raising those expectations myself.

Ramey had mentioned during the planning stages that she might try to come up with some "themes" for the pilot. I wasn't wild about the idea, but wanted to let her do her thing and didn't think too much about it. But now that I had experienced it, I felt more than ever that this had to be a show that essentially produced itself. It couldn't be like a regular talk show where most of the work happened before an inch of tape was shot: producers wracking their brains for fresh ideas; hitting the phones to book the right guests; researching the topic to prep the star; and then scripting, editing, and packaging the show to exploit that fresh idea to the max.

That couldn't be the process in *Crossing Over,* or whatever we were calling this. In this show, ideas would be what we got *after* we taped.

Booking only needed to mean opening the doors to the studio and getting everybody in a seat. The real guests would announce themselves, in their way, at their time. And we couldn't in any way think of the people who came to the show as vehicles brought in for our use. So Ramey had to abandon all the other ideas that were apparently being discussed: Families of victims of the Oklahoma City bombing. People with organ transplants who wanted to connect with their donors. And "Saturday Night Dead"—bringing in the families and friends of Gilda Radner, Phil Hartman, and other departed *Saturday Night Live* stars.

On those two days in December, we shot hours and hours of tape, trying different approaches to see what worked best. Ramey brought in an audience of about a hundred, and others much smaller. They tried some different lighting and camera positions, some different ways of introducing and closing the show. And of course there was the matter of my aura. I'm not speaking universally here. I'm speaking of my clothes. Did they want me in a suit or a collarless skintight shirt? Glasses or contacts? Did they want a cool medium for the cool medium? Or a regular guy for the folks in Cincinnati? My grandmother would have been so pleased—all these people concerned about the way I presented myself. I just did what they told me, wore the clothes they handed me, spoke the words they wrote for me, then did what I do. I was determined to ignore all the TV stuff and concentrate on not changing anything about the work. Bonnie just wanted to "capture it with cameras." I just had to make sure *I* wasn't captured by the cameras.

Spirits have never been known to wait for me to be ready, and they weren't impressed in the least that this was TV, where you start when the director says so. "Does anyone have someone who was murdered?" I asked the second I reached the stage for one session, having waited in the wings with this poor soul practically pushing me out there himself. "This is somebody who was stabbed. It was a brutal murder."

A man in the back row called out. "My brother Vincent was stabbed. Stabbed seventeen times."

"Did someone in the family have to identify him?"

"My mother and my sister."

"Mom is still here?"

"No, she passed."

"Okay, your mom is coming through. She's with your brother."

With that, the man in the audience tightened his lips, obviously trying to stay in control.

"Your brother walked into this," I said. "That's how it's being shown. Are you aware of that?"

"It was mistaken identity," he said. "He was mistaken for stealing something earlier in the day, but he didn't do it. It was over a radio."

"That's the way he's coming through. He's not taking any responsibility for this. He didn't do anything to bring this on. Do you have his blue hat?"

"Yes." Now the man was quivering.

"He's telling me . . . are you not going to computer class?"

"No," he said, looking taken aback.

"Why not?"

"Don't like it," he retorted defensively.

"He's telling me you should do that. It's supposed to be good for your career."

The man rolled his eyes with annoyance, a gesture that seemed to speak volumes about his relationship with his brother.

"He's making me feel like it's hard to get up in the morning. He's telling me there are so many opportunities in front of you and you're not taking them. It's like he's saying get over this and move forward. This is very important to do this."

The reason I am not naming this person is that he's been exposed enough. It turned out he worked in one of the back-office departments for Sci Fi and just happened to come by. I'm not even sure he knew what the pilot was for. But a tight shot of him at his most emotional and vulnerable later wound up being used not only for the pilot, but by a number of entertainment shows when they did stories about our show. So I want to protect his privacy now.

After two days of shooting, Ramey had the pilot edited and packaged. The name of the show? *Crossing Over with John Edward.* Nobody ever got around to revisiting the title, and it just sort of stuck. I liked the pilot. It was compelling but restrained, not overdone. But Bonnie thought it needed to be faster, more polished, to get it past her bosses in California. "You do a pilot for one reason," Ramey explained to me. "That's to get a green light. Once we get that, then you can move the show forward the way you want. But this is all about getting approval." So we were really only making this pilot for the one or two people who had the power to say yes or no. "We have to think of their sensibilities," Ramey said.

Ramey brought a box of videotapes home to L.A. and delivered them to Jean Wiegman, an experienced producer and editor who recut the pilot with an editing room full of young, fast video editors. The content of the new version wasn't a lot different from the first one, but the opening was glitzier and the segues between segments were New York-fast. A lot of rapid-fire cuts of the best moments from the upcoming segment, with hip Sci Fi music and glib one-liners—"You can argue with the living, but the dead get the final word"—laid over it. There was a celebrity reading with actress Kari Wuhrer, the star of *Sliders,* a Sci Fi show about a parallel universe.

My own parallel universe was now in the hands of the lords of L.A. Although Ramey had delivered the pilot quickly, there was no immediate reply from the network. I wasn't privy, of course, to the discussions between Bonnie and the people above her—and I don't mean parents, grandparents, aunts, and uncles—but I've since learned they had to do with making sure there really was a television show here, with a beginning, a middle, and an end. Closure. We were looking for some of that ourselves.

In January, Bonnie asked me to come to Los Angeles and appear at the annual conference of the Television Critics Association. This is where the network bigwigs, producers, and stars get up in front of writers from newspapers and magazines and talk about their upcoming shows and the state of their networks. Bonnie wanted me to get up in front of them, introduce myself, and talk about *Crossing Over.* That the show hadn't been approved yet was apparently a minor detail. So I went out on the stage by myself—as opposed to the panel discussions they usually had—and just talked about myself and the show, and then took questions. Then they showed a highlight reel on a large rear-projection screen.

As I walked out of the room, I saw that I was being followed by a group of people, and suddenly I was completely surrounded by about thirty journalists throwing questions at me and asking for readings. "Is Stephen seeing this?" Bonnie asked Ramey. "He's watching," Ramey said.

Ramey thought this was why Bonnie wanted me out here. "She's very smart," Ramey said later. "Bonnie knew that once you were presented it would give her a lot more heat. And Stephen let her do it. I'm sure he wanted to see, too. I think he intended to make this happen all along, but he just needed a little reaffirming. And he got it. Here were all these jaded TV critics, and they couldn't get close enough."

USA Networks made it official a few weeks later, announcing that *Crossing Over* would begin production in May and be on the air by summer. It would be on nightly at eleven o'clock, Sunday through Thursday, on the Sci Fi Channel. For thirteen weeks, anyway.

For Ramey, it was a bittersweet moment. It had never been her intention to run the show, only to develop and sell it and get it launched. So now that she and Adora had done what they'd set out to do, they would be returning to their other projects and turning their baby over to adoptive parents. From the beginning, our arrangement had a natural ending built into it. I wasn't going to move to Los Angeles to do the show, and they weren't going to move to New York. The funny thing about it was that this was news to me. We had never actually discussed what would happen if the pilot was picked up, so I had just assumed that Media-Savvy would be the production company, and Ramey and Adora would stay put as my TV spirit guides—my Girls. Maybe that's what Mary Jo McCabe, the psychic in Baton Rouge, was sensing when she said she detected a new female energy among my guides.

Ramey and Adora would have loved to be able to be there when the show began to crawl and then take its first wobbly steps. But they had been tied down by the daily grind of syndicated television for twenty years. It wouldn't make sense for them to jump right back in, no matter how exciting and innovative the show was, and no matter how emotionally invested in it they were. They would remain attached to the show as "executive consultants," but their final job—and they knew it was a crucial one—would be to make sure they put in place a production team they trusted, people they knew I would be comfortable with. Ramey and Adora had no fears at all about Bonnie Hammer; they told me I couldn't be in better hands. But Bonnie wouldn't be the only one I would be dealing with at the corporate level. And she wouldn't be producing the show. She agreed with the Media-Savvys that it was vital to make sure the key people were not even remotely cynical about the material. This couldn't be just another gig to them.

A few months earlier, when Ramey was looking for someone to direct the pilot, she had checked with Richard Lawrence, her agent, and he had recommended a New York-based director named Dana Calderwood. Ramey met Dana at her hotel, and both of them being extremely sweet souls, they clicked right away. Dana was very open to the subject matter. Although he didn't look or act particularly New Age-y, he was fond of noting that he and his wife had been married by a channeler in California (even if the channeler was a former TV executive). Dana was so eager to do the pilot that he tried to wiggle out of a commitment he'd made to go to Florida the same week to direct *Double Dare 2000* for Nickelodeon. He couldn't get out of it, and Ramey found somebody else. But now that the show was a go, she hoped he was available for more than a couple of days' work. Dana was a great director, with a solid list of credits and an Emmy nomination. He directed Conan O'Brien's late night show for its first two years, specials for CBS, and shows for Nickelodeon. He was also one of the few directors based in New York. Most important, he *got* the show. She urged Bonnie to call him.

Bonnie did call Dana, along with a few other directors and producers. Among them was Shirley Abraham, an experienced producer with a no-nonsense yet maternal style and a talent for assembling a solid staff. What Bonnie didn't know was that Dana and Shirley were partners. They and a third associate, Charles Nordlander, a writer-producer, had a company called Glow in the Dark Productions. Bonnie was talking to other people, but she liked the Glow in the Dark threesome and wanted to see what kind of chemistry we might have.

Dana, Shirley, and Charles piled into a car and drove out to Long Island for a meeting in my office above the hair salon on Jericho Turnpike. Like just about everyone else I had been involved with over the past couple of years, they were about fifteen years older than I was—smart, experienced professionals in their mid-forties trying to find a way to converge their world with mine. We spent two hours talking out the show as if the treatment had never been written and the pilot never shot. They needed to wrap their brains around what the show would be, how they could blend my concept with Bonnie's vision and their own ideas.

The first thing that was clear was that all three were intrigued and excited by the prospect of working on something so out of the mold. Having spent years in the trenches of the conventional, they thought this could be groundbreaking television, not a phrase they used lightly. I refer to people who have no experience with spiritual subjects as being "green." The Glow in the Dark producers were not that. All of them had at least some degree of belief and experience with the idea of the survival of the soul and after-death communication. What they needed to do was translate that to the tube. They needed to know who I was as a person and what I wanted to accomplish as a medium. What was the message of the show? Not a question often asked in television. And by the way, that question and a thousand others had to be answered very quickly. Sci Fi wanted the show up and running in less than three months.

I had never thought about what goes into the making of a TV show, but it wasn't exactly point-and-shoot. Not only would the producers have to hire more producers and a crew, but they would have to create a format and get it approved, find a studio, and design and build a set. And they would have to turn me into a TV personality. You know how I was pretty much assuming they'd give me my co-host so I could just come out and do readings? Not happening—Bonnie still wanted pure John. *Shit.* Didn't she know it wasn't so long ago that being asked to go on a radio show was enough to make me nauseous? *It's not how far we have to go; it's how far we've come.* Bonnie was adamant—"obnoxiously insistent," is how she later put it. "You don't need a crutch."

So that was that. My only crutches would be the people producing the show. I liked the guys from Glow in the Dark, and so did Bonnie, and so did Ramey and Adora. So Dana Calderwood, Shirley Abraham, and Charles Nordlander became the first three members of the production team of *Crossing Over with John Edward and No Co-Host.*

Right after that, the new producers went on a recruiting binge. The first person Dana called was a producer he had worked with at a show called *Fox After Breakfast.* The guy's name was Paul Shavelson, and Dana said he was incredibly smart and creative and funny. His name sounded familiar, but I couldn't quite place it. Dana said *Fox After Breakfast* didn't last very long, but it was preceded by a cable version called *Breakfast Time,* a wild, free-form show—the complete opposite of *Today* and the other network morning shows—that had gotten major buzz and positive press during the four years Paul had produced it. Dana said Paul would be the perfect person to help conceive *Crossing Over*. If we could get him. Apparently he was another one who was glad to be free of the grind of a daily show and enjoying the freelance life. He had moved his family to a great house overlooking the water on Long Island, and after getting axed from the Fox morning show for using puppets to make fun of his bosses, he had a great setup working out of a converted barn. He wouldn't figure to be in any rush to sign up for another round of fourteen-hour work-days plus a commute into the city.

Dana called Paul and asked him if he was interested in working on a show about a guy who talks to dead people, a guy named John Edward. "That's weird," Paul told him. "I was riding the train with a friend of mine a few weeks ago, and he told me about this guy. He saw a documentary on HBO and was telling me about him."

Paul had even more experience with spiritual subjects than Dana, even though he was married by a ferryboat captain, not a channeler. Although he was interested in the subject, he had to deal with a built-in bias against people who made a career of being a psychic. "I thought really spiritual people internalized it," Paul has since told me. "They didn't really preach, and they definitely didn't make money on it. It's almost like a 'professional psychic' is an oxymoron. You're psychic—you don't need money."

Paul wasn't so lofty on the subject that he didn't want Dana to send him the pilot. But when he watched it, he was skeptical that *Crossing Over* could be a credible TV show. "I'm fascinated by John, and I would love to meet him and see what's in his head," he told Dana. "But I don't see this as a TV show. It doesn't look real to me. It almost looked like magic. Like you could almost pop John out of that and put in David Copperfield. And it would be like theater. You would go and watch a big magic show. That's the problem I've always had with producing magic on TV. Who's going to believe it? We all know that magic is an illusion, and you can assume that on TV you can do anything you want. If you give me enough money, I can make my house float. I could levitate anything. So as fascinating as the subject is to me, I don't know if this ever will be a vehicle for TV."

Dana must have thought Paul was giving him a big, resounding no thanks. But what he was really saying was that there was only one way to make this idea work. And that was to find a way for viewers to take something from the experience of watching other people's departed relatives come through. As Paul later put it: "How can we grow from that experience of knowing that their souls are still part of our lives? How can *we* connect?" Paul said he'd like to at least see if this could be done.

Dana was hoping that Paul would say that. What he thought this project needed was a lot of careful thought by a group of smart people with integrity and a sure grasp of the subject. And fast. A lot of decisions had to be made quickly. "There's something here," Dana said.

"Well, the only way to really see what it is, is to see him work live," Paul said.

There was no time to waste. He would have to come and see me at my next event a few days later, but it would involve a little traveling. Paul and Dana would have to come to Barbados.

— CHAPTER 8 —

CROSSING OVER

CALL ME MICHAEL

In May of 2000, three of my favorite mediums—Shelley Peck and Suzane Northrop from New York, and Robert Browne from England—joined me for a retreat on one of my favorite islands. I gathered fifty people from all over the country, and a few from as far away as Australia, for a shorts-and-bare-feet event on Barbados. It turned out to be one of the most magical experiences I've ever had.

We did a series of psychic workshops during the day, led by Sandy Anastasi, one of my first mentors, and her husband, John Maerz. And then at night, we divided the participants into four groups—red, blue, green, and orange—for readings by the four mediums. We rotated each night so each group of about twelve would be read by each medium during the week. My hope and goal was that by the end of the retreat, every person would get a message from at least one relative. If I couldn't get something, maybe Suzane would, and if Suzane couldn't maybe Shelley would, and if Shelley couldn't get it, maybe Robert would.

Some phenomenal things happened that week—the first being that my colleagues agreed to join me. It was a lot of work for them, a major commitment of time. For the participants, meanwhile, it was a wonderful, emotionally satisfying bonding experience—both with their loved ones who had passed, and with each other. On the first night, each group was united by a color, but by the fourth, they were like a family. They could recognize each other's relatives when they came through—*no, no, that's your uncle, remember he came through with Shelley the other night?* The energy of these people was fantastic, and the setting was perfect.

One of the people who came was Terri Kaplowitz. She is the grandmother of Mikey DiSabato, the little boy who drowned in his family's swimming pool in 1993 when he was three and a half years old. Mikey and his family had become part of my life in the years since. He had come through many times during readings with his parents, his grandparents, and his aunt. And he felt comfortable enough to visit me regularly on his own. Pretty independent for a three-and-a-half-year-old. But of course, spirits aren't three, or thirty, or any age. They are timeless souls. The finer points of metaphysics aside, Mikey had a special place in my heart, and so did his family. He was Chapter 20 of *One Last Time*. I called it "Mikey and Me." It made his grandma a celebrity at the retreat. Everyone knew the story and wanted to talk to Terri.

"I can't believe how many people are in love with Mikey," she said. What they didn't know was the latest chapter. They were anxious to hear about it, and Terri was eager to share it with them.

In the summer of 1998, Terri had called from her home in Florida, saying she *really* needed to see me. By now I knew this meant that she wanted to connect with Mikey, but it was becoming difficult to do this objectively because I knew him and his family so well. Still, how could I say no to Terri? I told her she was in luck—Sandra and I were going down to Florida in a few weeks. I asked her to beep me the night I was to arrive, and we would set up a time to get together. But the night I was supposed to be in Florida, I called Terri and told her I had missed my flight and would be a day late. What I didn't tell her was the reason I had missed my flight, and why I was coming the next morning. Sandra and I had had a little, uh, disagreement, and I told her to go to Florida without me. Alone that night in my office, a picture of Mikey fell over. I heard a little voice say, "What about my grandma?" Okay, Mikey. I'll make a deal with you. If Sandra calls me in the next half hour, I'll go. No surprise: The phone rings and Sandra says, "John, come down."

I flew to Florida the next morning and arranged to see Terri at her apartment that afternoon. On the drive from my hotel, I began trying to connect with Mikey. I told him that he had come through for his family many times, but I needed him to come through differently this time. I needed validation that I could trust in order for me to do right by his grandmother. When I arrived at Terri's house, I said hello to her daughter Donna and Donna's husband, who were visiting from up north. I looked around for Artie, Mikey's grandfather, but figured he was out playing golf.

We chatted for nearly an hour, then I broke the formalities and attempted a reading. He did come through, but he didn't step forward like I expected him to. Actually, he stepped back and showed me his hand holding the hand of a male figure *above* him. The older male was wearing a military uniform. And then I realized why I hadn't seen Artie when I came in. Mikey was bringing his grandfather through—Terri's husband. "Terri, this can't be," I said, knowing it was. "Mikey is telling me that you lost your husband, and he's bringing him to you."

"Yes," she said sadly. "Artie died last month."

"Terri, I'm so sorry."

For a moment we weren't in a reading. Terri told me that her husband had died on the golf course. "He fell asleep in a golf cart and never woke up," she said. She didn't have a chance to say good-bye, so she called me right after the funeral. Sally, Terri's daughter and Mikey's mom, thought that she should tell me her husband had passed.

"If you don't, he'll think you're testing him," Sally had told her mother. Terri disagreed: "I think John would prefer not to know. If I told him and Dad comes through, John is going to feel he already knew it." I told Terri how right she was. She had given me the cleanest slate to work with. My logical mind told me Artie was out golfing. My psychic mind relied on Mikey.

Artie Kaplowitz was a Korean War veteran who was extremely proud of his military record but was very quiet about it. He had been awarded a Congressional Medal of Honor but never told anyone, even his wife, exactly how he had earned it. All Terri knew was that he lost most of his company. The first time I read them, some of his army buddies came through, walking on a battlefield. Artie never wanted to talk about the details of the war, Terri later told me, but it was the most unforgettable period of his life. So it made perfect sense to her that he would show up a few weeks after his death wearing his uniform but saying nothing more about it.

The first thing Arty wanted her to know, not surprisingly, was that he was with Mikey. That, of course, was what Terri wanted to hear. She was so glad that Donna was there to hear it, and couldn't wait to call Sally to tell her. Sally had told me years earlier that one of the things that disturbed her most was the fear that her little boy was all alone on the other side, with no one to take care of him. My feeling was always that Mikey was doing just fine, and in fact he was taking care of others. I remember that in 1995, Mikey told me during a reading with his aunt that he was going to be busy for a while, "going to school to help children cross over." About three weeks later, the federal office building in Oklahoma City was blown up. Still, no matter how well Mikey had made the transition, the fact that he was with his grandpa would give everyone in the family some comfort about Arty's sudden passing.

"Do you know why I sat here talking to you for an hour?" I asked Terri. "I know you always want to hear from Mikey. On the way over, I was trying to get Mikey's energy, but I couldn't. I kept trying, but it wasn't happening. That's because Arty had to come through." I'm sure Mikey was stepping aside to let his grandpa get his messages through.

Knowing how important validation is, Arty offered Terri plenty. "He's telling me that you said you'd be out of here if anything happened to him. But he says you should stay put." My God, Terri said. I had just repeated word-for-word a conversation she'd had with herself—and hadn't shared with Arty—a few days before he passed.

"You know how sometimes you get feelings, warnings?" Terri said. "The Wednesday before he died, I walked into the closet, and twice a picture flashed through my head of me taking his clothes out. I said, 'Arty, if anything happens to you, I'm outta here.' "

When Terri told the story at the retreat, she talked about how happy she was that her husband and grandson were together. "He's so happy to have his grandpa with him," Terri said. "I always thank you, John, for keeping Mikey alive. And now they're both with me." When I read Terri's group, Mikey came through to say that he would be at an upcoming celebration. Terri said her daughter and son-in-law were planning a big Sweet 16 party for Mikey's big sister, Cara. Mikey said he was coming with his grandpa.

Mikey's appearance on the island was the first time in a while I had heard from him. He had always come through as someone who wanted to grow and accomplish things and do his job—helping children cross over, for instance. So I wasn't surprised when he came through during my reading with Terri's group and said that he now wanted to be called Michael. It was his way of saying he was moving on.

"I feel like we're losing our little boy," I told Terri.

"John," she said, "I absolutely feel the same way." We both got tears in our eyes. "I think they stay with you more at your most vulnerable time," Terri said. "I don't know if you're ever really the same, but I think they say, 'They're okay now. They're functioning. So now I can go on and do my other jobs.' Not that they ever come out of your life."

No, they don't. I heard later that Donna, Mikey's—excuse me, *Michael's*—aunt, had gone for a reading with John Holland, a well-known medium in Massachusetts. Sometime later, the medium heard the voice of a little boy saying, "Tell my mommy I love her hair." He went to his appointment book and picked out Donna's name and called her. "I think this message is for you," he said. And sure enough, when Donna called her sister, Sally told her that she had gotten a new hairstyle and was upset that neither her husband nor her daughter had commented on it.

Mikey's story was so powerful that it inspired a song. It was by Annie Haslam, the former Renaissance singer Rick Korn invited to the World Hunger Year benefit at Town Hall and coaxed onto the stage to sing about angels. After we met that night in November of 1998, Annie took home a copy of the just-released *One Last Time*. Annie was recovering from breast cancer at the time and brought the book to an appointment with her oncologist. In one sitting in the waiting room, she read the chapter about Mikey—and wrote a song about him, which she later recorded. "This song is about the bond between a mother and child and the proof that there really are no boundaries to love, which will always exist between them," Annie wrote in the liner notes of her CD, *The Dawn of Ananda,* an album of songs about angels. "While I was singing this song I felt the presence of Mikey, which I believe you will hear . . ."

It was a beautiful, haunting song called "Precious One":

Unfolding as the storm clears, a woman left more wise
Someone standing by the door, the memory of a child
It feels like many years now, the scent that will not go away
It's really not that long, though, an empty shell, nowhere to play
Precious one, you cannot touch the ones you love now
Precious one, you try to make them see . . .

She knows he is waiting there, will always grace her sleep.
Her questions all answered now, no fear is left inside
Peace of mind returns a perfect gift of life
Precious one, your little hands are pure white wings now
Precious one, your voice at last is heard.

I've always considered song lyrics a great vehicle of communication between the spirit world and the physical one. So often, spirits use them to convey thoughts and emotions more eloquently than we mediums possibly can, sometimes using them as a powerful postscript—Roger's "Kiss and Say Goodbye" to Nicole being the most intense example I've experienced. It's like the difference between Morse code and T. S. Eliot. I found it tremendously rewarding to know that the spirits that have come through me aren't only using music; they're inspiring it.

On the last night of the retreat, we had what I called a "healing circle." Everyone came together and talked about their experiences during the week and what they had learned from them. We laughed and cried, a very therapeutic finale to an affecting week. And then I did something I had not intended to do. Before going to Barbados, I had thought about bringing a certain song by Celine Dion to play at the end of the retreat. But I had decided that it would be too emotional. For me, anyway.

The song is one that I associated with a friend of mine who had died eight months earlier. Clyde Corday was 62 when he died, and he had been with his partner, Patrick, for thirty years. Clyde was a truly compassionate person, funny, with an amazing energy. You couldn't help but love him. Until he got sick, he was very youthful-looking—he reminded me of the actor Nathan Lane.

Sandra and I had met Clyde through a friend when we needed someone to redecorate our house. But it was Clyde's mother who drew us together as friends. We were downstairs, talking about converting the basement into my office space, when Clyde's mother decided to "show up." She was very quick, very powerful—another surprise attack reading.

This is pretty much all you need to know about Clyde: At the height of my gloom in 1999, after I flew home from Dallas with my tail between my legs, I walked into my house to find Clyde and Patrick with a dinner they had prepared for Sandra and me, complete with soothing music and candlelight. When I walked in, Clyde said, "I know you're feeling like what you're doing is not being received well. But I needed to come and do this for you and tell you that you are loved, you're doing the right thing, and you're helping a lot of people. Look at me. I didn't believe in what you did. I thought this was a bunch of malarkey. And then after that day in your basement, I had no choice but to believe in what you did. It took me a couple of weeks to recuperate from that experience, but I'm back, and anytime she wants to come through again, I'm open for it."

A few months later, I was just home from another trip when I heard that Clyde had been diagnosed with terminal cancer. I went straight to the hospital. I hadn't seen him in a while. He looked so old. He opened his eyes and looked at me.

"Hey, Clyde," I said, still standing near the door

"Who are you?" he asked. My heart dropped.

"Clyde, it's John."

"John? John Edward?"

"Yeah, John Edward."

"Shit."

"What's the matter, Clyde?"

"Did I cross over?"

"No, Clyde."

"Good. I just figured you'd be the only person I'd still be able to talk to if I did."

We laughed about it, and I walked over and took his hand. I asked him how he was doing. He looked at me and shook his head. He asked about Sandra, and about my assistant, Carol, and her kids. They're all fine, I said. And how's the Lion King? he asked. I called my friend Joanne "King of the Forest." Clyde could never get it straight and always called her the Lion King. He wanted me to say hi for him. Then he said he was tired and wanted to rest his eyes.

"I think I'm leaving, John," he said.

Driving home from the hospital, I put in Celine Dion's new CD, *All the Way*. Near the end, there was a track called "Live," a song about a beautiful starry night, "not a night to die," and the feeling of wanting to live for the one you love, loving as no one has ever loved before.

I drove home in tears. Listening to these words after saying good-bye to my dying friend just destroyed me. *Live your life as best you can, and love like you've never loved before.* Clyde died soon after that. At the time, I was beginning to write a short novel called *What If God Were the Sun?*. There was only one purely nonfiction passage in the book. It was about Clyde's memorial service.

Packing for the retreat eight months later, I thought of ending the healing circle with the Celine Dion song, but I didn't think I could do it. I left the CD home. One morning I walked down to the house my Uncle Joey was renting for the week of the retreat. It was right outside the hotel complex, and I decided to lay out in the sun next to the pool. He put on a tape he had made, and the song came on. "Johnny, are you listening to this song?" Joey said. I couldn't speak. "Johnny, are you listing to this song? Johnny! You need to play this song at the end of your thing." He didn't know the story behind the song—didn't know I had contemplated bringing it down just for that reason.

"I want to end tonight in a special way," I announced as the healing circle and the retreat drew to a close later that week. "I want to prepare you, because I think it's going to be extremely emotional. But I can't think of any better way for me to end what we've all accomplished here this week." I dimmed the lights, and we all sat in a circle, everyone feeling a connection to the people who were strangers to them six days earlier. They understood the bonds they had lost through death, and the rejoining they felt that week was magic. I started the circle by asking each person to make an acknowledgment of those who had crossed over, and I could feel the emotion rise in the room. When it was my turn, I said, "This is in honor of my friend Clyde." I stopped and tried to get the words out. "I know he's watching us. And the rest of our family and friends who we all have spoken to this week are here watching us."

I started the song, and as it echoed loudly off the walls, everyone in the room started to break down, one by one. There was a woman, a beautiful lady who was always laughing and smiling. Her son committed suicide. She trembled, and everybody around her drew close and hugged her. There were two young women, Kathy and Andrea, both from upstate New York. One had lost her husband, the other her boyfriend. In separate readings, the men they lost came through, but for the partner of the other. They didn't know each other, but it brought them together. As the song played, Kathy started to cry hard, and Andrea ran across the circle and threw her arms around her.

When it was over, I knew I would make retreats both in the United States and abroad part of my life in the coming years. But I knew that this first experience was so perfect that it would forever be special to all of us, both on this side and the other.

THE TALENT

TWO LAST-MINUTE GUESTS had dropped in on the retreat midway through the week. Dana Calderwood came down with Paul Shavelson, the producer he and his partners in Glow in the Dark Productions were trying to bring on to *Crossing Over*. Bonnie Hammer wanted us to be shooting our first shows in six weeks—basically a barn-raising—and Dana was hoping that forty-eight hours in paradise would present Paul with the evidence he needed to bring him into the fold. Meanwhile, Dana brought a portable digital video camera with them to shoot some readings for the show.

Back in New York, Dana and his partner, Shirley Abraham, were well into creating the show by this time. They'd found a studio, had a set designed, and were in the process of forming the backbone of the show's staff, recruiting the producers who would do the day-to-day work of turning out segments that honestly reflected fifteen-minute readings in less than five minutes of tape. This wasn't your regular TV show, so for Shirley and Dana, hiring these producers wasn't as simple as collecting resumés or calling people they had worked with before. The people who would work on *Crossing Over* had to be considered not only for their TV work, but also for their cosmic attitudes. They didn't have to be in the 20 percent who are True Believers. But they couldn't be in the 20 percent on the other end of the scale, either. My usual standard held: Skeptics are fine; cynics need not apply.

Of course, Paul was coming to Barbados with a suitcase of skepticism that had nothing to do with a belief in a conscious afterlife. He was down for that. What he wasn't convinced of was the viability of a television show about the subject hosted by a psychic medium. But it was just that conflict that put him on the plane. He believed in the topic. He was interested in me. And he wanted to see if there was a way to make this marriage work.

Paul found the challenge so irresistible, in fact, that he was blowing off CBS just to have a look. They wanted him for a new show called *Big Brother*. Someone from the network tracked Paul down in the Caribbean and asked him what he was doing there. "I told you," he said. "I'm checking out the psychic." Really? the guy said. "He thought I just told them that as a play for more money," Paul told me later. "They couldn't believe

I was going to do a psychic show on Sci Fi instead of the big network spectacular. They just could not believe it." Paul and I shared a belief in the way the universe works. When people ask me what books they should read about spirit communication and the afterlife, I always tell them to just go to a bookstore—the right books will find them. Paul felt that way about projects. The right ones had a way of finding him. And they were usually not the obvious ones.

Paul watched me read a group the night he arrived, and he was struck by how straightforward the readings were. "It's like you're just a guy giving someone directions—make a left, make a right—just matter-of-factly mapping it out," he told me. "This is no mumbo-jumbo." I didn't have much time to talk to Paul and Dana during the retreat, and I changed my mind about letting them shoot the nighttime readings. It felt like too much of an invasion. Paul didn't care. He wanted to see me in action, and just as important, he wanted to see how the readings affected people. To him, they represented the core audience of *Crossing Over*. He pulled many of them aside and, with Dana rolling the digital camera, talked to them about their readings, trying to understand what was going on between us and whether he could discern from that the essence of the show. "What difference did it mean to you that John knew your father's name—why is that important?" Paul would ask someone. "It wasn't so much that he knew his name," he would be told. "It's the fact that he knew that we used to go shopping at John's Bargain Stores and that he loved clams casino. It means there's this presence. I'm not cut off from him like cold turkey. He's still a part of my life and my growth, my journey."

Paul heard story after story like this—as if this was a big focus group—and by the end of the first night, he knew he would do the show. He says he came into this skeptical, but you could have fooled me. At our first few meetings back in New York, he talked intensely about building the show around the kinds of people he and Dana had met at the retreat. He liked the way I did my work and delivered information, but he thought it was *their* stories—and what viewers might take from them— that would make the show fly. "The readings are the vehicle, and they have to be shown in as genuine a light as possible, but it all has to be with an eye toward connecting the viewers with the spirits in their *own* lives," Paul said. "To show you just making psychic statements that these people react to isn't enough. I'm more interested in the subject of continued consciousness and how to use a psychic medium's talents to deal with grief and make your experience here in this lifetime richer."

Thinking about the unique connection this show might have with its viewers—and how the people in the studio could be seen as their surrogates—it occurred to Paul that calling them an "audience" didn't do justice to their role. He had an idea. Let's call it the "gallery," he suggested. "Each person you read will be a portrait in the gallery." Everyone loved the idea.

Paul was on a roll. The only obstacles for him now were his other clients. He was in New York helping create a show about people connecting with their loved ones, who happened to be dead, when he was supposed to be in California making specials for the TV Guide Channel about celebrities still very much alive. Paul is the type of person who loves to become completely consumed by a project and then complain about how overwhelmed he is.

One night after a meeting, I offered him a ride home to Long Island, and we wound up sitting on the FDR Drive for two hours waiting for a car fire to be cleared. It was the first quality time I'd had with Paul, and we spent it, naturally, talking about the show. It was the beginning of what became regular commutes to and from the city, during which we got to know each other's backgrounds and motivations, and discovered we shared the same irreverent sense of humor. I began to feel that Paul's energy was like manna from heaven. Paul was right: He was perfect for the show. It wasn't just that his vision was the same as mine. It was that he helped clarify what my vision *was,* and how we could get it to the screen. I loved the irony of the short shrift Paul had given me two years earlier when I called him trying to get on his *Fox After Breakfast* show. "You blew me off," I razzed him. He denied ever having talked to me—that was his story, and he was sticking to it.

During one of our rides, I got some insight into why Paul seemed to have such a deep feeling about this show. Five years earlier, he had gone through the devastating loss of his father, Marty. Paul cherished his father, and even after he passed, he felt his presence in his life every day. "He was a pharmacist," Paul said one day during a conversation for this book. "And he totally had purpose in his life. He grew up on top of his father's drugstore, and he opened up that store at seven o'clock in the morning and closed it at ten o'clock at night. He was just a beautiful person. When I got into my thirties and forties, we didn't spend a lot of time together, but we were connected daily. We'd talk on the phone two or three times a week, and his energy and spirit were with me. And it really didn't change much after he passed. Of course I grieved. But when I think about him, I still get inspired by him, and I still feel his love and his commitment to me. So when I was thinking about what the show was about, I had a very personal experience to draw from."

In television, anyone who gets in front of a camera is known as "the talent." Paul got right away that while it was an unusual talent that got me here, I wasn't to be confused with an entertainer. I wasn't doing this for the money, and I sure wasn't doing it for the fame. As corny as it sounds, I was doing it to reach people, so many more than I could by doing what I was already doing. Of course I wanted a lot of people to watch the show, but what concerned me most were the lives that the show would touch. At an early meeting, I introduced everyone to my favorite phrase: "Honor the process." I expected it to be the guiding principle of the show. No matter what pressures they felt from the network or from within themselves, no matter what the numbers were, they had to resist whatever TV instincts they had to do anything hokey or exploitative. "You really don't care about TV," Paul said in the car one day, as if I were a member of some species he'd never encountered before. "That's why this is going to work."

With Paul's arrival, Ramey and Adora felt ready to cut the cord. "It was like an open adoption," Adora said, "where we all just kind of sat in a circle and said, okay, this baby is yours now. Call us, keep in touch, let us know what we can do."

The baby needed a roof over its head. Shirley found an available studio on the West Side of Manhattan, a converted old theater at the corner of Ninth Avenue and 55th Street that had once been the home of *Sesame Street*. It wasn't fancy, but it seemed somehow fitting that it was a big old place with history. I wouldn't be surprised if the ghosts of actors and actresses from the twenties started coming through. My dressing room had one of those star mirrors with lights around it and a barber's chair where Maddy the makeup artist would use Preparation H to hide the lines on my face that were sure to develop after three straight days of shooting. The dressing room was upstairs. If you went across the hall and through a door, you found yourself in the dark, looking down at the set from a wide-open area filled with unused lighting and camera equipment. It took a few seconds to realize you were standing in the old theater's balcony.

Shirley and Dana rented a floor of office space down the block. The first time I went to the office, I looked around and realized I was seeing an entire company of people in offices and cubicles, everyone on the phones or at computers or in little meetings, getting ready to help me put the work out there. This was my dream: to teach about spirit communication on a big scale. And now it was a reality. At least for thirteen weeks.

Dana's main task these months was to create the show's look. He knew it couldn't be set up like a traditional talk show. Applying Paul's gallery concept, his first thought was to borrow a look he remembered from the Broadway show *Candide*. It had little pockets of audience on and around the stage. For *Crossing Over,* he had in mind an asymmetrical set with stairs and assorted platforms holding gallery members. The idea was that I would go from place to place as the energies drew me from one area to another. But the lighting and set designers talked Dana out of it, saying it would be almost impossible to shoot, with all those different light patterns and camera angles. Eventually, he settled on a lit disk as my stage—inspired by the set he worked with on Nickelodeon's *Double Dare*—and the gallery members sitting in a semicircle in three or four rows of these sort of built-in cushioned benches.

Dana had a model made of the set and brought some Polaroid shots of it when he came to Barbados with Paul. We sat poolside in bathing suits as I flipped through the pictures, looking at them blankly and saying nothing. Dana took my nonreaction to mean I hated the design and that he was going to have to start all over, a frightening thought at this stage. But what he was actually seeing was my mind being blown. The first thing I noticed was that all around the set were large, irregularly shaped swatches of stretched nylon. These white "sails" would be backdrops, and the two biggest ones, front and center, would serve as screens to project the first few seconds of taped pieces as segues. When I do a reading, I focus on something blank—a wall, a floor—so that when I see quick flashes of information, they're not overlaid on a busy image. It's like seeing it on a movie screen. The set Dana had designed had these all over the studio. No matter where I looked, I would see these clean white sails. But I hadn't talked to him about the set design—hadn't even had one conversation—so he had no idea that the one he came up with fulfilled my only need. I told Dana that not only did I like the set, I thought it was perfect.

The show would be made up of three basic elements. Readings in the gallery would be the centerpiece. Then there would be private one-on-one readings that would be shot on the set but without an audience. Some of these would be with celebrities. And then the producers would do what they were calling "post-analyses," when they took the people who had been read into a separate room and asked them to explain the messages that came through, what made sense and what didn't, and to talk about the loved ones who came through and what the experience meant to them. They would be sent home with a prepaid FedEx® envelope to send us pictures that we could use in the finished segment. Dana came up with a creative way to keep the whole thing running efficiently. The post-analyses would be shot in evocative black and white, while the main cameras were upstairs shooting the next gallery segment.

There was only one big question left. The co-host question.

I wasn't the only one who believed I shouldn't be alone out there. Dana agreed that I needed a second banana, as he put it quaintly. Apparently buying into the "Honor the process" theme, he said he wanted to keep me from having to "sell soap." He thought all the TV stuff would be bad for my credibility, and the show's. Paul thought so, too. He wanted someone to act as a buffer—a "facilitator." They weren't thinking of a crazy cutup like Todd Pettengill. More like a combination of George Feneman, Groucho's straight man on *You Bet Your Life,* and the guy outside the courtroom in *People's Court.* And they were thinking this person ought to be a woman. One of the ideas he and Paul came up with was to have the facilitator whispering things like, "We'll be right back with more of this reading," as I continued talking in the gallery in the background. Dana called this the golf-announcer idea. It grew out of a discussion about how we could make the show look and be more authentic and you-are-there, and less packaged and edited. Doing the show live was even considered for a few seconds.

Facilitator, co-host—whatever you call it, Bonnie Hammer was still dead-set against having anyone on the stage but me. She let Paul and Dana interview people and even shoot some test shows with someone doing all the housekeeping. But in the end, she insisted, "This is your show. Don't dilute it. I don't want a sidekick, I don't want someone for you to bounce humor off. You are funny enough, you are honest enough, you are interesting enough."

I begged to differ. Really—I begged. "I'm not an actor, I'm not a performer," I protested. "I won't be any good at this." I resisted until the last possible moment, coming up with every excuse imaginable until they practically had to throw me out there to get me to read the openings and closings and segues for our rehearsal and test shows. Charles Nordlander, the show's writer, tried to make them easy and casual, and Dana explained why I had to do it. "You need to have at least a moment to make a connection with the audience," Dana said. "You can't just go out and start doing readings." But I couldn't see how reading from a TelePrompTer would make a connection with anyone.

Finally, we compromised. "You don't have to come out and read," Dana said. "You can just talk to the gallery, and we'll capture that. Just go out there and explain what you're going to do." That I could handle. I'd been doing that in my lectures for years. Eventually, after a bunch of rehearsal shows, they got me to introduce taped segments and give the show a final thought by sitting among the gallery and reading what Charles had written for me on the TelePrompTer. Charles was working hard to capture my voice and make the introductions natural, and even I was beginning to see their value. The openings, closings, and segment introductions he wrote gave the readings context and the show more meaning. There was some discussion of whether there should be a "writer" listed in the credits that rolled at the end of each show. For the producers, as well as the network, the show's credibility was the undercurrent of virtually every decision they made. They wanted to avoid even a subtle implication that the show might be cooked up. It didn't take a rocket scientist to figure out that if the show got any attention at all, that's what skeptics, reporters, and viewers would be looking for. Would listing a "writer" suggest a lack of spontaneity, or even that the readings were staged?

It was the kind of question that the producers realized could come up again and again and only bog the show down in other people's cynicism. There was no reason to hide the fact that the few seconds of material that were obviously not spontaneous—and which had nothing to do with the authenticity of the readings—were written by someone other than me. I've always said I would not defend my work because if I did I would be conceding that it needed to be defended. The same would go for the show. It was smart to be careful about how things were presented. But as long as it was done right, I would have nothing to defend.

— CHAPTER 9 —

CAMERA ONE CLOSES IN

WHAT *IS* THIS?

On the morning of June 14, 2000, I stood in the darkness outside the white sails cloaking the set of the first television show devoted to communication with the dead. My eyes were trained on Doug Fogal, the stage manager. He had been stage manager for *The Lion King* on Broadway, among many other things, and a couple of months earlier he had gotten a call from his old friend Dana Calderwood asking if he wanted to work on a TV show with a psychic. Why not, Doug said. It's a job. *Three . . . two . . . one. . . .*

Doug pointed to me, and I bounded out for the first time before a live gallery and cameras rolling tape, knowing that some of what was about to happen would find its way onto television screens across the country. *Crossing Over with John Edward* was launched, and my life would never be the same. Even if the show were a colossal flop, more people would see me in a single night than in a lifetime of lectures.

I managed to get through the opening, and welcome the first official gallery, and by extension, the first few hundred thousand viewers, or whatever number would be tuned in to Sci Fi or stopping by on their way to a tearjerker on Lifetime or spinning wheels on the Game Show Channel. I rubbed my hands together, focused on the sail beyond the last row, and silently delivered the welcome to the *other* gallery, the one that really counted.

The first few weeks I felt like a little kid bicycling with training wheels and still falling every time I turned. But as Ramey pointed out, we were starting out in relative obscurity—compared to the syndication she had been shooting for, we were practically doing this in private—so if there was a time to tumble, get back on the bike, and find my balance, this was it.

I wasn't the only one trying to find my way—there was a whole staff of people trying to find my way. And theirs. We were all struggling to figure out how to do a show that was so different from anything ever attempted on television that most of the fifty-six people hired to produce it weren't even sure what this was. If I was so psychic that I could read everyone's mind, here's what I would have heard those first weeks: *Is this for real?* That's what a lot of them were asking each other in private conversations. Jim Scurty, a camera operator for thirty-one years, pulled

Dana aside and asked for the truth: "Is this on the level, or is it a gimmick?" Dana basically told him that all he had to do was look through his camera lens. Eventually, he'd see the truth for himself. A few people on the staff wondered if they were participating in a hoax so sophisticated that no one working on the show knew about it. One crew member took producer Allison Blecker aside and asked bluntly, "Allison, is this bullshit?" She said she didn't think so, but she really didn't know. Not yet.

Allison was recruited to work on *Crossing Over* when she was a producer on *The Aimsley Harriet Show,* "a dancing chef singing variety show," as she described it, that was ending after a one-year run on NBC. She got a call from Paul Shavelson, with whom she had worked on the Fox breakfast shows. "Want to work on a weird show?" Paul asked. Allison wouldn't have expected anything less from Paul

"All right, keep your mind open," Paul said. "It's this guy. He speaks to the dead."

"Oh, great, Paul," Allison said. "From a dancing chef to a guy who speaks to the dead."

Allison had two reasons for not wanting to work on the show, and only one in favor. The upside was Paul. She loved working with him, as it seemed everyone did. The downsides were that she had a big, big problem with death—didn't want to think about it, and definitely did not want to work with it—and two, she didn't believe there was a guy who speaks to the dead. "I can't think of a more depressing show to work on, people all the time saying, 'My son died, my daughter died,'" Allison told Helen Tierney, her colleague at the dancing chef show, who had also worked with Paul, and also got a call from him wanting to know if she wanted to work on the guy-who-talks-to-dead-people show.

"I was totally skeptical," Allison recalled during a conversation for this book. "Not cynical, because I wanted to believe it so bad. But I was so afraid that I was going to manipulate these people who were grieving. I knew Paul would never work on something cheesy. But I came from a place where I just didn't believe this stuff. I vaguely thought, *Oh wow, that would be so amazing if that was possible.* But what's the trick? There must be a trick. There's either a trick or we're going to have to get in there and give him information. I thought maybe Paul was getting involved in something that, you know, we'll find out when we get there."

Helen had been going to psychics for years. "She was like, 'Yeah, I'm in,'" Allison said. "I'm like, 'You're in? Wait a second.'" Helen told her to think about it. So she thought about it and figured she'd give it a month. "Worse comes to worse, if I think it's completely bogus, if I feel like we're taking advantage of these poor people, then I'll just leave. I think the major thing that made me decide to give it a try was that I really, really hoped I would be convinced that it was true. I am afraid to die. Time is going so fast, and there's nothing else when you die. So my reasons for coming here were completely personal. It had nothing whatsoever to do with television. It was: Imagine if he can completely make me believe that there is something else, and that the fear I've had my whole entire life would somehow go away."

When I first met Allison, I thought she wasn't going to last on the show. She really looked like she was in the wrong 20 percent. But her attitude began to change after she saw me work live for the first time. The tapes she had seen were intriguing, she said, but not convincing. Weeks before we started taping, Allison and her associate producer, Christine Cipriani, walked up the block to the studio to watch a rehearsal show. "The two of us were like, yeah, whatever, we'll watch this gallery. And then we were bawling, we were completely crying in the gallery. I was just completely amazed by the things that came through. Like crazy, specific things. In my whole life, there was never anything that ever made me believe this was even a slight possibility. And then in one second . . . I mean, it's hard to erase thirty-two years of being a complete skeptic. But you can open your eyes a little bit." Months later, she said, "I wouldn't believe it if I didn't work on the show myself."

With half the first season already shot, we finally got on the air in July, and that was like turning on a switch. The mail started coming in, people wanted tickets to the gallery or to get one-on-one readings, and the show began to gather energy and take on a certain rhythm. A little before nine o'clock three mornings a week, the day's gallery would line up outside the studio doors on Ninth Avenue. Then Jesse Shafer, our friendly gallery coordinator (and an aspiring actor who came in one day and announced he had gotten a bit part in an episode of *Law & Order*), would bring our guests inside, get them seated, and tell them what the show was all about. Then Maddy would make me up, and Risa, the wardrobe stylist, would present me with my clothes for the day. I would take the stage at around ten and welcome my first guest from the other side.

The goal was to get three half-hour shows (twenty-two minutes of actual show, leaving room for eight minutes of commercials) out of each day's gallery. Paul, Shirley, and Dana had devised a system of leapfrogging producers that was a marvel of efficiency and order—as long as those in the great beyond stayed with the program. Which, of course, was something that couldn't be counted on. "Can we go now? They're starting," I've said to Dana more than once, standing on the set and talking to him in the control room as we prepared to start shooting. As Charles wrote one day, the real control room is on the other side—not an easy concept for producers used to scheduling everything down to the bathroom breaks.

On any given day of shooting, three producers—Allison, Helen, and Lisa Tucker—were responsible for one show each. The way it worked was that the producer of the first show, say it's Allison, would sit in the back row of the control room watching the first series of gallery readings on a monitor, scribbling copious notes of everything being said. After two or three readings, Shirley would turn around and ask Allison, "Do you have a show?" At the first break, Allison and her associate producer would dash from the control room to the set to pull out the people who had just been read. They would escort them behind some curtains, through a door, and down a narrow stairway to a small room where they would do the "post-analysis," or simply the "posts," as they became known. These were whole new terms in the psychic medium field. These were debriefings with cameras. *What did the blue sweater mean? Did you understand when John talked about the sonogram on the refrigerator? How did it make you feel connecting with your son?*

Allison would interview the people in black and white, while upstairs I would be back with the gallery in living color, doing the next set of readings for the second half-hour show. Those would be the responsibility of the next producer, Lisa, who would take the seat in the control room just vacated by Allison and begin taking notes on what *she* was seeing on the monitor. When Lisa had enough for a show, she'd grab the people in the gallery who had just been read and do her posts, while Helen took her seat in the control room and repeated the process once more. Mediumship for the masses.

This system yielded plenty of good readings—and not all of them were for the people in the gallery. In case anyone was under the impression that spirits knew and cared that we were making a TV show here— a show whose credibility we wanted to establish quickly and firmly—they wasted no time setting everyone straight. We had a hundred people in the gallery, but we also had half that number working on and around the set and in the control room. The inevitable happened almost immediately. One day, an older male figure came through claiming he had developed some kind of technical device.

"I have a cousin who worked on a water purifier," a man in the gallery said.

"No," I said. "This is some kind of health-care procedure. Invasive surgical practice or procedure."

I looked around the gallery. No takers. Then a voice from beyond. "My godfather worked on the first heart transplant." I looked up and saw that it was Doug, the stage manager. I just laughed and shook my head. "Nobody's safe."

"Has he passed?" I asked. Doug said yes.

"Godfather's here." Just then, another spirit stepped forward. I felt that Doug's godfather was there as an escort. "But I feel like he needs to announce what he's known for."

"That would be my godfather," Doug said wryly.

"By the way, he almost didn't get credit for that transplant thing. I feel like he was passed up."

"The credit went to someone else," Doug acknowledged. (When he was posted later—yes, everyone gets posted, even the posters—Doug explained that his godfather was a cardiovascular thoracic surgeon as well as a mechanical engineer. When the first heart transplants were being performed in the 1960s, his godfather developed a machine that kept patients alive during the few minutes when they had no heart. Doug said his godfather was "very egocentric and didn't feel that he got the credit he deserved.")

The person Doug's godfather was bringing with him had an even stronger energy. This was a younger male who was acknowledging either a Marge or Maggie and who wanted to thank Doug for "taking care of his art." As Doug later explained, the person coming through was a friend named Michael, an artist who died of AIDS. Maggie was Michael's close friend—"like his wife but not his wife," Doug said—who had nursed him as he was dying. Doug and his partner had loved a reproduction Michael made of a painting by Donald Roller Wilson, an artist known for his oil paintings of chimps in dresses. The one they liked was a picture of a chimp named "Naughty Betty," dressed like a woman with a huge floral headdress and pickles flying through the air. Doug commissioned Michael to reproduce another of Wilson's paintings, but then Michael got sick and never finished it. After he passed, Maggie gave Doug and his partner Michael's original "Naughty Betty" reproduction. They had it framed and put it up in a featured spot in their front room.

There were several other major validations, thanks to Michael being as demonstrative in spirit as he was in body. He showed me a cat being held by its tail so I would talk about how everyone despised his cat. And he got me to flip my wrist in a swatting motion, a mannerism that Doug said was a perfect rendition of "Michael's 'don't even . . .' gesture." After we wrapped that day, Doug went home and called Maggie and told her, "Michael came to visit me at work today."

IT WAS LIKE THIS throughout the first two months of the show's life, one staff member after another doing their jobs on the set or in the control room and slowly realizing that the names and details coming from my mouth were not for anyone in the gallery. Some of the more veteran crew members came into this job thinking they had seen and done it all. The work had long since lost its glamour. Jim Scurty, a camera operator for thirty-one years, and a multiple Emmy winner, had heard that this was a talk show with a medium. *Fine, whatever. It's a job.* I'll never forget the sight of Jim peeking out from behind his camera viewfinder and saying, "Uh, I knew a guy in high school named Gaspare who committed suicide."

One day a few months later, I was getting some information that included a name that sounded like Gehrig without the last "g." Like Garesh. When no one claimed the information, Dana broke in over the studio speaker, saying that he thought that Garesh was the first name of the father of one of our associate producers, Nina Bhargava. Nina's father had been to the show when we needed people for the gallery in the beginning, and Dana had met him and remembered his name. Nina was usually in the studio, but today for some reason she was back at the production office up the street, where Dana called from the control room. "John's saying your dad's name," he told her.

"What?" Nina said. "I just got off the phone with him."

"You have to come down here."

"Oh, God. What if it's not me? All these people will be staring at me."

Nina ran down 55th Street to the studio and came out onto the set still wearing her coat. "I think your dad's dad is coming through," I told her. But Nina said she didn't know him and would have trouble with names and details. Someone brought a phone out, and Nina called her father. The only thing bad about these spontaneous phone calls is Call Waiting.

"I'm on the phone with EZ Pass," Nina's father told her. The next thing Nina heard was a dial tone. She called him back and told him what was going on. I passed on the information I was getting. Some of it was from an older brother of Nina's father who died when Garesh was five or six, when the family was in India. Her father was able to validate it.

These neighborhood excursions didn't have to involve someone connected to the show. One day, I was badgering a poor group of women who were sitting in the back row, diagonally to my left. I couldn't understand how they didn't know that they had a male to the side who passed in a car accident who was making references to someone named Richard, another named Tony or maybe Timmy, and that there was a connection to a teacher, to a falls somewhere, and to the number 16. "Guys, please think," I implored. I was sure of the information, and pretty sure of the area of the gallery it was meant for. "I'm in the back row. Or I'm behind them. Is there anyone behind them?" But the women in the back row just kept shaking their heads. They couldn't validate a single thing. And there was nobody behind them. Finally, the energy was brushed aside by others trying to come through. I just left the information with the women and asked them to please go home and try to validate this unfortunate soul who was trying so hard to make a connection. I went with the other readings.

At the end of the show, Dana came over the PA: "John, I think we figured out what was going on in the back row," he said. Just then, Paul came onto the set with a man wearing a red parking attendant's shirt. His name was Basil, and he worked in the garage adjoining the studio. "The garage attendant thinks this might be his story, so can you just spend a couple of seconds with him?" Paul asked.

I was totally baffled. "Um, how did . . .uh." My stammering made the gallery giggle. "What exactly did they explain to you?" I asked Basil. "What did they say?"

"You're getting a signal there's a Richard involved," Basil said in a strong Jamaican accent. "It happened when he was sixteen."

"Okay, wait. Explain to me why you think this makes sense for you."

"I have a brother Richard who died at sixteen in a car accident," Basil said. "I was a teacher in Jamaica."

There was a collective gasp from the gallery. I just stood there, agape.

"I was teaching at the school that he was attending," Basil continued. "A particular evening, he was riding his bike and he got in an accident and hit his head on the asphalt and died."

I had to know how this happened. "Who found Basil?" I asked the producers.

"Tjeerd," someone said. He was one of the production assistants.

"That's damn impressive," I said.

"John, we *work* with you," Paul said, as if nothing was impressive anymore. All in a day's work here at *Crossing Over.*

Tjeerd explained that he had been watching me point toward the women in the back row, and noticed that I didn't seem to be pointing right at them. It was more like past them—and in fact, at one point, I did ask if there was anyone behind them. "I felt compelled—*compelled*—to go out the back door, where you were pointing," Tjeerd said. His first stop was a group of police officers who were standing on 55th Street. He related the information about the male who had passed in the accident, and asked if this made sense to any of them. No, this didn't make any sense to them. In more ways than one. Then, Tjeerd went a few steps down the street, to the parking garage. That's where he found Basil. Stunned, he recounted his brother's passing.

"Wow," I said, then turned to the women in the back row. "You're definitely off the hook." I turned back to Basil and asked him who had the "T" name.

"My brother. His name is Tonto."

Back to the gallery: "Was there anything we missed?" We were rolling tape, of course, but there was an after-show informality to this.

"Falls," people called out.

"Any type of falls connection?" I asked Basil, but as soon as the question left my lips, I had the answer. "Oh—Dunns River Falls. That's freaky, even for me. I think the hair on my legs is standing up. I think you've seen the ultimate pull-in. I've never gone through a brick wall before."

What was amazing about this for me was how it drove home how *not* about me this process is. I dropped the ball for Basil's brother. And Tjeerd, a production assistant, picked it up because Basil's brother saw his opportunity to get this message through. You could almost imagine him handing Tjeerd a little note and then whispering, "Would you mind going next door and giving this to my brother?"

Then there was the wild morning when I was getting all kinds of information but no clue to where I was supposed to go with it. Nobody in the gallery was acknowledging it, and I wasn't being pulled anywhere. Then Dana came on the studio speaker and said that it might be for someone in the control room. I looked at the gallery and said, "Don't go anywhere." I hustled back to the control room, cameraman in tow, like one of those routines on Jay or Dave. When I got there, I saw Paul, and he had this half-smile on his face.

"Who's the Merv or Marv?" I said.

"My dad was Marty," Paul said. He had been listening in the control room and connected with enough that he had one of those "Well, it could be for me" moments. Later, when the tables were turned and Paul sat in the post-analysis interview chair, he said he was both dreading and awaiting this moment. "I was very scared this was happening," he said. "I was trying to push it away because I don't want this show to be part of my personal experience, but part of my professional experience and what's best for the show. And I'm thinking while this is going down, *Well, I'm not going to use this on air because this is not going to add to the credibility of what John does.* On the other side of my brain, I'm thinking, *Well, screw the credibility, my father's coming through!*"

But it wasn't Marty after all. I went out of the control room to continue the search. I wound up back on the set, talking to the control room again over the speakers. Now I got a Kimberly. We have a producer named Kimberly Dunn, who was back in what we were now calling the out-of-control room. But we quickly ruled her out. "Who's to your left?" I asked from the disk, not wanting to make another trip back there.

"Liz," Kim said. "Liz Arias." She's our coordinating producer, the one who takes care of, basically, everything. Now the camera was back in there.

"Pass the mike to Liz," I said. "Liz, are you in the corner?" She was. "It's for you," I said.

It wasn't. Now Dana had the scene in the control room projected onto the big white sail behind me. "Oh, how cool," I said, momentarily distracted from the ongoing confusion. Be careful what you ask for: I had stressed to the producers that I didn't want the show edited in such a way that all the viewers saw was a highlight reel every night, all hits all the time. I wanted them to see reality: Sometimes I'm right, sometimes I'm wrong. Well, this could be a highlight reel of the other kind. All confusion. The camera following me on this ludicrous search for someone willing to claim a Merv, five siblings, and a "C" name. Of course, a cynic watching this—or any of the other psychic treasure hunts that were becoming almost commonplace around our set—would think these were the most ridiculous charades. But what we say at the beginning of the show is true. It's all real.

Just about the only person left was Helen Tierney, who was sitting in the control room taking notes for her show when she realized what she was writing made sense to her. "This might be all your fault," I joked, looking at her projected image on the sail.

"I'm so sorry," she said, embarrassed to find that she was now starring in her own segment. Would she have to post herself?

As I gave her information, she started to cry, and I could see somebody's hand rubbing her back. I couldn't imagine what this must be like for all these people on the staff who were being read, having to go back to work after these emotional experiences. It got to the point where everyone—camera operators, producers, utility guys, security guards—would come to work wondering if this was their day to hear from Grandma. Some started brushing up on family history, just in case. They saw what it was like when I got in someone's face, insisting that they had an older female named Sarah with a beagle named after a car. Cameramen would have to focus both on their subjects and on my words—just in case. Even Bonnie Hammer, the head of Sci Fi, was not immune. She sat in the gallery one day and had to stand up in front of the national audience that she was personally trying to build, and have me tell her that her ex-father-in-law was here saying, "I knew the marriage wasn't going to last."

After a few months, it seemed that the only people on the staff whom I was in regular contact with but hadn't read were Shirley Abraham, Charles Nordlander, and Jesse Shafer. They joked that they should start wearing big badges that said "U." They were the Unread.

Working on *Crossing Over* means knowing that at any given moment you might wind up crying on the job. There have been readings that have left nearly everyone in the control room in tears, passing around the box of tissues Liz always has on hand. One of the most unforgettable moments since we've been on the air—one that brought a flood of letters and e-mails—was a reading of a young widow named Catherine, whose brother and husband came through together. Her brother had died at thirteen, and her husband, Steve, at thirty-two. Catherine had a young daughter named Megan, who was not yet three when her father died of lymphoma in 1996. They'd had difficulty conceiving, and for them, Megan was a beautiful gift. Steve "adored Megan, he lived and breathed Megan," Catherine said later. Catherine had been dating someone when she came to the show, and she was nervous. She desperately wanted to hear from Steve, but she was worried he would disapprove of her seeing someone, let alone that she was contemplating marriage. Steve put her at ease, coming through with a literal symbol: a green light.

But it was Steve and Megan who had everyone in tears. In this work, I try not to evaluate the relative tragedy of deaths or judge the weight of their loved ones' grief. But two kinds of death are particularly heart-breaking: One is that of a child and the grief of the parents. And the other is the death of a young parent, and the loss, not yet completely felt, suffered by a young child. I don't know about you, but, like I said, I wouldn't even want to think about which is worse.

"Why is Niagara Falls significant?" I asked Catherine.

"We were just there," she said.

"You were just in Niagara Falls. Okay."

"With my daughter."

I concentrated in silence for a few seconds. Catherine's husband was showing me something important.

"Did you find a feather there?" I asked her.

"Yes, and . . ." Catherine was crying.

"Did you tell your daughter that was from Daddy?"

"Yes." She buried her face in her hands.

"This is a validation that he was there for you. Because he's showing me the feather." I told Catherine it was a good thing that feathers are my mother's symbol to me. She leaves feathers for me. "That was definitely him there for her."

"Thank you," Catherine said. She later told us that she and Megan had gone to Niagara Falls to visit friends of hers and Steve's from college. Catherine and Steve met in college and had gone to Niagara Falls to visit these friends. They hadn't seen each other since Steve passed.

"By acknowledging stuff like that to her, it's allowing her to know that even though Dad's not here physically with her, spiritually he's still connected. So that she's moving through. She's not going to feel like she doesn't have him."

But perhaps no one has been more moved than Jim Scurty, the camera operator who came in thinking this was just another talk-show job. He took the job because it was a job and he liked working with Dana. He barely even noticed what the show was about. Pretty much point and shoot. And then the weirdest thing happened. It occurred to him that this job was changing his life.

In the gallery one day was the family of a fourteen-year-old boy named Louis Acompora, who had died in a freak accident a year earlier when a lacrosse ball hit him in the chest between heartbeats. Louis was an exceptional kid, and his death devastated his school and community. His mother, father, and sister were in the gallery, and when I started validating Louis's presence, they became understandably very emotional. Their pain struck a chord that no one on the show will ever forget. As I gave them the facts and details that Louis was giving me—ultimately that he died from an impact to the chest but not from a weapon—Jim Scurty's camera was trained on the father.

"This man was bottled up with death," Jim recalls. "I was shooting the close-up and watching the expression on his face, watching him begin to fall apart. First the tick and then the trembling in the chin and the kind of embarrassment, the eyes shifting while seeing if anybody's watching. And I literally watched this person fall into this grief and surrender to it publicly. It was very hard to watch."

Jim continued shooting through his own tears. It wasn't the only time that he was left emotionally drained by what he photographed. Sometimes he would walk up to people in the gallery when we were finished taping and put his arm around them, offering some comforting words. Paul loved this—all these seemingly jaded crew guys falling into a job that made them go home and tell the people in their lives how much they loved and appreciated them.

I'M OVER HERE

I BEGAN TO REALIZE SOMETHING VERY COOL. I was forming a really special bond with the producers and crew members of the show. It felt a little like the way I connect with spirits, by raising my own vibrations as they lower theirs so we can meet somewhere in the middle. These were *TV people*, but there wasn't an ounce of cynicism in them. They were real people who wanted to do a meaningful show. And I was a *psychic medium guy*, but I wasn't so serious that I couldn't have fun with it or appreciate the bizarre nature of what we were doing. I mean, a TV show about universal spirituality? Forget *Millionaire* or *Survivor* or *The Weakest Link*. This was like a cosmic game show. We joked about the promo lines: *Whose dead relative is going to come through tonight? What's going to be today's Big Validation? Stay tuned as* Crossing Over *continues.*

Right from the start, we knew we were doing something really different. Something so affecting it could make you cry the fifth time you saw it. And something so funny even the grieving widow had room to smile. Tissue boxes everywhere—onstage, backstage, and in the control room. And the staff keeping a *Crossing Over* Quote Board. "When you marry someone, you marry their family. Even their dead family." I began holding ballroom-dance classes for the staff on the set after each taping. Producers pairing up with security guards, the assistant director with the stage manager, as a Latin beat played over the sound system—nobody could recall doing that on their previous jobs. It was a way of bringing us together.

And yet, none of us was so naïve that we didn't feel the inevitable clash of cultures that was in the air these early months. The network didn't completely buy my operating principle that we weren't really making a TV show; we were just televising what I do. Even if all the people working with me on the show believed that—which they didn't, at least not at first—they couldn't completely ignore either pressures from above or their own impulses to *do TV*. In other words, to do what producers do—orchestrate, arrange, plan, *control*. In this case, it meant occasionally doing those things to the makeup of the gallery to maximize the chances that good, dramatic, and packageable stories would emerge.

The operative concept was Theme Show. Bring in the golf announcer: *John Edward doesn't know it, but he's walking into a gallery filled with people who have had organ transplants. When we come back, we'll see if their donors come through.*

Paul was an amazingly creative producer who loved to have fun and try new things—it's more or less why he was doing the show in the first place—and his initial instincts were that there were *a lot* of cool things you could do with this. Nothing that would compromise the integrity of my work or the credibility of the show. Just *cool ideas*. But done responsibly. So the producers called organizations of people in dangerous lines of work—the police and firefighters' associations, the movie stuntmen's union—and asked if they would be willing to supply some grieving friends and relatives of members who had died in the line of duty. *Click.* They invited members of Mothers Against Drunk Driving to the gallery. Theme shows. The studio wanted them, and the producers couldn't see why not. It's the way things were done.

To me, this was dangerous territory—the biggest, thorniest, and most persistent issue associated with this project since Ramey had first pitched it. It's important to state very clearly that the danger wasn't deception or fraud. There was never, ever any suggestion from anybody that we do the kind of thing Elmer the infomercial man wanted to do a year earlier—feed me information and try to get me to make the host cry. Those guys weren't even living on the same planet as the people working on *Crossing Over*. It was decided very early on that we would state before every show that I am never given information in advance about people I read. In the TV industry, each show has its "bible," something that captures the essence or guiding principle of the show. That assurance was our bible. So, no, the danger of orchestrating the makeup of a gallery was not a perception of trickery. It was that the show would no longer be about the work. It would be about TV. We wouldn't be honoring the process. And we might be getting a little too close to playing God.

"Do you want to play the game of whose death experience is more important?" I asked Paul during one of our drives into the city. "Do you really want to get involved in that?"

Paul considered this for a moment. "That's a scary thought," he said. But rolling tape without having any idea what you'll find on it at the end of the day? Even scarier.

"So you mean like if on Elvis's birthday we had an audience full of Elvis impersonators, you would have a problem with that?" Paul asked, deadpan.

"How sick are you?" I replied, laughing hysterically as we drove on the Long Island Expressway. "We're talking about dead people here!"

Paul was kidding, of course, but he wasn't kidding. He knew that some studio person somewhere would be thinking, *Hmm, Elvis imper-sonators—I can promote that.* They wanted something they could blurb in *TV Guide.* Wasn't "man talks to dead people" enough?

At first, I dealt with this by not dealing with it. All I said was: Don't tell me what you're doing. Just make sure it's not horrible. And if it's a celebrity, don't put anything on paper that I might come across, and of course don't talk about it in front of me. Once I walked into an office and saw a board listing ideas for segments. I stopped, turned, and literally ran out. I think it's safe to assume that none of these producers had ever worked on a show in which they constantly had to be on guard against telling the host what was going on—on orders from the host. They took this seriously. I found myself walking into offices and having people abruptly stop talking. I don't think they were planning a surprise party for me. I would find out soon enough what they were talking about.

One day I walked out onto the disk, and was overwhelmed by an incredibly heavy, depressing, negative energy. There was a suicide in here. And then I saw the same thing, and then again. It confused the hell out of me until I realized what was going on. It was like TWA 800 again—but much, much worse. It seemed like most of the gallery was filled with people who had suicides in their lives. That was all I was going to take. I stormed into the control room and showed a side of myself that my new colleagues hadn't seen. I was beyond furious. I felt like my brain was exploding and oozing out my ears. *What is that out there? If you ever to do this to me again, I'm going to put your face through a wall. Don't you ever, ever stack the deck like that again. That is so unfair to these people. So, so unfair. You're manipulating emotions out there. You cannot do that.*

"We're just trying to give them the same opportunity—" someone said.

"Don't be putting that bullshit on me. You're not giving anybody any opportunity. You're trying to do a theme show."

It was as if we really were doing the cosmic game show Paul and I had joked about: *Whose Death Is It Anyway?* Contestants in the gallery competing to hear from their lost souls. Paul and Dana admitted that they were under pressure to deliver, at least occasionally, the kind of thing Ramey and Adora had promised in their original proposal, the one that offered Saturday Night Dead. Bonnie Hammer said she wanted an organic show. "If you stay true to what John does, the show will succeed," she told the producers. But by that she meant that the essence of the show had to be what happens between me and the people I'm reading. It didn't preclude the producers from having a hand in deciding who those people were. So for a while there, our concepts of "Pure John" were not totally in sync. There was no getting around the fact that this was a television show. But that didn't stop me from trying to get everyone to pretend it wasn't.

"I know you're trying to do the right thing by the show," I told Paul. "But you can't control the other side. They don't work like that. They're not going to come through telling you what you want to hear because you're doing a TV show. They can give a rat's ass about the show. It has to happen naturally. And it will."

After my diatribe in the control room—which was seconded by Suzane Northrop, who happened to be in the studio that day—the producers talked among themselves about how they were going to reconcile a conflict that seemed to be on a collision course. They had to concede that mixing in the occasional theme show felt more natural to them than letting fate run the show—and that's what the people paying them wanted. So they had to decide whose culture this show was living in: theirs or mine. I was just the host of the show, the "talent," getting a paycheck like everyone else. Unless you're Oprah, the talent works for the show, not the other way around. I wasn't Oprah, but I had to act like I was. "I have to be militant about my process," I told them. "I have to really, really care, and I can't bastardize what this is or sensationalize it. Because if I do, it'll have an effect. They won't stand for it." I pointed upward. "The show will be cancelled." When I said this couldn't be like any other show, I wasn't being arrogant or egotistical. I didn't see it as trying to pull a power play. I thought I was just stating the obvious.

"You know what I think we have to do?" Dana said to Paul. "We have to surrender our egos, and surrender our control as producers, and just jump off this cliff. Let's just take this leap of faith. We may get our butts kicked by the network. They may bounce us out of here. But you know what? I don't believe I could make a good TV show by forcing something down John's throat. And we wouldn't want our jobs if we have to do it that way, anyway."

Driving home that day, Paul said to me: "We're really not producing this show, are we? We're really just waiting and seeing what comes out and then post-producing."

The man put a smile on my face. "You got it," I said.

Out of this came two decisions. One, that we would not do anything to orchestrate who was in the galleries. We would fill them the same way I scheduled my private practice. I open the phone lines once a month, and whoever gets through gets through. With the show, people would write in for tickets and get on the list. It was a fair and simple system that didn't involve any decisions on our part. That left the question of theme shows. We had another simple solution. We wouldn't do them. Or rather, we would do them *after* the fact. Sci Fi gave us an hour on Sundays to do special shows, so the producers would create compilation shows, following a certain theme. For example, gather up all the segments involving surprise-attack readings on staff members and package a show about that. Or do a show about pets that came through. You didn't need to fill the gallery with members of the American Kennel Club.

Somehow, the entire issue faded. The show was starting to get a buzz, the numbers were getting strong, and we as a team we were evolving, gradually coming around the concept that this really was a show that essentially produced itself. My guides have always given me great analogies and metaphors to explain what our world is all about—they just show them to me in pictures, and I say them. Now it seemed that the staff and I were playing out a metaphor after each taping. The after-work dance classes on the set symbolized how we were getting in step with how to do the show. *One-two-one-two-three, now change partners . . .*

It was the unpredictability of the universe that was making the show work. Keep it truly organic—no artificial ingredients—and see what happens. We didn't need to go find great stories, I said to Paul one day. They will find us.

"I'M OVER HERE," I said one morning, pointing toward a couple in the back row of the gallery. "Who has the background of either Brazilian or Portuguese? "

"I had a good friend who's Colombian," the woman said.

"No, this is Portuguese. My wife's Portuguese, so I know it's definitely Portuguese. I'm back here. I think I'm on this back row. One of you is either connected to someone who's Brazilian, Portuguese, or just came back from one of these two places. There's a Portuguese connection here."

What followed was a classic *Crossing Over* tug-of-war.

"God, there's a major Portuguese or Brazilian connection here."

"Really?" said the man's wife. "Never."

"Oh, yeah. Who comes from Europe? Whose family did not come from here?"

"My father came from Europe," the man said.

"Any ties to Brazil or Portugal?

"Not to my knowledge."

"Are you sure?"

"No, I'm not sure."

I was getting frustrated, trying so hard to make this connection—but I wasn't angry or annoyed, as I have been known to get. On the tape, you can hear me make a deep groaning sound, like I was trying to force these two pieces together. "Okay, they're not stopping. I refer to this as a hostage crisis. Me being the hostage. Okay, I gotta go up." I climbed the steps of the gallery and got right in front of the couple.

At that point, another energy pushed in. It was a woman who had been in a coma, which the man's wife acknowledged as her mother. And then they were back: "Who the heck is from Portugal?"

"I don't know," the woman said, to giggles from a few of her gallery-mates.

"Well, your mom's hanging out with somebody who's from Portugal."

"No kidding."

"Did she have a friend who's from Portugal? Somebody's telling me, '*Fala Portugues?*' which means 'Do you speak Portuguese?' " There was a name that sounded like Fernando or Ferdinand, and somebody was involved in politics or government—two governments, actually. Somebody had a weird name that started with "B." And somebody's arm was either missing or deformed. He was making me feel like the arm wasn't there.

"I don't know," the man said to everything.

"Are you guys *sure* you have no Brazil or Portuguese connection?"

"Honestly," the woman said. "That's the truth."

"Not even like somebody just came back from vacation there? Where's your family from?"

"My father was from Germany, my mother was from Hungary," the man said.

I went back down the steps to the disk, and as soon as I hit the middle, I spun around back to them. "Who has the 'H' name?"

"My mother, Helen," said the woman.

"Okay, this is all connected for you. You guys have some type of Brazilian or Portuguese connection here. I have no idea what it is, but it's coming through around you guys. So it's probably something you're overlooking. It's something you're not even realizing. But it's directly connected to you. They're giving me all kinds of specific symbols. So if you get out of here and somebody starts talking to you about their father Ferdinand or Fernando who passed, it's going to be connected there. Then call us back and let us know. Okay? Promise?"

"Promise."

"Cool."

THE MAN'S NAME was John Shauder. In the post-analysis interview, he said that his father, Hans, had been deported to Germany in 1946—that might have been the connection to the two governments—and he and his mother never saw him again. John was two years old when his father left. That may have been why he couldn't validate any of the information I gave him. "We have no information as to where he may have ended up," John said. "It could very well be that from Germany he went on to Portugal or to Brazil. I'm certainly going to check that out more thoroughly."

John Shauder was in the gallery that day for the same reason you might expect a fifty-six-year-old man who runs a construction supply business to be there: His wife dragged him with her. He wasn't afraid, just not that interested. The last thing he expected was to be sitting there getting badgered by this guy trying to get him to acknowledge something Portuguese. And being told that he was connecting with the very person whose absence had left a deep scar. "It was a tremendous void, not having a father to look up to, to give me advice," he said. "As a young boy, playing Little League baseball. Having my friends going on vacations with their mother and their dads. I never felt fulfilled. I always felt like there was something missing in my life, and there was. I was certain that he had passed away in the war. But only years later did I discover that he wasn't killed in the war. He was sent back to Germany." John tried to get help from several federal agencies, but came up empty. At one point, he found a man named Hans Shauder in Munich, but it wasn't his father. It was another Hans Shauder. He told John he was sorry that he couldn't help him.

Leaving the studio that day, John was determined to try again, and as he promised, he called us back to tell us about the developments. When he said he would check all this stuff out, it was music to my ears. Neither John nor I knew it, but he was about to become a model of the Delayed Validation. And from this day forward, follow-ups would be the element that would seal the deal we'd made. To deliver closure.

As it happened—and I don't believe in coincidences—John Shauder had a close friend who had a visitor from Germany who was a lawyer. John told him his story and gave him whatever paperwork he had. When the lawyer got home, he called John and said he had some bad news. John's father had passed away in 1985. But there was also some good news: The lawyer had found that John had two younger half-sisters in Germany. He gave him their phone numbers, and John called them immediately. Soon after that, he was flying to Hamburg. When he landed at the airport, they were holding up a sign that said "Welcome, Big Brother John," in English.

The first thing John asked, of course, was about the Brazil and Portugese references. His sisters told him their father had worked in Brazil. He had learned Portuguese there. And he spent time on an island off the coast of Brazil called Fernando Island. His father had a brother Bruno—the "weird 'B' name." And his father had a stroke before he passed away that took away the use of his right arm. Before he left, his sisters gave John a ring that had been on their father's finger. He put it on and looked at it, and he cried.

"When I look at the photographs of my father, I try to look into his eyes and try to feel what he may have been feeling," he told our follow-up producer, Lauren Bright, during a visit she made to the Shauders' home in New Jersey. "I have his ring now. I put this on the day they gave it to me, and I will never take it off. I would like to think that he knows I have it on. Maybe he sees it, also. I'm convinced that what happened to me in the studio that day was his tremendous energy trying to find me. He was able to communicate and say to me, 'I'm here,' and even though I may not be on this earth now, I'm here and I'm looking for you. And I'm waiting for you, and we'll meet someday. Never to part again."

There was even more to the story, and we invited the Shauders to come back to the studio and share the best—though most bittersweet—part. In Germany, his sisters told him that their dad always told people that he had a son in America, and he was looking for him. They gave him a letter he had written in 1983 and sent to an address where John and his mother had once lived. "Dear Helen and John," it said. "I wrote and wrote, and all the letters came back. Maybe I have better luck this time." But this one had come back to Germany like all the others. John finally received it seventeen years later.

In the letter, John's father said that he had met a man in a beer garden in Munich, and they had introduced themselves and toasted each other. "My name is Hans Shauder," the man said to John's father, to which John's father replied: "*My* name is Hans Shauder." And then the other

Hans Shauder said that he had gotten a call a few years back from a man from America who was looking for his father: Hans Shauder. "I told him I couldn't help him."

So John's father knew in 1983, two years before he died, that his son was looking for him. He hoped that this letter would be the one to make it through so that John would know that his father was looking for *him*. Now, finally, he did know. For John, the confirmation was in a videotape he brought back from Germany and showed to us. He had gone with his sisters to the same spot on the harbor in Hamburg where they had taken a picture of their father years ago. "I found you, Dad," John said quietly, too softly for the video camera to pick it up. "I don't know if you know I'm here, but I'm here and I found you." The next day, before leaving to return home, they stopped at the cemetery where their father was buried, and John stood over the grave and said a prayer. He wanted his father to know he was there.

When he got home and watched the videotape, John was astounded. Both segments—at the harbor and at the cemetery—were totally distorted. All the colors were mixed, and there was a kind of pulsing glow through the frames. The rest of the video was perfectly normal. "He knew I was there, and there's no question his spirit was there," John told me. "He was telling me, 'I know you're here, and I'm going to show you *I'm* here.' To know that he searched for me is bittersweet. Unfortunately, I didn't have the opportunity when he was alive to sit there and talk with him and hold him and look into his eyes and hear what he had to say. And yet it's very fulfilling."

When I thought about this story, I marveled once again at how powerful the spirit world is. The soul doesn't just have consciousness, it has will. When I looked back on the tape of the Shauders' original appearance in the gallery, I was struck by my last words to them: "Call us back and let us know. Okay? Promise?" I pass on information every day that doesn't seem to connect. But I don't think I've ever made someone *promise* to call us back and let us know if they figured it out. But that's how strongly Hans was pushing the Portuguese connection— how much he wanted his son to pursue the mystery that he knew would finally give him some peace.

"It's really been a life-altering experience," John's wife Brenda said.

"He's totally changed. There's no void in his life."

When I think about John Shauder, this man who lived with a hole in his heart for half a century, I understand why I'm here in this ghostly old theater with its gallery of portraits, talking to Camera One. There is, of course, nothing like a personal experience, especially one so rare and special as John's. But it's not necessary to run out and find a medium to have a revelation about the unbroken bonds we can have with those we've lost. We can all take heart and learn through John's experience.

After we wrapped the last day of taping of our first season, Bonnie Hammer came down to the studio and gathered everyone around the set. Congratulations, she said. You're coming back. The news was even better a few months later. Studios USA had decided we were ready for syndication. Sci Fi would remain our home, but the parent company would begin talking to broadcast channels around the country about adding the show to their daily lineups. By the winter of 2001, stations in more than 90 percent of the country's major markets had signed on. Whoever made the decisions about whether to do the show or not a year earlier, however they made them, I now knew that this was the way it was meant to be. The worst thing you can tell someone in television is that something is out of their control. But sometimes it's the only thing I know for sure.

I remembered that rock on my desk. Trust.

— CHAPTER 10 —

THE MEDIUM
AND THE MEDIA

GOTCHA

"Reality TV is the buzz word now. But that's really what this is," Paul Shavelson, who by this point was sharing the title of Executive Producer with me, was saying one night in early March of 2001. We were sitting in the green room at CNN in New York, where I was waiting to go on with Larry King. I had plenty of company. Besides Paul, Dana, my collaborator Rick, and Jean Guerin, the Sci Fi Channel's publicist, there was Angela Mancuso, then the executive vice president of USA Cable. She just happened to be in town during what some deemed a *Crossing Over* crisis. The emergency? It had something to do with Paul's observations about the authenticity of the show *Crossing Over*. "I made documentaries for years and years, and that's what we're doing," he said. "You can't use that word because it won't make money. But we're showing exactly what John does. This is exactly how these people feel. This is exactly how it's affected their lives."

The five people with me at CNN were a virtual entourage, but still not as big a crowd as the one gathering on two continents to talk about *Crossing Over* and whether other mediums and I were legitimate. "Tonight: On his hit show, he claims that he can talk to the other side," Larry announced as the show went on the air. "But are psychics for real?" This was my fourth time on *Larry King Live,* but it was the first time I would be asked if I was perpetrating a hoax. The week before, no less prestigious a publication than *Time* magazine had printed an article claiming just that. It caused a fury in our production office and got the network's attention, to put it mildly. But somehow—and this never would have happened a couple of years earlier—I was relatively unruffled by it. Partly because I wasn't surprised. I knew this day would come. I didn't know it as a psychic. I knew it as a psychic who has been dealing with perceptions of his work on a daily basis for fifteen years. And now I had a national TV show that was getting ready to go into syndication. The bigger the stage, the bigger the target.

I learned a long time ago that it's impossible to do this work in any kind of public way without taking hits, fair or not, intelligent or inane. So I've tried to limit the kinds of things that I will let get me worked up. I never lose sight of this reality: I am a member of the only profession in which the work will always be questioned and can never be proven. As Bonnie Hammer says, people either believe it or they don't. Everyone in the public eye—politicians, actors, athletes—is subject to scrutiny. But all those guys have to worry about is being gossiped about or criticized for their performance. At worst, they might be accused of being dishonest politicians, greedy athletes, or lousy actors. But nobody will claim that their entire life is an illusion.

My attitude is this: You want to attack my profession, go ahead. You want to say mediums are doing cold readings and playing guessing games, fine. People are going to say that because they can't wrap their brains around what we do. It's futile for me to try to convince them otherwise. But what does get me upset is when people try to define my motivations or attack my personal character. Saying I'm in it for the money or that I'm taking advantage of people or that I'm a phony—those things bother me. I know it's hard for some people to separate their opinions about the field from what they imagine to be the motivations of its practitioners, but there are limits to how strong my emotional armor is. Call me silly, but I don't appreciate being called a fraud.

One approach I've taken is to pay attention to how journalists and professional skeptics work so I understand how they think. It's not enough to be wary, and it's counterproductive to be antagonistic or unapproachable. Sometimes it's a good idea to just step back, appreciate other people's perspectives, and acknowledge that their motivations might actually be honorable. When I was taking my first baby steps into the media in the mid-1990s, a radio host named Steve Harper asked me to go on his morning show on WBLI, a station in my home area of Long Island. The only thing I had done to that point was a radio show in Miami arranged by my cousin and Naomi DiClemente's early-Sunday-morning show on WPLJ in New York. When I got to the WBLI studio, Steve Harper told me that he felt a great responsibility to his listeners, and while he took what I claimed to do seriously, he didn't know me and hadn't seen me work. So before going on the air, I would have to prove myself. We took calls, and he taped the readings without putting them on the air. And when Steve felt satisfied that what I was doing was credible and helpful to his audience—and that it made great radio—he put me on live. To me, he was doing the responsible thing. Along with Naomi and

Todd Pettengill, Steve became a great supporter and friend, and I still go on his show.

The first time I was attacked in the press was in New York's *Village Voice*, after I did the Andy Warhol séance. At least I thought it was an attack at the time. It was actually just a lighthearted tease by a gossip columnist that looks quaint now. I wasn't that well known then, and maybe I was offended, and maybe I also thought it was kind of cool to be mentioned in the *Village Voice*. I guess you could say that, and a few other little stories about the Andy Warhol thing buried in a few newspapers, was my first brush with celebrity.

I've never gotten completely comfortable with being well known. I have a hard time even saying the word "famous." My initial instincts about liking radio because it meant nobody had to see my face have never really gone away. I realize that's a weird thing for someone with a TV show to say, but unlike most people on TV, *being* on TV was never my goal. It's just the best vehicle I have to teach and help legitimize spirit communication.

I was walking through an airport once with some colleagues, and one of them was muttering, "Recognize me. Recognize me." I'm sort of the opposite. I hope they don't. I can always feel the energy when I *am* being recognized, even if the person is not even within eyesight or isn't being obvious about it.

It's not that I don't appreciate people saying hello to me, especially if they have kind and encouraging words, but sometimes I wish I could take a break. It's nice to have fans, I guess, but seeing serious, endless discussions on the Internet about what my motivations are, that Sandra is pregnant when she wasn't, what my real name is, is kind of creepy. Some of this transcends celebrity. Even among my friends and relatives, I can feel like The Medium. *What's he going to come up with next?* It's not their fault—that's how it is being around someone who, at any given moment, might say, "Who's the 'R'-sounding name with the heart problem?" I appreciate my ability and its potential for helping people, but sometimes I wish I could just unzip the skin I'm in and be like everyone else for a while.

In 1999, I began talking to a producer from *Dateline NBC* named Deborah Trueman about a story she was wanted to do about mediums and spirit communication. It had become a hot topic for the network news magazine shows, and the publicist for my Learning Annex tour was negotiating with several that were interested in doing segments with me. But it was *Dateline* that I was most interested in working with. I liked Deborah Trueman, and after several meetings with her, I decided to go with it. "I want to be clear with you," she said. "If we do a piece—and I don't know if it's going to be approved—but if we do a piece on this, it will be done with journalistic integrity. It will show both sides." I asked her if that meant there would be skeptics on the show, and she said yes. I told her I respected that and appreciated her honesty. Just as long as the story was balanced and didn't attack me personally. I had just done the HBO documentary, which I considered a good experience, and I liked Deborah Trueman, as I liked Lisa Jackson, the producer of *Life After Life*. I also thought that Deborah's last name was a good sign.

Deborah thought that the right correspondent for the story was John Hockenberry, and she waited for him to be available. Meanwhile, I invited her out to Long Island to sit in on a day of private readings so she could get a feel for the work. Only one person of the five booked for that day didn't want her in the room. The first reading was a struggle. It was for a woman who left unhappy, obviously disappointed that I didn't get what she wanted. The others were just as difficult. One I couldn't even read. Of course, the only good reading of the day was for the one person who didn't want Deborah to sit in. Was this a big heads up—don't do this? I don't know. I tried to look at the bright side: At least Deborah wouldn't think I brought in a bunch of setups to make me look good. *Really* looking on the bright side—and flattering myself—I told her that I was glad she got to see this because now she knew there's a process here, and it's not always bang, bang, bang, hit, hit, hit.

Deborah's enthusiasm about John Hockenberry had me looking forward to meeting him. I imagined he was a pretty open-minded guy who wouldn't figure to be waiting to ambush me. So imagine my disappointment when one of the first questions at our first interview was, "How much guesswork is involved with what you do?" That set the tone. His questions seemed designed to challenge me and challenge me again, and to get a reaction. I found I was answering most of the questions the same way: "Like I said, I see, hear, and feel my information. Some I get right, some I get wrong. But I get it." He showed a clip from the *One Last Time* video, in which I got the name of a woman's son who had passed. "You guessed the kid's name," Hockenberry said. I don't know if he was trying to get me riled up. I wasn't going to let him, but I had to politely challenge him: First of all, I didn't guess. Second, do you know how insulting it is to that woman to suggest that because I got her son's name right, she was going to validate the other details if they weren't true?

I hoped the slant of the story would change after Deborah's crew filmed me doing readings and Hockenberry got an up-close and personal view of how this worked. We arranged for a crew to come to the Holiday Inn on Long Island and shoot a group reading I already had scheduled. But before that, they wanted to get some footage showing my non-medium life, and stopped in at Sandra's dance studio, where a cameraman named Tony taped us dancing.

A few people dropped out of the group reading because the camera crew was coming, but most agreed. When the *Dateline* producers arrived, I asked them to talk to every person and verify that I had not spoken to any of them beforehand. The night went well, as far as I was concerned. It was a typical group session—a lot of information connected, and some didn't. Toward the end, I got a sequence of information that nobody acknowledged. Finally, the cameraman, Tony, said, "I think that's for me." At that instant, I had a weird push-pull feeling, like this could be a bad thing to do, or a good thing. I decided to go with the information, and Tony claimed it. It was his father coming through. He took the camera off his shoulder and became the focus of the moment. He was visibly upset as I relayed the information.

Deborah arranged a second interview with John Hockenberry a couple of weeks later. This time, he showed me a short clip from the Holiday Inn and asked me if I considered it a good reading. "Are you asking me if what you're showing is a good reading, or if what actually happened was a good reading?"

"Well, I should say this has been edited for time," Hockenberry said.

"No, you've edited for content. What you're showing is not good. What actually happened, yeah, I think that was good."

Then he showed me giving a woman a sequence of information, none of which she acknowledged. What he didn't show was that all of it was meant for the person sitting next to her. "You're not showing that," I said.

And then, the climax of the interrogation. Hockenberry showed me the clip of me telling Tony the cameraman that his father was coming through.

"You've met Tony before, right?"

"Earlier that day, yeah."

"You spoke to him."

"Yes."

"Were you aware that his dad had died?"

"I think earlier in the day he had said something."

"That makes me feel like that's fairly significant. I mean, you knew he had a dead relative, and you knew it was the dad. So that's not some energy coming through. That's something you knew going in. You knew his name is Tony, and you knew that his dad had died, and you knew he was in the room, right?"

"That's an awful lot of thinking you got me doing," I said.

It was true that Tony had mentioned in passing at the dance studio that if anyone came through for him he hoped it would be his father. I realize it's futile to say this to a tough skeptic, but I really don't remember things like that when I'm working. I just say what I get as soon as I get it, half the time not connecting it to something I've heard or said a minute before, let alone hours before. What happened at the Holiday Inn was that I got a bunch of information—more than Tony had told me at the dance studio—and he understood it and raised his hand to claim it. Did I know it was for him? No! I realized now why I was getting that push-pull feel when that information was coming through. My decision to pass it on was good for Tony. Not good for me. Maybe what I was feeling was a little tug-of-war between my guides and Tony's dad. *Say it. Don't say it.* The idea that there are no spectators to the process—if you're in the room with a medium, you're a participant—was, of course, nothing new. But this was months before *Crossing Over*, so doing a surprise reading of a cameraman wasn't routine yet. So it didn't occur to me to avoid talking to him earlier in the day. And when the information came through later, I definitely was not thinking about how this would seem and whether I should keep it to myself. I just get the information and pass it on. That's what I do. In this case, what I did was give *Dateline* its "Aha!" moment.

For reasons I never knew, the story didn't air for a year, until November of 2000, by which time *Crossing Over* was hitting its stride and giving me a much higher profile than I had when I was taping the story. I never saw the show. I don't read or watch much of what's reported about me because I find it impossible to judge it objectively. I'd rather hear what people around me say about the stories and use that as a gauge or the response. The story was a lot longer than I expected, about two-thirds of the hour-long broadcast, and according to most of my friends—who are admittedly protective of me and not probably not much more objective than I am—it wasn't pretty. But they didn't think it was terrible either. They showed both sides as promised.

I was shocked—shocked!—that I hadn't done anything to move John Hockenberry. He thought the session at the Holiday Inn was "an often tedious four hours with many, many misses." He summed up: "What if we could have a snapshot of all the people John Edward said were clamoring to send a message to the living? What kind of people would we find that they are? Well, they're not angry folks. They're not bitter at being taken too soon. We heard no stories of pain and suffering, no calls for revenge or settling scores. These dead people are *nice*. And maybe a little boring. But as we saw here, even a nice, boring word from the dead beats a whole sermon from anybody in this world."

Hockenberry came down on the side of the professional skeptic they used as my foil. He was identified as Joe Nickell, a member of the Committee for the Scientific Investigation of Claims of the Paranormal, which likes to simplify things and call itself CSICOP. He did the usual sound bites: that modern mediums are fast-talkers on fishing expeditions making money on people's grief—"the same old dogs with new tricks," in Hockenberry's words.

Some people thought that except for the snideness of some of Hockenberry's comments and his big Gotcha! moment, the show was right on balance; that Deborah Trueman kept to her word to show both sides. They thought it was the man from CSICOP who was the same old dog, and he didn't even have any new tricks. The show must not have been all bad. Studios USA was using it to help sell *Crossing Over* into syndication.

And it wasn't until after *Dateline* aired that the paperback version of *One Last Time* made it onto the *New York Times* bestseller list.

THE *DATELINE* PIECE and some stories that appeared in respected publications left me with the feeling that there's a lot of inaccuracy in the media. Hey, stop the presses! But beyond regular old bad reporting, there's the added problem that few who write about this phenomenon seem able to do so without catering to somebody's belief system—either their own, or the people they work for. It seems that the bigger and more prestigious the news outlet, the less chance there is that it will take what is evidently a big risk and present spirit communication honestly and openly, without the inevitable elitist, mocking tone. Maybe that's why *Star* magazine's story on me was more accurate than the one on NBC. There are exceptions, of course, the story by Bill Falk in *Newsday* in 1997 being the most notable. But some reporters see this as a free ride. Write whatever you want—hey, he's just some goofy TV psychic. It's libel-proof.

And now we have the Internet. I hate the Internet. Sure, I'd be lost without e-mail, and it's amazing the kind of stuff you can find online. But that's also the problem . . . it's amazing the kind of stuff you can find online.

"Why is *Crossing Over* all that bad?" somebody named Viki Reed wrote in November 2000. "For the same reason that when a child is abducted in a small town, no one can sleep with their doors unlocked again. When you poison the already depleted well of human trust, you taint it for all. . . . How much love is caused by someone who takes grief and turns it into zeroes on a contract? . . . I have some questions for John Edward and company: Have The Dead given you an approximate date as to when you'll be exposed, and what foreign country it feels like they're suggesting you should fly to?" There are endless discussions filled with erroneous statements on the skeptic websites. Somebody claimed my mother isn't even dead.

I'm not looking for one of those free rides. I'd be more than satisfied with simple, unbiased accuracy. If Deborah Trueman had reported that she sat through a day of one-on-one readings and that I had struggled so much that one of the people had practically left in a huff, that would have been accurate. That happened. I have no insecurity about people knowing that—as long as they also know the whole story. Even on *Crossing Over*, I want whatever happens to be reported accurately.

In the context of a half-hour TV show that's boiled down from hours of tape, that means the kind of careful editing that doesn't leave false impressions. From Day One, I was very concerned that we not edit the show so that all the unvalidated information and slower moments disappeared, essentially leaving a highlight reel of one jaw-dropping read after another. I knew going into this that this was the TV instinct—I couldn't expect our producers and post-production staff to instantly unlearn everything they knew. But I did expect them to adapt what they knew to what I did.

Editing an entertainment show to make it flashy is fine. Editing *Crossing Over* in a way that distorts what actually happened—that's not fine. Besides being dishonest, it goes against the grain of what I want to accomplish. Making myself look good is just not something I care about or need to do. I want people to know the truth about this. The last thing I want to do is raise expectations so high that people come to the gallery expecting their socks to be knocked off every five seconds. I can't deliver that. So the law in our editing room is this: *Edit for time, not for content.*

BUGS

SO ABOUT THOSE FREE RIDES. I used to pretty much assume that the top institutions of American journalism had minimum standards that they rarely slipped from. They made mistakes, everyone does, but they were honest ones and usually not monumental. They had systems of checks and balances—editors, I think they call them—to make sure they adhered to basic accuracy and fairness. So a reporter from, say, *Time* magazine, couldn't just make stuff up or write whatever he wanted without checking it out just because it happened to fit with some personal bias or belief he had. Could he?

In mid-February of 2001, a call came to my office from a reporter from *Time* named Leon Jaroff. Carol, my assistant, took the call, and Jaroff told her that he had written a story about *Crossing Over* that he imagined we would want to comment on. Carol was confused. First, how could he have written a story? This was the first she had heard of him. He hadn't been to the show or interviewed me or anyone else. And she knew that someone else from *Time* was supposedly doing a story. It was a woman, and the last Carol had heard was that she was making arrangements with Jean Guerin, the publicist for the show. Carol asked Leon Jaroff if he was working with this other reporter. He said he wasn't. He was already finished with the story and, as he was saying, he wanted to get a comment. He said he was on vacation on Florida, in case she was interested.

She still didn't understand how he could have written a story. "Where did you get your information?" she asked. Jaroff said he had watched the show, looked at my website, and interviewed someone who had been read on the show. "So you haven't spoken to John and you haven't been to the show?" Carol asked, demonstrating a greater appreciation of the journalistic technique and a higher level of professional curiosity than Mr. Jaroff. And, really, how surprising was that? As we later found out, Jaroff was a science writer with decades of experience reporting on things like human genetics. So you wouldn't expect him to be very big on finding things out. One of the high points of his career was a story claiming to expose spoon bender Uri Geller twenty or thirty years ago. So there wasn't much he didn't know.

Jaroff repeated that there were some things in the story that we would be concerned about. Carol asked him to fax the article, but Jaroff said he couldn't do that. "Then how can we comment?" she asked. He said he wanted to read it to her over the phone. At this point, Carol decided this was getting strange. This guy says he's from *Time* magazine and he's got this story we would be "concerned" about, and he still hasn't asked to speak to me, or even asked Carol who she is or whether she is the person he should read his thousand-word story to and get a comment from. Carol asked him to hold on, and came back to my office. Definitely something for Jean to handle, I told her. Give the guy her number.

Jaroff did call Jean Guerin—but not immediately. When Jaroff said we would have concerns, he wasn't kidding. He told Jean that someone who had been read on our show had told him that staff members gathered information about people in the gallery and then passed it on to me during a supposed "technical difficulty" delay. This person also was saying that we had microphones around the studio that picked up conversations among the people in the gallery before I came out. Jean was flabbergasted. These things were ridiculous, she said—who was this person? She told Jaroff that as a rule, I don't respond to criticism—an interpretation of my "I have nothing to defend" policy. But she tried to set him straight and invited him to the show to see for himself—we have a wide-open-door policy—and interview me. He said that wouldn't be possible. He was on vacation in Florida, and the story was going to print the next morning. *The next morning?* Well, Jean said, at least correct those false allegations.

The headline was the first clue that he didn't: *Talking to the Dead. To reach those who have 'crossed over,' John Edward may have crossed one line too many.* The first paragraph described me as "a fast-talking former ballroom-dancing instructor who is cleaning up" on his supposed abilities to connect with the dead. It went downhill from there. Jaroff went on to list my various sources of income and proclaim that I was "one of the few growth industries in an otherwise lackluster economy," thanks largely to my heavy reliance on "posing a series of questions and suggestions, each shaped by the subject's previous response." Cold readings, in other words.

If Jaroff's story had been limited to one more clueless description of my work or a predictable overstatement of my net worth by someone whose mind was narrower than the ties that were fashionable the year I was born, you wouldn't be reading about it here. But what the people who toiled over *Crossing Over* found when they opened *Time* that Monday in March was a different kind of surprise-attack reading. After producing this groundbreaking and delicate TV concept with the highest order of integrity for nearly a year, they found themselves accused of being the worst scoundrels in television since the quiz show scandals of the fifties. As for me, I just want to make one thing clear: I am not a *former* ballroom-dancing instructor. And if you don't believe me, just show up on the set any day after we tape.

Here's what seems to have happened: A man named Michael O'Neill had come to the show with relatives who had an extra ticket and were hoping to connect with Michael's grandfather. An older male figure did come through and pulled me toward the area in the gallery where O'Neill was sitting. He validated enough of the information to indicate that we had connected with his grandfather, and he apparently went home reasonably impressed. But when O'Neill saw the show on TV weeks later, according to Jaroff, he "began to suspect chicanery." He believed that the reading was edited so that he appeared to be nodding yes to information that he remembered saying was wrong, and that most of the other "misses" in his reading and those of others were edited out.

"Now suspicious," Jaroff wrote, "O'Neill recalled that while the audience was waiting to be seated, Edward's aides were scurrying about, striking up conversations and getting people to fill out cards with their name, family tree, and other facts. Once inside the auditorium, where each family was directed to preassigned seats, more than an hour passed before show time while 'technical difficulties' backstage were corrected. And what did most of the audience—drawn by the prospect of communicating with their departed relatives—talk about during the delays? Those departed relatives, of course. These conversations, O'Neill suspects, may have been picked up by the microphones strategically placed around the auditorium and then passed on to the medium."

What does it say about the state of American journalism when validating information is more important to a fast-talking ballroom-dancing psychic medium than to a science writer for the country's premier news magazine? To those of us on the show, of course, the charges were beyond ludicrous. Yes, we preassign seats. Pretty much the way they preassign seats at the rides at Disneyworld. And about those "technical difficulties:" They're called Producing a Daily Television Show. When Paul looked back at the log for the day that Michael O'Neill was in the gallery, he found that the morning gallery had run later than usual, which delayed the lunch break for the crew and the taping of the afternoon gallery, which included O'Neill. I guess I wasn't the only one who thought it was just point and shoot.

And, yes, it's true that a lot of people on the show—I'm sure they don't appreciate being called my "aides"—do a whole lot of "scurrying about." That's practically the job description of most people who work on TV shows. But as much as they might like to go around striking up conversation with members of the gallery, with all this scurrying about they don't have time do that *and* hand out all those cards and get all that family information down and then collect the cards and scurry backstage so I can read the cards and memorize all that fascinating family information while the aides are lining up to tell me where the people who filled out the cards I was reading are sitting. And I really have to do that fast, because there are more aides waiting to relay all the information they have just written down after listening in to all the chatter being picked up by those strategically placed microphones that apparently we didn't place strategically *enough* that eagle-eye Michael O'Neill couldn't detect them, or at least detect that he *suspected* he detected them. Of course, how could Leon Jaroff know any of this? He hadn't had time to come by our "auditorium" and have a look around.

Whether or not Michael O'Neill wanted to believe his grandfather came through that day was for him alone to decide. But whatever button the experience pushed, it led him to e-mail his suspicions to the James Randi Educational Foundation in Fort Lauderdale, Florida. Leon Jaroff heard about O'Neill from Randi, his fellow Skeptic. Or rather, Selective Skeptic. He wasn't at all skeptical of Michael O'Neill or his "suspicions." Randi quoted O'Neill liberally in his column in *Skeptic* magazine. "I think the whole place is bugged somehow," Randi quoted O'Neill as saying. "My guess is that [Edward] is backstage listening and looking at us all and noting certain readings. When he finally appeared, he looked at the audience as if he were trying to spot people he recognized. He also had ringers in the audience. I can tell because about fifteen people arrived in a chartered van, and once inside, they did not sit together." On that, *Time* magazine based its story on *Crossing Over*.

I had expected something like this to happen, ever since the *New York Post* ran a story on its TV page raising the possibility that I was the Devil Himself—illustrated by a *huge* picture of me with computer-generated horns. If I didn't know it already, that confirmed that psychic mediums are what's known in the media as Fair Game, which is a nice way of saying Raw Meat. Jaroff's story was so over-the-top absurd that on one level I thought it was actually funny. I mean, did this guy—or any of the army of editors they supposedly have at the news magazines—actually think we would go around gathering information about people before the show and expect nobody to say anything about it for nearly a year? What was so special about Michael O'Neill, "a New York City marketing manager," that he was the one who finally cracked the case?

Jaroff's story lit a series of brushfires on two coasts. At the show itself, staff members were outraged and upset, and I was angry on their behalf, much more so than for myself. These were professionals, and this was a despicable and groundless attack on their integrity. Their commitment to the show and to me was not something I took lightly or for granted. They didn't deserve this. It was all the more disturbing because we knew almost immediately that the network was very concerned, and we weren't sure what that was about. We could feel the rumblings three thousand miles away, and we only hoped it was parental concern we were feeling. I didn't want them to "defend" the show, but I did want them to show us support and fight back somehow. On the other hand, it was clear pretty quickly that there were some higher-ups who seemed to be realizing that, come to think of it, they didn't know a whole heck of a lot about how this show was produced. For all they knew, we *were* bugging the place and doing who knew what else.

Paul was ordered to prepare a detailed report of our procedures: everything from how the gallery was picked to where every microphone was. They wanted to know everything that happened to members of the gallery from the moment they wrote in for tickets to the moment they left the building when taping was over. Who talked to them, and about what? Did they fill out any forms? What information were they asked to give? For the record, the only paperwork that gallery members are asked to give us is a legal release granting us permission to include them on the show, and contact information for post-taping interviews. The only thing our gallery coordinator, Jesse Shafer, talks to them about is what's going to happen in the next few hours and where the bathrooms are. Neither the producers nor I have anything to do with the process of filling the gallery.

Meanwhile, just in case someone asked, Paul and Dana tested the microphones that are indeed "strategically placed" above the set—to pick up applause and "ambient noise." They found that if they listened real closely in the control room, and everyone was real quiet, they could hear people talking. But it was difficult to make out much of what was said. It was hard to imagine anyone of any intelligence thinking that an entire television show would be dependent on producers straining to hear snippets of whispered conversation and hoping they picked up enough to fill three shows.

Paul and Dana carried out their little investigations with a mixture of annoyance and amusement. "I've been on game shows that have more to hide," Dana said. When he and Paul watched the raw tape of Michael

O'Neill's reading and compared it to the show that aired, it confirmed what we knew: There was no creative editing to make it look as if O'Neill was answering yes to information he couldn't validate. Cynical people like Leon Jaroff are so willfully ignorant of the reality of what I do and of how *Crossing Over* is produced that they wouldn't even consider the possibility that manipulative editing is the very symbol of what the show is *not* about. Unfortunately, Jaroff is in a position of tremendous power because he happens to write for *Time* magazine. Had he done the most basic journalism, he would have learned that in our continuing effort to make the show a mirror of the process, we were doing even less editing than when we started, even for time. We were letting the readings breathe a little bit more. The real problem was that the editors of *Time* allowed someone with such an obvious bias to write about the show in the first place. Instead of printing the shoddy, lazy "reporting" of a confirmed skeptic—the kind of reckless junk you expect to find on the Internet—why not assign the story to a reporter who would approach the story like any other: with eyes and mind open, and with fairness and accuracy the first priority?

Larry King, right on top of the story, invited me on his show to talk about the controversy. He also had Sylvia Browne and James Van Praagh in Los Angeles, along with a variety of skeptics, including Paul Kurtz, a professor of philosophy at the State University of New York at Buffalo and publisher of *The Skeptical Inquirer*. And Leon Jaroff himself.

"By the way, Larry," Jaroff said, after James, Sylvia, and I were introduced as authors of books, "I have written a book, too, but it's on a real subject, the human genome project. I thought I would throw that in."

When Larry asked Jaroff if I and other mediums are frauds, Jaroff said: "I will say two things. One, I think they're very good at what they do, but I think what they do is baloney." When Larry asked him why, Jaroff said, "Because they use a technique that has been known to magicians for years. It is called cold reading, and then there are variations of it which are called warm reading and hot reading."

A few days later, the network sent out the lawyers to have a look around. This was so they could state publicly what the show's procedures were. And so they would have all the information they needed should they decide to take legal action. Paul showed them around one day. "There's John's bathroom," he said when he brought them into my dressing room.

"His boom box. His socks. Nothing to hide." There were long, involved discussions of what procedures could be instituted to guarantee that nobody got information about members of the gallery in advance—not that anyone thought we were doing that. It was all about perception. There were ideas about code numbers and computer systems to ensure that the hands of no one directly connected to the show ever touched a ticket request. "At a certain point, how much time, energy, and money do we want to spend on something that we're doing legitimately in the first place?" Dana said.

There was definite sentiment for a lawsuit around the show, and it did seem that one was being seriously considered. The studio had a lot at stake with syndication. Two months before, *Crossing Over* had been the talk at the National Association of Television Producers and Executives annual meeting in Las Vegas. By then, the show had been picked up by stations in more than 90 percent of the country's major markets, and wherever I went at the convention, people wanted to talk to me about the show. Now, two months later, word was that competing syndicators were spreading the *Time* story in the hopes of getting stations to drop us before they aired even one show. But weeks later, none had pulled out, which seemed to cool any thoughts that USA Networks would sue no less than Time Warner AOL over whether Psychic Boy over here was cheating.

Charles Nordlander wrote a letter to *Time*, which was published heavily edited—for space, I guess they would say, not for content. And Bonnie Hammer wrote an angry letter to Norman Pearlstine, the editorial director of Time Incorporated, lodging "the strongest possible protest over the grossly negligent and irresponsible journalism by writer Leon Jaroff." She demanded a retraction, which never came.

After the tempest died down, I thought about why I was doing the show in the first place. It was to reach people. The audience was my only real concern. And they were the ones hurt the most. It pained me to think that anyone who had sat in our gallery over the past nine months and gone home more aware and connected than when they arrived might wonder if it had all been a grand illusion. Would John Shauder question, for just a second, if we'd had his name on our list and dispatched our staff of researchers to dig into his past? Would Catherine start to wonder if it was possible that while waiting for the taping to begin, she had been standing near some hidden microphone and mentioned the feather that fell at her daughter's feet at Niagara Falls? And what about all those people watching at home? Would some of them think it was just a magic show after all?

Yes, I could look back and see how far we had come. But that didn't mean we didn't have far to go. Or still don't for that matter.

EPILOGUE

Unitel Studios, New York City
May 2, 2001

I'm standing on the luminescent disk that has been my second home for nearly a year, about to say good-bye and thanks for coming to the last gallery before we get a two-week break. The rest isn't for the weary. It's for the backlogged. Too much tape is piling up in the post-production department, so Paul has decided to take some time off from shooting to let them catch up. I love the show, but I can use the break. We all can.

I glance at the signal from Doug Fogal, my faithful stage manager, that it's time to wrap up. Seems like a lifetime ago that Doug was counting me down as I waited uneasily offstage, about to go out and greet my first official gallery. Now, all these galleries later, I look out and see what I always see at this moment: disappointed faces, people wondering why their families didn't come through, why they weren't among the lucky ones, like soldiers who've come up empty at mail call. I tell them I wish I could have read them all.

But among those disappointed faces are many others who may not have gotten the messages they wanted to hear but who got the bigger message: that the *experience* was as much for them as for the people who were read. They got comfort and insight through the readings of those sitting nearby, and I feel their appreciation. And I hope they—and the people watching at home—accept my take-home message: Always remember to communicate, appreciate, and validate the people in your lives, past and present. And you don't need a medium to appreciate and communicate with those on the other side. Nor should you get fixated on the other side at the expense of your life here on earth. If there's one thing those on the other side want us to know it's that you don't have to worry about them. Move on with your life, enjoy it, value it, and don't make it about waiting for that reunion in the great beyond. There's a reason they call it the *after*life.

I turn and bound off the disk, feeling good about the day's work. I stop for a series of little chats before heading off the set and up the stairs of the old theater to my dressing room. There's a *Time* magazine on a table along the way, and for a second, I'm jolted back to the reality that no matter how much work I do, this will never be easy, or easily accepted. Even I had my doubts at the beginning. *Should I even be doing this on TV? I'm not sure it's honoring the process when what I'm doing is called a "show."*

I knew that doing this on national television would be like painting a big bullseye on my back. Those who see mediums as con artists making money off people's grief would be lining up to take their shots. But if anything's become clear to me, it's that while the cynics and snipers may never go away, they are becoming more and more outdated and irrelevant every day. They're still marching to the same old beat of disbelief. They say they want scientific proof, but it's hard to see evidence when you've got your blinders on, your back turned, and your mind closed to everything but what you have always believed. I have to chuckle at the irony: Whose position is really based on faith (or lack thereof), and whose on evidence? But like I said: They're not going anywhere.

Not long ago, I was on a flight to San Diego, reading Shirley MacLaine's book, *The Camino*. There was a passage in which she was musing about how the media cover spiritual topics, and her analogy was pointed, if not original. She thought they were like a pack of dogs. At that moment, my Boys kicked in with an "oh, by the way" comment. And it was that I would be a "warrior" for my field. Instantly, I let out an expletive. The man who had the luxury of sitting next to me looked over as if I suffered from Tourette's syndrome. I smiled painfully with an apologetic glance, and then just stared straight out at the clouds. All I could focus on was that word. *Warrior.* It implied struggle, if not outright battle. How could that be possible when I refuse to defend what I do? I much preferred "ambassador."

I understand their message more clearly each day. While finishing up this book, I attended the bat mitzvah of a friend's daughter. We arrived late, and while Sandra went to the ladies' room, I sat outside in a chair. Just then, a swarm of teenage boys and girls came flying out of the party room, heading for their respective bathrooms. The boys kept going, but one after another, the girls noticed me and stopped to try to figure out how they knew me. Finally, one of them said, "Oh my God! That's the man who talks to God!" Another girl corrected her. "No—he's in the movies." The girls swarmed around, looking at me as if my spacecraft were parked outside. I really wanted to know what was taking Sandra so long. "Well, what *do* you do?" one of the girls asked.

Suddenly I found myself in my own episode of *Touched by an Angel.* "I don't talk to God," I said. "Well, actually we can all talk to God. He listens to all of us, not just people on TV. I'm on a show that deals with psychic stuff." One darted another a look.

"You believe him?" Her friend—red hair and freckles—leaned forward, hands on hips. "I think you're a *big fake!*" she said, then turned and marched off to the ladies' room.

I'd just been dissed by someone in junior high. The last time that happened was when I made a date with a girl, only to have her show up with her boyfriend. Yes, I get the warrior message.

ALONE NOW IN MY DRESSING ROOM, taking off my makeup and hanging up my wardrobe, I'm not in a fighting mood. There's a stack of letters nearby from people writing to say how much *Crossing Over* has helped them. Many of them have included photos of their loved ones or little tokens of appreciation. There's a letter from a mom and dad saying thanks for giving them a One Last Time with their son. They want me to have a framed Special Olympics-type medal he had won. When I read letters like these, it takes the sting off the attacks. I'm finding myself getting less and less angry at the cynics. More and more, I feel sorry for them.

But I don't need letters to feel validated about the past year. I only have to flip through my mental file of memorable moments. I think of Carla and Vincent, newlyweds who were sitting in the gallery one day. Carla's dad came through saying he danced at her wedding. Carla said she had his picture pinned inside her gown. I think of the woman who connected with a little boy who drowned in front of her eyes when she was a little girl—and I think of how much it moved Diane Wheeler-Nicholson, one of our producers.

"I swear that when this boy came through for this woman, her energy became that of a small, scared, sad child who had carried the trauma and guilt of this boy's death her whole life," Diane wrote me in an e-mail. "There was something so moving about the moment when the message came through that she should let it go. I felt like I saw her be released of something. It took my breath away."

And I think of the note I got three years ago from one of the closest people in my life, my best friend, Mark Misiano. In my lowest moments after *One Last Time* came out and I was contemplating going to vet school, it was Mark who helped get me back on track. This may not sound surprising, but he might not have been able to do it just a few years ago.

In July of 1998, I gave a seminar on Long Island that Mark attended. Seeing him in the audience was a strange experience for me. Mark had been to the first seminar I ever gave, about ten years earlier on Staten Island—and none since. What impressed him the most at that first event wasn't my psychic ability—that was nothing new to him—but the fact that I was able to stand up in front of people and talk. In fact, at that event, all I did was talk about psychic theory. I didn't do any readings, because I wasn't ready to do it in public, in front of a lot of people. Over the next decade, Mark had little interest in coming to events where I was appearing. He knew what I did, and he thought it was pretty interesting. But when I tried to explain to him why it was so important, he really didn't get it.

That all changed when he came to the seminar in 1998 and saw for the first time how people are affected by communications from loved ones on the other side. We were both a lot older now, and Mark could see how I had changed and how he was ready to understand my work. He himself was moved to tears that night, and sat down to write me an e-mail about how he had been affected. "Being at the seminar, I felt the pain that these people were going through, and at the same time, I could see and feel them healing or at least becoming more at peace," Mark wrote, crying as he typed. "No one close to me has passed away. The first person I was really close to that passed away was your mother. She treated me as if I was her son, too. But I was away at school in Buffalo when she passed, and one of the things that really bothered me was that I was coming home to see her that weekend, but I never got the opportunity. Before tonight, I never understood how what you do could help people. Now I understand."

Mark's message was a signpost for me. It told me that I was finally becoming the teacher that Lydia Clar said I would, and that my guides had affirmed along the way. Now, three years later, I feel as though I've traveled miles more. I've crossed over one more bridge . . . on the road to the next. I know it may be a difficult one at times, but I can finally appreciate my grandmother Mary's favorite saying, all these years after her daughter offered it to me as we made our long way back to our ship in St. Thomas.

I can now turn and see how far I've come, and look forward to the distances I have left to travel.

ABOUT THE AUTHOR

John Edward is an internationally acclaimed psychic medium, and author of the *New York Times* bestsellers *One Last Time* and *What If God Were the Sun?*. In addition to hosting his own syndicated television show, *Crossing Over with John Edward,* John has been a frequent guest on *Larry King Live* and many other talk shows, and was featured in the HBO documentary *Life After Life.* He publishes his own newsletter and also conducts workshops and seminars around the country. John lives in New York with his wife and their two dogs.

For more information regarding John Edward, see his website at: **www.johnedward.net**.

THE JOHN EDWARD APPRECIATION PIN

Many of you have heard me talk for years about how important it is to take the opportunity to communicate, appreciate, and validate the people in your life today. Many people come to me as a medium to do it for them, but there's nothing like doing it in the present. The John Edward Appreciation Pin is just that symbolic gesture. For those who do not have the words, let the pin do it for you.

For Someone Special

To order your pin just fill out the order form. It's free with the purchase of *Crossing Over,* the book.

Just send $2.95 for shipping and handling for one *free* pink rose pin. In order to purchase additional pins, go to **www.johnedward.net**.

Due to overwhelming demand, you must send in the original form, not a copy:

Name_____
Street Address_____
City _____State_____ Zip _____
Phone_____E-mail address_____

Please make check payable to **Get Psych'd Inc.,** and mail your order to:

P.O. Box 383

Huntington, NY 11743

Allow 4 – 6 weeks for delivery.

We hope you enjoyed this Jodere Group book.
If you would like additional information about
Jodere Group, Inc., please contact:

JODERE
GROUP

Jodere Group, Inc.
P.O. Box 910147
San Diego, CA 92191-0147
(800) 569-1002
(858) 638-8170 (fax)
www.jodere.com